Socially Restorative Urbanism

The need for a human-orientated approach to urbanism is well understood, and yet all too often this dimension remains lacking in urban design. In this book the authors argue for and develop socially restorative urbanism – a new conceptual framework laying the foundations for innovative ways of thinking about the relationship between the urban spatial structure and social processes to re-introduce a more explicit people-centred element into urban place-making and its adaptation.

Focusing on this interplay between humans and the built environment, two new concepts are developed: the *transitional edge* – a socio-spatial concept of the urban realm; and *Experiemics* – a participative process that acts to redress imbalances in territorial relationships, defined in terms of the awareness of *mine, theirs, ours* and *yours* (MTOY).

In this way, *Socially Restorative Urbanism* shows how professional practice and community understanding can be brought together in a mutually interdependent and practical way. Its theoretical and practical principles are applicable across a wide range of contexts concerning human benefit through urban environmental change and experience, and it will be of interest to readers in the social sciences and environmental psychology, as well as the spatial planning and design disciplines.

Kevin Thwaites is a Senior Lecturer at the University of Sheffield.

Alice Mathers is Innovation Manager at the Tinder Foundation and a Visiting Scholar at the University of Sheffield.

Ian Simkins is a freelance lecturer, a Chartered Landscape Architect and the Managing Director of Experiemics Ltd, the consultancy of Experiential Landscape.

Socially Restorative Urbanism

The theory, process and practice of Experiemics

Kevin Thwaites, Alice Mathers and Ian Simkins

Routledge
Taylor & Francis Group

LONDON AND NEW YORK

First published 2013
by Routledge
2 Park Square, Milton Park, Abingdon, Oxon OX14 4RN

Simultaneously published in the USA and Canada
by Routledge
711 Third Avenue, New York, NY 10017

Routledge is an imprint of the Taylor & Francis Group, an informa business

British Library Cataloguing in Publication Data
A catalogue record for this book is available from the British Library

Library of Congress Cataloging in Publication Data
Thwaites, Kevin.
Socially restorative urbanism : the theory, process and practice of Experiemics / Kevin Thwaites, Alice Mathers and Ian Simkins.
pages cm
Includes bibliographical references and index.
1. City planning--Social aspects. 2. Urban ecology (Sociology) 3. Landscapes--Social aspects. I. Mathers, Alice. II. Simkins, Ian. III. Title.
HT166.T454293 2013
307.1'216--dc23
2012043951

ISBN: 978-0-415-59602-2 (hbk)
ISBN: 978-0-415-59603-9 (pbk)
ISBN: 978-0-203-46749-7 (ebk)

1006924051

Typeset in Bembo Std 11/14pt
by Fakenham Prepress Solutions, Fakenham, Norfolk NR21 8NN

Printed in Great Britain by Bell & Bain Ltd, Glasgow

Contents

Authors   ix

Preface   x

Acknowledgements   xv

INTRODUCTION   1

PART I BEYOND BOUNDARIES: DEVELOPING THE CONCEPT OF
SOCIALLY RESTORATIVE URBANISM   13

Introduction   13

1   New Age-ing Cities: in search of a new discipline for socially orientated
    urban design   17

    Introduction   17

    The nature of boundaries: professional, spatial and social   28

    Addressing boundaries: some thoughts on material, spatial and social
    integration   33

2   Balance of control at the margins   37

    Introduction   37

Contents

Evolutionary urban morphology and socially sustainable urban design   38

Control, territoriality and the balance of form, place and understanding   42

3   The socially restorative urban environment   51

Introduction   51

Developing the socially restorative environment   52

Social restoration: issues of social exclusion and participation   59

Mine, theirs, ours, yours: a framework for universally inclusive
communication   60

PART II IN SEARCH OF THE EDGE   69

Introduction   69

4   The edge as socio-spatial concept   73

Introduction   73

The phenomenological nature of transitional edges   74

The social significance of the edge   78

The segment hypothesis: a socio-spatial framework for transitional edges   101

Segment as socio-spatial structure   106

5   Transitional edge anatomy: extent, locality and laterality   110

Introduction   110

Spatial porosity   115

Localised expression   119

Coherence and adaptation   123

Transitional edges, Habraken and Experiemics   128

PART III EXPERIEMICS   **133**

Introduction   133

6   **The need for participative processes**   **137**

Introduction   137

Exclusion in environment   138

Development of social design strategies   140

Participation within limits   142

Participation and professionalism   143

Social innovation   147

Community capacity building and localism   148

Summary   150

7   **Experiemic development**   **152**

Introduction   152

A place to begin   153

A responsive approach: 'Our Parks and Gardens'   154

Moving into the edge: 'Excuse Me, I Want to Get On!'   167

Employing Experiemics: 'What's the Fuss, We Want the Bus!'   177

The Experiemic Process   182

Process completion: end of the journey?   191

Summary   193

8   **Developing the practical application of Experiemics**   **195**

Introduction   195

Case Study 1 Development of the 'Insight Method'   196

Contents

Case Study 2 Research into practice: applying a person-centred process to environmental and social change in a primary school, North-East of England   199

Case Study 3 Playground and field project: primary school, North-East of England   203

Case Study 4 Development of the Experiential Landscape mapping methodology   207

Summary   211

9   **Conclusion: life on the edge**   **216**

Notes   228

Bibliography   230

Index   241

Authors

Kevin Thwaites teaches and researches socially responsive landscape architecture and urban design at the University of Sheffield. Research interests centre on the development of Experiential Landscape, the theory and philosophy of urban landscape design and particularly how spatial and experiential dimensions of urban life converge to influence human psychological health and well-being.

Alice Mathers is Innovation Manager at the Tinder Foundation and a Visiting Scholar in the Department of Landscape at the University of Sheffield, UK. Her work is driven by an interdisciplinary approach to people–environment interactions, which straddles the academic boundaries of landscape architecture, planning, sociology, disability studies, human geography and environmental psychology. Her doctoral and post-doctoral research with disabled people seeks to challenge current professional and societal constraints that inhibit the involvement of under-represented communities in environmental planning and design, and has received considerable attention from policy-makers and the international academic community.

Ian Simkins is a freelance lecturer and Managing Director of Experiemics Ltd. the consultancy of Experiential Landscape, whose overall strategy is to develop and apply an integrated approach to teaching, research and practice. The work has developed theoretical principles and practical methodologies focused on socially inclusive approaches to landscape and urban design, participative practices and experiential mapping methodologies.

Preface

This book presents socially restorative urbanism as an exploration towards the development of a new disciplinary position which places human experience at the forefront of how the urban places that people occupy are understood and made. It follows and is underpinned by our earlier work in Experiential Landscape (Thwaites and Simkins, 2007) and represents the most recent stage of an ongoing journey involving research, teaching and practice onwards to what we might hope to be a growing understanding of the relationship that people have with the routine environments they inhabit and use. Like Experiential Landscape, we present this very much in the spirit of ongoing enquiry. We hope that it will provide a platform from which further discussions and avenues of exploration might arise.

The content of this book owes much to opportunities provided by the UK Leverhulme Trust who, through the award of a research grant in 2008, allowed us the time and space to work through some ideas about how we might further develop the ethos of Experiential Landscape and some of its methods more effectively for use in practice. At the time we imagined this as a 'toolkit' of methods and procedures that would give practitioners the necessary know-how and practical means with which to empower a larger cross-section of society to express their environmental experiences and influence processes of change to places they use. We decided that the best way to do this would be to work in partnership with some of the most voiceless of the voiceless in society: those who most often have their environmental circumstances imposed upon them by specialist professional processes that can often overshadow the value of authentic lived experience. We felt that if we could develop a participatory toolkit that would not only bring out the voices of these groups but also make them influential as inclusive partners in the processes of change, then we might have something that would be equally applicable, and effective, for other, perhaps less extremely disenfranchised sections of society. The story behind the development of this process, which has come to be called the Experiemic Process, and the huge debt of gratitude that we owe to our participant groups of young children and people with learning disabilities, is told in Part III of the book.

But other, less expected, things occurred along this journey. Our work in Experiential Landscape had always highlighted that, echoing the words of E.F Schumacher, 'Small is Beautiful' (Schumacher, 1973). At the level of ordinary lived experience, it is seldom the grand environmental gestures that impact the most, but the small, often almost invisibly small, differences that make the greatest impact on the quality of a day-to-day life. Moreover, it is the experience of having some level of control over these differences that can matter even more and this depends crucially on being able to experience our routine surroundings at a human scale. The impact and perhaps the wider significance of this awareness came into vividly illuminated focus by the work that we did with our participant groups. It is not the experience of participation itself that counts, even in its most well-meaning and empathic form, if all this leads to is the delivery of information back into professional arenas for re-interpretation. While clearly better than nothing at all, in many instances, this simply represents a lesser, but nonetheless equally invidious form of disenfranchisement. Voices may be heard, but control is once again shorn and returned to professionalised processes. Gradually, to greater or lesser extent, society as a whole comes to accept the belief that decisions about the form, fabric and management of our everyday surroundings are almost entirely a matter for professional concern. There are three lessons that we learned from our experiences here that we would like to draw attention to before beginning the book.

One is that we must somehow learn to value more explicitly the social gains implicit in participatory acts. Done well, it is not just about informing better material changes, it is also about recognising and giving value to the gain in self-esteem, self-confidence and environmental competence that participants derive from their experience as inclusive partners in participative activity. Even when little or perhaps no immediate material change results, there are still gains at individual and group levels which raise the sum total of social capital available in localities. Part III will explain this in relation to our learning disability and school children colleagues.

Second is that if small is indeed beautiful, and that if a measure of control must somehow pass back to people, whoever they are and in whatever circumstances they find themselves, then change must be made possible at often very small levels of human scale, and, moreover, it must become possible for such small acts of change to be visible, and be a meaningful and valued part of the public realm: human self-esteem depends on this, at least in part. Working alongside our architectural and urban design colleagues, we believe this requires a radical re-think about the scale of urban place-making and the extent to which this can, once again, be made more time-conscious, bringing it within reach of adaptability and change at local levels under the, at least partial, control of individuals and groups who inhabit and use it. Here, again we realise that participation is not enough: even participation that sets out to empower and transfer decision-making. Control is only effective if the infrastructure is configured in ways amenable to such small and localised acts of adaptation. Simple common sense supports this: many people will happily, and often with impressive levels of ambition, cultivate and manage a front garden, display goods for sale on a streetfront, assemble tables and chairs in a courtyard café, for their own benefit and that of their community, but few would willingly set about such expressive acts within the sort of wide-open, mown grass wilderness spaces typical of many UK 1950s and 1960s housing estates. In simple terms, if a job looks manageable for people, it is likely to get done, if it doesn't, the chances are that nothing will happen, despite the need or desire: it will simply be left as someone else's problem. We will try to demonstrate in what follows that this is as much a matter of urban morphology as it is of citizen participation and empowerment. Our contribution to this is to discuss the importance of what we have called here *transitional edges*. It means, in essence, accepting loose and ambiguous margins at the interface of material form and human occupation as a fundamental component of socially responsive urban environments.

Third, and finally, is perhaps the most challenging lesson of all. This is that the kind of participatory processes and the approach to urban morphology that we have sketched out here cannot be understood as discrete matters: they must, somehow, come to be understood as two mutually supportive elements in an integrated system. The major challenge here as we see it is that of disciplinary divisions. The kind of 'real world' we see here is one in which the physical and spatial infrastructure of the built environment continues to deliver necessary stable structures that can then be occupied and used by people: clearly, we will need appropriately trained and skilled professional agents for this purpose, but of a different kind to the ones separated by artificial professional and disciplinary boundaries. Equally important, however, is the need for occupiers to be able to express themselves in this process. This is so that their occupation, place-making and subsequent community development is not simply 'accommodated' but becomes an integral part of the way the locality establishes itself, grows, adapts and changes according to prevailing local circumstances to create 'belonging'. In other words, people should be able to have more control over how and what their places 'become' and how that 'becoming' expresses its uniqueness and identity (Figure 0.1).

There is in this an implicit balance of 'top-down' professional planning and design decision-making and 'bottom-up' processes of local empowerment and self-organisation. This is not a question of either one or the other, as is often implied in discourse on these matters, but of a need for mutually accommodating and supportive approaches to both: a closer integration of sociological and psychological issues and the environmental planning and design professions. Achieving this may also require a shift in the focus of attention in relation to urban form

Figure 0.1: The socially restorative urban environment is spatially porous, absorbent of diverse social activity, expressive of human habitation and adaptable to changes in space and time. Cooking in old Delhi, India.

away from the present duality of built form and open space towards a more holistic socio-spatial conception of the interface between material form and processes of human habitation. Collectively, this may imply that progress towards more socially sustainable urban solutions may need modifications to, or even new directions in, our prevailing professional structures.

Acknowledgements

This book brings together a wide range of ideas and experiences drawn from an ongoing process of exploration, through our research, teaching and practice, into the relationships people develop with places they use in the course of everyday life. In many ways it is a collective work which tries to bring thoughts and ideas developed over several years from many places and with many people into a framework for further discussion, research, teaching and practice that we hope will help make the human urban habitat better. We are indebted to our many friends and colleagues who have freely contributed the time, ideas, expertise, wisdom and often extraordinary insight that have made this book possible. We pay particular tribute in this respect to Sergio Porta and Ombretta Romice at the Urban Design Studies Unit, University of Strathclyde, who have been with us every step of the way with boundless and unreserved collaboration, helping to shape our ideas about urban spatial organisation in particular. Especially important in this respect is the Urban Design Studies Unit's work on the formulation of plot-based urbanism, a radical human-orientated approach to urban morphology and an intrinsic influence on many ideas developed in Part I.

From the work with Ombretta and Sergio came the opportunity to develop and convene a symposium for the 'Continuity and Change of Built Environments: Housing, Culture and Space across Lifespans' conference in Daegu, South Korea in October 2011. This provided a valuable chance to bring together some developing ideas about urban spatial order and to have the opportunity to weave these together with the work of our symposium contributors. In this respect, in addition to Ombretta and Sergio, we are especially grateful for the expertise and generosity of Lineu Castello (Universidade Federal do Rio Grande do Sol, Brazil), Aleya Abdel-Hadi and Kaled Hawas (Helwen University, Egypt), Sabrina Borgianni, Nicoleta Setola and Maria-Chiara Torricelli (University of Florence, Italy), Julia Robinson (University of Minnesota, USA) and Sergio Porta (University of Strathclyde, UK). We thank our colleagues and hosts in Daegu, The Architectural Institute of Korea, for providing this opportunity.

We are also very grateful to continue to share enjoyable and fruitful discussions about a range of topics in the book with our friends and colleagues in Scandinavia. Our thanks and appreciation, in particular, go to Mari Sundli-Tveit and Helena Nordh at the Norwegian University of Life Sciences, and to colleagues at the Swedish University of Agricultural Sciences, especially Susan Paget, Petter Akerblom and Caroline Hagerhall. We are particularly grateful to Susan for the help and collaboration in case study fieldwork detailed in Chapter 8 and also in this respect to Guy Rawlinson, UK Chartered Landscape Architect. Guy has also worked for several years with us on the design studios described at the end of the book, bringing the reality of professional practice to bear on the academic developments.

We would also like to thanks the school communities in the North-East of England and South Yorkshire, from whom we learnt a great deal helping to progress the Experiemic Process in 'real-life' situations. Also our thanks to Professors Allison James and Penny Curtis of the Centre for the Study of Childhood and Youth, University of Sheffield, for their support in other fieldwork opportunities.

We are, of course, immeasurably indebted to John Habraken, Professor Emeritus of Architecture, Massachusetts Institute of Technology, who was kind enough to invite Kevin, Ian and Sergio to his home in the Netherlands. The inspirational conversation and hospitality extended to us left a sustaining influence on all our thinking and provided the lynchpin through which our ideas have been able to be brought into focus here. We would also like to thank Sjoerd Soeters of Soeters Van Eldonk Architects, Amsterdam, for making our visit to John happen.

Much of the research work underpinning the development of this book, particularly in Part III, was made possible by a research grant awarded by the Leverhulme Trust and we are extremely grateful to have had the opportunities made possible by this award. Again, in this pursuit, we are grateful to have benefited from the steadfast help of our collaborators in this research programme; Sergio and Ombretta once more, and also Barbara Golicnik from the Urban Planning Institute of the Republic of Slovenia.

Mention and thanks must also be given to the ESRC for award of a +3 Studentship (PTA-030-2004-00895) to Alice Mathers, which supported her PhD work, enabling our initial development of participatory tools and approaches. In association, we are indebted to the communities with whom we had the joy and privilege to build up strong working relationships and friendships over a considerable number of years. Without their commitment, insight and energy, Experiemics would not be possible. In particular, we would like to thank the members and staff at Sheffield Mencap Day Services, the students and tutors at Dilston College of Further Education, Northumberland, the members and staff of SUFA (Speaking Up for Advocacy, Sheffield) and the trainees and staff of WORK Ltd, Sheffield.

In addition, we wish to acknowledge the important support we have received from policy-makers and practitioners. This has ensured that Experiemics can achieve the social impact that underpins our research ethos. Their active contribution and openness when working with communities demonstrate how effective true partnership working can be. As such, thanks go to Emma Cawley and the Sheffield City Council Mobility Strategy Team, to Damian Dutton and the South Yorkshire Passenger Transport Executive and to the management and staff at the First and Stagecoach transport companies.

As people working in Higher Education, we are uniquely privileged to be able to share ideas as they develop with our students and it is beyond doubt that their enthusiasm and creativity have helped immeasurably to clarify and refine our thinking. We are particularly grateful to students on the Masters in Landscape Architecture course at the University of Sheffield who elect to take part each year in an Urban Landscape Design programme. They never fail to deliver high-quality, innovative and thought-provoking interpretations of our developing ideas, and although too numerous to mention individually here, you all know who you are and our gratitude to all of you is boundless. We must, however, single out for particular mention, John Edwards, who graduated with the Masters in Landscape Architecture in 2011. John's dissertation research contributed significantly to Chapter 4.

Introduction

Socially restorative urbanism seeks to operate at the interface of human and material realms, removing the duality maintained by current disciplinary categorisation. In essence, it has two mutually interdependent concepts: *Experiemics* – a participative process that acts to redress imbalances in territorial relationships; and *transitional edges* – a socio-spatial concept of the urban habitat.

The essence of what we are trying to do with this book is to articulate a new conceptual framework, called socially restorative urbanism. We hope this will provide a foundation for discussion, debate, new directions of thinking, research and practice which can re-introduce a more explicit human dimension into the decisions we make when shaping our urban habitat. The idea to do so, and indeed our belief that it is important to do so, have their roots in a number of increasingly convergent issues. These arise from our ongoing work in Experiential Landscape (www.elprdu.com) and how this relates to wider concerns, evident in professional and academic contexts, that contemporary approaches to urban place-making may be insufficiently responsive to the ordinary daily lives, needs and aspirations of urban communities (Urban Task Force, 1999; Cuthbert, 2007; Gehl, 2010).

Calls for more human-orientated responses to urban regeneration and design issues are not new. They have in fact had an almost constant presence in the development of elements of urbanist thinking at least since the work of Jane Jacobs in 1961. Although there is no shortage of well-intentioned design guidance meant to embody this ethos in professional decision-making arenas, there remain reasons to be concerned that this has not yet taken root in the mainstream. Perhaps one of the more dramatic and widely popularised of these can be found in Andrew Marr's television documentary exploration of the global growth of megacities (*Andrew Marr's Megacities*, 2011). But there are also practitioner voices, Lord Rogers of Riverside among them, questioning the human value in much of what is delivered by professional processes (Urban Task Force, 1999), and also academic voices which point to a conspicuous lack of sociological and psychological awareness in design decision-making (Cuthbert, 2007).

We are now entering a political environment in the United Kingdom which is promoting a strong 'localism' agenda (Cameron, 2010). Yet many of the processes and practices adopted in urban place-making remain steadfastly top-down, driven by aesthetic and economic agendas which seem to privilege rapid delivery and visual spectacle over social value. Our work in Experiential Landscape emphasises the importance of local values, the uniqueness of the individual and the importance of community, and we have tried to integrate spatial and experiential dimensions into new structures of thinking and practice in response. Although in many ways an over-simplification, and certainly incomplete, Experiential Landscape principles intentionally seek to deliver new ways of thinking about the relationship between human experiences and their spatial expression in the routinely used environment: an intrinsically localist perspective. Against the challenges of contemporary urban development and the possibility of a leaning toward more localist agendas, we feel there is justification for further new thinking and this is essentially what this book sets out to begin to deliver.

In what follows we will talk about some of the socio-spatial structures developed in Experiential Landscape and about more recently developed participative processes that may form some tentative foundations for such new thinking. In particular, we will try to show how this aligns with the interests of some commentators who see at least a part of the way forward in the development of new forms of language: processes of communication that not only can bridge present disciplinary divisions, but also, and more importantly, bridge the divide between urban communities and the professional agencies that design and manage the places they use (Habraken, 1986; Sanoff, 2000; Cuthbert, 2007).

In our development of the socially restorative urbanism framework we will try to express this as a holistic relationship of urban morphology and participative process. Conventionally, these are not generally closely related, but here we will try to show that, if participation and processes of self-organisation are accepted as socially and environmentally beneficial, then certain morphological conditions are more likely than others to encourage it. The concept of socially restorative urbanism, therefore, sees morphology and participation as necessarily integrated in a mutually supportive framework.

In Part I, 'Beyond boundaries: developing the concept of socially restorative urbanism', we will explore in more detail how we see limitations in prevailing approaches from a perspective of boundaries: urban form-related boundaries, especially those at the interface of interior and exterior realms; disciplinary boundaries; and social boundaries. We will try to explain how we have found that, by taking a different approach to talking about place from a uniquely human, rather than professional, perspective grounded in territorial experience, we can begin to build bridges across these boundaries.

One of the cornerstones of our discussion is the exploration of the structure of the ordinary built environment presented by John Habraken (Habraken, 1998). Important here is that Habraken shows that the way in which ordinary built environments came into being, before a post-Palladian growth in professional architectural influence, had more to do with social processes based on a balance of levels of control. These environments tended to reflect local social relationships, conventions and norms, and were adaptable, changing and developing to reflect the social forces at work locally. Habraken conceptualises this in terms of a relationship of form, place and understanding. We will relate our discussion closely to this structure to highlight that currently prevailing approaches are significantly out of balance, heavily privileging form-based solutions which may be obstructing sufficient expression of place and understanding in much of our contemporary urban development (Figure I.1).

We will try to show that this has implications far beyond simply the appearance of the urban realm. In their essence, Habraken's place and understanding reflect the levels of control that inhabitants express through their occupation and use of their surroundings. They can be closely related to territorial behaviour and represent the extent to which people are able to express ownership and personalisation of places they use. This has significant implications for the relationship between professional practices, which deliver urban infrastructures, and the social processes they accommodate.

Taking our lead from Habraken, we will argue that this represents an excessively over-professionalised approach to urban place-making which, at extremes, may ultimately be detrimental to the well-being of some urban communities. Despite well-intentioned motives for urban regeneration and development in recent years, economic and time pressures appear to have increasingly de-humanised the way

Figure I.1: Excessively *form*-dominant infrastructure can inhibit expression of place occupation beyond the confines of the private interior space and so weaken the development of common *understanding* necessary to encourage and sustain the sense of belonging and mutual cooperation necessary to the embedding of community. On the left, ubiquitous form-dominant apartment block, Amsterdam; centre, human-scale urban edge encouraging temporary territorial occupation, Uppsala; right, expression of mutual cooperation and understanding, Dehli flower market.

we create much of our urban habitat. As we will show in Part III when we discuss research carried out with school communities and communities of people with learning disabilities, at these extremes such de-humanised approaches can lead to social exclusion, which in turn obstructs the capability to develop important environmental and social competencies.

We relate particular characteristics of this detriment to the opportunities people have to develop and sustain a sense of self-esteem. This depends at least in part on the extent to which people can develop an understanding of themselves as valued individuals and contributors to a community with shared interests. We will try to show that the prevailing over-professionalised approaches and their concurrent form-led solutions can be an inhibiting influence in this respect. In response, we suggest that what is needed is an approach capable of recognising that fulfilled lives depend on achieving a subtle balance of self-assertion and belonging.

In this book we will draw on our research and wider explorations to discuss what we believe to be some necessary components in the delivery of such a balance. At a fundamental level this includes the form of language used to talk about the human–environment relationship, emphasising a strong territorial leaning, which we refer to as relations between awareness of *mine, theirs, ours, yours* (MTOY). It will also include some implications for practice and participatory processes, emphasising a much more inclusive approach which recognises the importance of social gains as well as material changes (*Experiemics*). It will also include ideas about the socio-spatial anatomy of the urban realm, developed from Experiential Landscape principles, highlighting the importance of edge settings which define the interface between human habitation and material form (*transitional edges*). These social, participatory and structural components are interwoven in the new conceptual framework of socially restorative urbanism as a foundation on which to try to overcome boundaries, form and spatial, disciplinary, and social, by building a more localist perspective, and to redress the imbalance in professional and social influences on the development of the urban realm.

Developing the foundations of our conceptual framework will begin with a brief discussion on restorative environments and how we see this developing and influential area of research relating to contemporary urban environments. Our argument here is that more emphasis now needs to be placed on exploring a more social conception of restoration which can embrace the more dynamic and challenging settings that often characterise urban environments. We use this discussion to speculate that there may be a more territorial perspective on human restoration, perhaps more relevant to the compact, multi-use urban settings promoted today, but which has thus far not been extensively investigated.

Throughout the course of our work we have come to believe that territoriality is of critical importance if we are to develop more localised, inclusive and socially restorative approaches. Inclusivity, as we will demonstrate, is in fact a key issue here and we suggest that true inclusivity begins by paying attention to how these important territorial concepts are communicated. In professional architectural and landscape architectural arenas, such concepts are usually dealt with by using terms like *space* and *place*, and in particular the relationship between the two. However, these terms mean little beyond specialised professional contexts and are therefore not inclusive. Although the concept of 'place' is now generally acknowledged as capturing human behavioural and emotional attributes, once transposed into mainstream professional architectural and urban design contexts, for example, it remains far too narrowly form-centric where it fails to capture the complex nature of territoriality reflecting authentic lived experience.

With this in mind, our discussion moves on in response to describe how we can understand this complex, multi-dimensional and territorial human–environment relationship in terms of an integration of experiences derived from how all people come to know what is 'mine', 'theirs', 'ours' and 'yours'. These terms and, more importantly, the ever-changing relationship between them as we make sense of our routine surroundings, reflect the fundamentals of human social and therefore spatial organisation. They also help to extend concepts beyond the narrow confines of material form by embracing territories of ideas, values, shared concerns and other intrinsically socially orientated human attributes that impact on the way we identify, control and personalise our surroundings. MTOY relations are, therefore, the socio-spatial building blocks of socially restorative urbanism and tools with which new understandings of human–environment relationships can be articulated and related to decision-making processes.

MTOY provides us with a basis with which to discuss in more detail issues of human self-esteem based on the need for a certain breadth of territorial opportunity to be available to us. We then move on to discuss how we see this weaving together with Habraken's tripartite concept of the structure of the ordinary built environment (Habraken, 1998). This enables us to make an important intellectual bridge between an intrinsically social concept to one that has direct implications for shaping the built environment, emphasising the importance of social structures and especially the human and built environment interface in achieving socially beneficial outcomes.

MTOY relationships enable us to look at the issues concerning urban development from a different, much more humanistically driven perspective. Building on this, Part II, 'In search of the edge', will concentrate mainly on the development of socio-spatial understandings of the urban realm to try to show how the territorial and social concept embodied by MTOY relationships can be related to certain kinds of urban form. In his exploration of the structure of the ordinary built environment, Habraken (ibid.) talks about the importance of margins. These are understood as the usually linear features of the urban realm defined by what happens at the interface of human habitation and material form. What Habraken focuses on here is that when people occupy structure, they make places by controlling access and egress, and through use of these places are able to express something about themselves in the surrounding world. Social value and therefore social sustainability are, according to Habraken, related to the empowerment people have to express these processes of occupation and have them recognised in the way that urban form becomes manifest.

In essence, what this suggests is that where material form in some way inhibits such territorial expressions, social value is likely to be lower than where material form encourages, and indeed becomes a part of, territorial expressions of inhabitants. In this way, Habraken makes it possible to conceptually differentiate between margins which are socially rich and those that are less so, suggesting that the former may have looser, adaptable characteristics more easily amenable to change through occupation and use. As Jane Jacobs (1961) also demonstrated almost 40 years earlier, and Jan Gehl (2010) more recently, these characteristics are usually more observable where built form and the public realm overlap, giving special significance to the capacity of these elements of urban structure to sustain the social life of cities. Emphasis on the social significance of edge environments is evident in the wider literature and we will draw on key aspects of this later in this section. But here, the important thing to establish, as Habraken, Jacobs and Gehl advocate, is that in order for them to support life and be socially sustainable, they must enable human activity to become a part of how they appear. They cannot simply be prescribed in static and finite form entirely through professionally prescribed interventions.

Focus on the socio-spatial significance of such marginal settings can be related directly to Experiential Landscape principles, first conceptualised in 1999. In doing so, we will move on to show how this can form the basis for developing an understanding of their anatomy in ways relevant to more socially orientated design decision-making. Experiential Landscape seeks out ways to understand the structure of the human–environment relationship by recognising its holistic nature as a fusion of spatial and experiential dimensions, developing from the phenomenological perspectives of Merleau-Ponty (1962) and others (Norberg-Schulz, 1971; Alexander *et al.*, 1977; Dovey, 1993, 2005). In order to try to move this beyond a philosophical position, however, and make it operationally viable in educational and practice arenas, a range of fundamental human experiences and their spatial expressions, have been developed into an integrated system of four components: *centre, direction, transition* and *area* (CDTA). This now forms the basis of an established mapping methodology used in academic and practice contexts as a means of visual representation for people's place experience.

In Experiential Landscape, the term *transition* is associated with spatial experience that signals change. We will explain how CDTA, as an integrated system for understanding different characteristics of spatial experience, can be used to further develop the structural qualities of Habraken's margins by recognising the intrinsically transitional quality afforded by their defining dynamic and adaptable nature in both space and time. Specifically we will show how this can be related to territorial themes at the centre of socially restorative urbanism by drawing on a specific type of transition defined in Experiential Landscape as a *segment*: a more complex kind of transitional experience, forming where distinguishable realms merge.

Segments represent elements of urban form that have particular spatial properties related to their varying capacity for territorial occupation and expression: capacity that we understand as the social absorbency inherent in different kinds of segments. We demonstrate in Part III how this is activated by the Experiemic Process: a special participative process developed through Experiential Landscape research. Before doing so, the remainder of Part II establishes the key structural foundations for socially restorative urbanism through the establishment of a typology of segments relating to their potential to deliver different intensities of social absorbency. The key outcome of this is to establish segments as the principal components in the formation of transitional edges: components which, through a collective rebalancing of MTOY relations, activated by the Experiemic Process, optimise the social absorbency of transitional edges. The wider significance of this can be appreciated when we apply the segment principle to the analysis of contemporary urban development. What we find is that we currently tend to build in ways that deliver a relatively narrow range of segment types: usually those with low intensity and therefore low potential for social absorbency. We suggest in response that we need to find ways to deliver urban settings much richer in their range of segment types, and in particular those that can offer greater levels of social absorbency.

As alluded to earlier, the significance of urban edge environments to the social life of towns and cities is far from new, from Jacobs (1961) and Lynch (1960) in the 1960s to Habraken (1998) and Gehl (2010) in more recent years. *Active* and *inactive* edges are terms frequently used in the urban design literature to refer to the capacity of edges to attract and hold social activity and therefore bring life to urban environments. We argue here, however, for an explicit understanding of transitional edges as socio-spatial components of urban fabric. We seek to be able to identify spatial properties which relate to their capacity for social absorbency, but also seek to recognise and respond to these properties as the expressions, at least in part, of social processes that bring them into being and drive their adaptation and change.

With this dual characteristic in mind we address the former by concluding this section with an exploration of the properties of urban edge settings that appear in the wider literature. In doing so, we wish to be able to locate our developing conceptual framework within this wider knowledge area, using it to build a more consistent picture of the properties and characteristics that are associated with their social value. For the purposes of illustration, we can show through a range of international examples, that segments of all types that we identify are observable in the built environment. We will use these to illustrate some of their spatial and physical qualities and discuss some of the social and other environmental benefits that may accrue from the implementation of this conceptual structure. We will then move on to Part III of the book in which we seek to address what we mean by transitional edges and their constituent strings of segments as expressions of social processes, to show how this might be activated and with what material and social gain.

Part III, 'Experiemics', deals with another underpinning motivation of the book which is to recognise the often de-humanising impact of prevailing approaches to urban place-making. We argued earlier that this can have damaging consequences on the well-being of urban inhabitants because of a tendency to unwittingly deliver solutions which polarise territorial experience into a dualism of 'mine' and 'theirs' at the expense of encouraging the experience of 'ours'. Without a sufficiently established sense of belonging, people can become socially isolated, selfish, territorially confrontational, and we find evidence of this at all scales of urban habitation. Although we have tried to show in our development of an anatomy for transitional edges that rebalancing this to give greater prominence to the experience of belonging does have spatial and material implications, which the urban planning, design and management agencies can readily respond to, this is far from all that is required.

A genuine concept of belonging inevitably requires those that belong to be able to participate, at some level great or small, in what they belong to. Being able to exercise the innate human instinct to territorialise, we will show, is vital to the achievement of self-esteem. Identifying, occupying and marking territory is intrinsically participative, yet much of our over-professionalised approach to urban design makes genuine participation extremely difficult to achieve. Specialised language sets up barriers, as do perceptions of superiority of expertise, and even the most enlightened attempts to inject participation into design and development processes through 'consultation' often achieves little more than tokenism.

This final section of the book has, then, two aims. The first is to establish the crucial need for genuine participative processes to be at the core of urban place-making. Not simply because the opinions and values of urban communities need to be heard and heeded by professional agencies who make the places they use, but because there are significant social benefits which are shrouded, obscured and which remain undeveloped without them. This has detrimental consequences for individuals and for society at large, and we argue that, in the context of the current localism agenda, such loss will become increasingly visible.

The second purpose is to discuss the development and application of a participative process, called Experiemics, which we hope may provide a basis from which to begin to develop more socially aware approaches. Experiemics arises from our research into the development of effective participative approaches which aim to develop environmental competence and self-worth in participants as well as helping to inform the shaping of the material and social worlds forming the habitat of ordinary daily life. Specifically, Experiemics provides a means to develop MTOY relationships away from polarisation towards a balance emphasising the importance of achieving belonging (ours).

In Part III, we will outline what we mean by participation in this context, how it relates to the need to deliver a better balance of territorial experience and how it relates to the spatial structures developed previously. We will do this by focusing on the idea of participation as something much more socially significant than as a means to deliver local information into the hands of professional agencies. Instead, we are concerned with the role that participation has in individual and community capacity building, how this may then facilitate more effective development and distribution of social innovation and how this corresponds to a localism agenda. By doing this, we seek to show that participation is both an end in itself and also a means by which individuals and communities can express something about themselves in the surroundings they use and see how this influences its form and fabric.

We then move on to discuss the research work behind the evolutionary development of the Experiemic Process across a range of key themes which include: participatory processes; evaluation; the concept of seeding; methods; language; and operationalisation. The resulting Experiemic Process is then outlined in detail, using examples of its application in the contexts of research-led practice and research-led teaching. Through these examples we will show how significant social and environmental gains can be achieved, often through the accumulated impact of interconnected small-scale interventions, or by the identification of the key interventions necessary to then enable processes of self-organisation to take hold and evolve.

Experiemics is, then, a person-centred process enabling professional agencies, individuals and communities to make socially sustainable solutions in outdoor environments. It is a means to reveal and understand issues often hidden from conventional planning and design processes and addresses an imbalance which often places material and aesthetic considerations before social benefit. Experiemics recognises the value of social networks and the roles of individuals within them. It unlocks their capability to influence change by responding to the way urban settings form around the daily rhythm of social association. The process builds socially restorative environments by revealing and interpreting present experiences and aspirations in the patterns of people's daily life and their potential to influence environmental improvement. The way change progresses is necessarily incremental and time-sensitive, conceptualised as a process of fine-tuning during which minor modifications generate a mutually influential dialogue between gradually changing patterns and management of occupation and social relations, and their physical and spatial context.

The final chapter, 'Conclusions', will reflect on the three parts and how they work together as integrated components of a new conceptual framework for socially restorative urbanism. We suggest that this may form a starting point from which to consider the development of new and better integrated disciplinary systems, with implications for both education and practice. This would recognise the specific importance of transitional edges to the social sustainability of the urban habitat, their understanding as socio-spatial components of urban fabric and the centrality of inclusive participation in their realisation and adaptation.

PART I

BEYOND BOUNDARIES

Developing the concept of socially restorative urbanism

Introduction

> In too many cases, we design for places and people we do not know and
> grant them very little power of acknowledgement ... This floating profes-
> sional culture has only the most superficial conception of particular place.
> Rootless, it is more susceptible to changes in professional fashion and theory
> than to local events.
>
> (Jacobs and Appleyard, 1987, p. 115)

In 1987, Jacobs and Appleyard warned about the potentially damaging consequences that might arise from an increasing influence on urban place-making
from a professional culture which seemed to be increasingly distant from the urban
inhabitants who used it. Their perspective, delivered as part of an attempt to draft
out an urban design manifesto, highlighted that the delivery of urban environments in the latter part of the twentieth century had increasingly been perceived
as a problem requiring professional solution. In consequence, urban dwellers were
seen as recipients of aesthetic and technical expertise and less as acknowledged
participants in the generation and management of places that they used. Some
22 years later, Lord Rogers of Riverside expressed a similar concern about one
of the cornerstone challenges facing progress towards an urban renaissance in
the UK. 'Many of the current problems in English towns and cities lie with the

development professions and businesses, alongside those who regulate them. We have tolerated a lazy over-use of off-the-peg designs and layouts' (Urban Task Force, 1999, p. 50).

In a recent evaluation of the Urban Task Force impact after its first decade, Punter singles out ubiquitous apartment developments as representing a particular failure:

> Undoubtedly the biggest design failing has been the medium and high-rise apartment buildings, which have been widely criticised for their poor architecture, build quality and urban design, lack of energy efficiency, inadequate space standards, amenities and management ... many have had problematic impacts and presented significant failings in terms of liveability, streetscape and neighbourhood amenity.
>
> (Punter, 2011, p. 16)

In too many cases in recent years we seem to be witnessing an increasing number of urban developments that exhibit few of the social ideals embodied in the now widely accepted 'liveable cities' concept (Figure PI.1).

Some argue that we should not perhaps be surprised about this because of a continuing theoretical vacuum in urban design. Cuthbert (2007), for example, suggests that urban design, because of its state of being situated inbetween architecture and planning, has so far been characterised as a fairly chaotic, anarchic, unfounded sequence of creative ideas bearing little or no coherence with each other, and has consequently failed to establish a relationship between design and societal processes. Furthermore, it has failed to create meaningful relationships with important disciplines such as social sciences, economics, psychology and geography. In response is a call to draw on the social science disciplines that have not been brought into mainstream urban design thus far. Urban design, in Cuthbert's view, needs to respond to the fact that the organisation of cities reflects the organisation of society, and space cannot be separated from its social production in specific urban forms.

One of the aims of this book is to offer reflections on how we might make some of the processes of urban place-making more orientated to the human element. There is, of course, nothing particularly new or novel in this aspiration. Indeed, much of the development of urban design theory in the Western world could be said to be characterised by such an aspiration, with many influential and enduring

Figure Pl.1: Striking icon of urban regeneration but what about liveability, streetscape and neighbourhood amenity? Salford Quays, Manchester.

contributions taking an explicitly socially responsive approach in theoretical development and practical advice. By no means an exhaustive list, but among those of particular significance to us here would include: Kevin Lynch (1960), Jane Jacobs (1961), Gorden Cullen (1971), Christopher Alexander (1979), Ian Bentley and colleagues (1985), John Habraken (1998), Karen Franck and Quentin Stevens (2007) and Jan Gehl (2010). In Part II of this volume, we will present a summarised account of a wider review of work relating in particular to the conception of transitional edges, one of the principal components of socially restorative urbanism. In writing this book we acknowledge a deep debt of gratitude to this body of knowledge and how it has inspired and shaped the development of our own ideas. We hope that our own contribution here may usefully add to this by drawing some common threads into sharper focus and possibly introduce some new interpretations.

In pursuit of this aim, one question which continues to crop up time and again in various facets of our work is, why it is that, with the benefit of such influential, evidence-based and generally consistent wisdom, we do not see more contemporary urban development with these human-orientated qualities? It seems that in spite of the presence and application of well-intentioned approaches, concern remains about a lack of sufficient human understanding embedded in the mainstream of urban place-making. This seems to now take on additional significance in light of a growing attention to localism, which aspires to deliver social as well as material and economic solutions, and requires greater degrees of community empowerment.

It seems from our own research and inquiry, however, and from our inter-pretation of the work of others, that the central issue lies with the relationship between professional processes of urban place-making and the capacity of urban inhabitants to experience a sense of belonging within it. Trying to explore, therefore, the nature of the boundaries that inevitably arise between the profes-sional delivery of urban form, essentially a design-related matter, and the processes of occupation and use, an essentially social matter, provides a benchmark for our enquiry. We begin in the South Korean city of Daegu.

Chapter One

New Age-ing Cities

In search of a new discipline for socially orientated urban design

Introduction

In 2011, in the UK, the BBC broadcast a short documentary series presented by journalist Andrew Marr called *Andrew Marr's Megacities*. The programmes were meant to highlight the unique challenges and opportunities to come from the 'greatest social experiment that humanity has ever undertaken': that of unprecedented migration from the countryside to cities. Marr highlighted that this has now accelerated to such a pace that the world is seeing the emergence of increasing numbers of urban agglomerations of more than 10 million inhabitants. Whether these megacities serve humanity for good or ill depends on the decisions we will take in shaping, managing and using them.

One of the things that Marr talks about in this respect is that, despite the huge size of their collective populations, megacities seem to work best when they can operate and be experienced as interconnected accumulations of village-scale communities. Where this happens, the overwhelming, and potentially isolating, impact of the megacity is tempered by a sense of belonging to a more localised collective with its own sense of identity and purpose (Figure 1.1). Marr highlights that this is not necessarily related to contemporary notions of economic prosperity, the drive behind much of our approach to urbanisation, but has more to do with the need to cooperate and share, sometimes to mitigate crushing desperation and poverty, or to simply satisfy a need for social contact and affinity with those around us.

Figure 1.1: Two faces of modern Daegu. The sterility of form-dominant city-edge residential development (left) and the kaleidoscope of tradition and cultural expression in the city market (right).

As Marr points out, these opportunities can be all but obliterated by often well-intentioned, but heavy-handed, planning interventions which see the solution to urban growth and development as purely a matter of decision-making by state or commercial agencies with highly professionalised and bureaucratised levels of control. Through numerous examples, Marr suggests that this can lead to sterile machine-like solutions that, at extremes, have a profound impact on the social and psychological well-being of inhabitants as well as the scale of resource consumption, waste and energy management. In contrast, however, are examples of small-scale enterprise and creativity, of social innovation occurring in hidden corners of the urban fabric, for the most part untouched and ignored by the larger political and development infrastructure, pointing the way to more socially and environmentally sustainable solutions. Marr highlights that optimising the chances that the growth of megacities will lead to socially beneficial outcomes requires identifying the delicate balance of top-down professional levels of control with bottom-up locally generated levels of control.

Against this background, and in the interests of stimulating debate and new directions of thinking, we were delighted to have the opportunity to accept an invitation to convene a special symposium at a conference called 'Continuity and Change of Built Environments: Housing, Culture and Space across Lifespans', hosted in Daegu, South Korea, in October 2011, jointly by the Architectural Institute of Korea and the Housing and Culture and Space in the Built Environment networks of the International Association of People–Environment Studies. Through convening this small symposium we wanted to begin to explore what those concerned with urban design decision-making could contribute to achieving this delicate balance. In particular, are there spatial dimensions to this balance of control that we can identify, describe and ultimately apply that will give the greatest social experiment of humanity a better chance of delivering socially sustainable outcomes?

The symposium was developed and organised by me (KT) and Ombretta Romice, Director of Urban Design at the University of Strathclyde and, at the time, President of the International Association of People–Environment Studies (IAPS). We called the symposium 'New Age-ing Cities', reflecting that social value in the contemporary urban habitat may need to reconnect the form of the urban environment with processes of evolutionary growth and adaptation: a more time-conscious form of urban development amenable to ageing through time, rather than one delivered intact through processes akin to industrial manufacture (Figure 1.2). In many ways a development from our earlier book, *Urban Sustainability through Environmental Design: Approaches to Time–People–Place Responsive Urban Spaces* (Thwaites *et al.*, 2007), the symposium theme and its contributing papers sought to show that this requires a radical rethink of priorities for design in the urban environment; for the way we understand the urban human–environment relationship; and for the professional agencies that currently

Figure 1.2: Mounting global evidence of cities no longer seen as settlements evolving and changing with time. Clarence Dock, Leeds (left); Java Island, Amsterdam (centre); Daegu, South Korea (right).

deliver our urban habitat. We hoped to be able to begin to address the hypothesis that making towns and cities more responsive to social processes may also mean that they become more adaptable in consequence. Through this we sought to promote the restoration of a kind of urban realm characterised by localised change and adaptation through time: a reflection and expression of the social forces that help shape it, rather than simply the static expression of the designer imagination.

We began by defining the concept of New Age-ing Cities as a symbolic antidote to some of the potentially dehumanising consequences of prevalent approaches to urban design, often characterised by: the large scale of development interventions; the commercially led and rapid pace of delivery; a focus on lifestyle over community; and increasing levels of professionalised control in design, delivery and management. Our central assertion was that whatever benefits might initially accrue from these solutions to urban development, they will soon be outweighed by threats to social value.

Central to the concept of the New Age-ing City is the idea of social absorbency, an exploration of urban morphology and the processes of its generation that can increase, rather than decrease, the capacity to attract and hold social activity. Achieving this, we believe, requires disciplinary re-orientation away from the currently segregated architecture, landscape architecture and urban design disciplines towards a professional position in which these fields can become better integrated and recast to embrace wider sociological and psychological aspects of urban human–environment relations. The contributors to this symposium began to provide a foundation from which such a re-orientation might take place, and some of the emergent themes relevant to this book are summarised here. We are, of course, indebted to our friends and colleagues, the symposium contributors, whose work helped us to achieve this. They are: Professor Lineu Castello (Universidade Federal do Rio Grande do Sol, Brazil); Professors Aleya Abdel-Hadi and Kaled Hawas (Helwen University, Egypt); Sabrina Borgianni, Nicoleta Setola and Maria-Chiara Torricelli (University of Florence, Italy); Professor Julia Robinson (University of Minnesota, USA); and Professor Sergio Porta (University of Strathclyde, UK).

Intuitively, and indeed largely supported by observation and experience of urban settings, is that the kind of socially orientated ideals that we seek to achieve are more easily associated with settings that have an inherent human scale about them. As Lineu Castello highlights, this is a major challenge in contemporary cities, and especially those of the scale that Andrew Marr discusses, made all the more problematic by the fact that changes are often marked by the introduction of large interventions which bring about dramatic and abrupt 'new-ness' to the local environments. Frequently, these interventions do not pay enough attention to the cultural and social sustainability of localised situations, entailing changes that provoke serious disruption to socio-spatial structures. In contrast to this, Castello provides examples where he believes that the introduction of such changes can, in certain circumstances, enliven the social value of their locality because of a capacity to give rise to the generation of transitional spaces at their edges. Usually there by accident rather than design, Castello witnesses enthralling opportunities to investigate strategies for transmuting such edges into coherent socio-spatial domains (Figure 1.3).

Castello calls this property *placeleaks*, a kind of energised catalytic character-istic possessed by some edge settings, causing them to become magnetised to

Figure 1.3: Liverpool's Albert Dock. Once a large expanse of disused dock buildings and warehouses, now adapted to accommodate a diversity of social life at its transitional edge.

social action. Very reminiscent of the kinds of 'loose space' discussed by Franck and Stevens (2007), such energies accumulated at interfaces have an aptitude to produce unusual human–environment experiences due to the unsmooth collision of social forces associated with the changes and adaptations inherent therein. There is an evident friction, but this friction generates energy. As a consequence, that energy can be used to enhance the production of lively urban environments, 'there', not by design, but as a consequence of often unplanned appropriation of what Castello refers to as their intrinsic 'between-ness': an ambiguity of interior and exterior, social and material realms, open to interpretation and occupation.

We can, of course, identify many more examples of large-scale building interventions which do not achieve such social status or value, becoming, instead, monumental presences which appear to repel, rather than attract, new social experiences. Ultimately, then, how can spatial organisation contribute to accelerate the transition between built forms and societal processes? Perhaps, then, one of

Figure 1.4: The soul-less edges of Manchester's Spinningfield development.

the key issues lies not with the presence of the building itself, iconic landmark or otherwise, but with the qualities of its interface with its adjacent public realm (Figure 1.4).

Something of the essence of Castello's observations about the significance of emergent 'between' places is echoed by Alexander Cuthbert (2007): 'The need at this point is to move from an intellectual position which discriminates *inside* from *outside* ..., towards a more unified logic' (ibid., p. 210). Such logic would provide the basis from which to explore the 'between-ness' identified by Castello in a more comprehensive and structured way: no longer a haphazard by-product of archi-tectural intervention, but instead a coherent component of urban fabric defined in terms of its capacity to weave together spatial and social dimensions of urban order. With this in mind we began to further develop some collaborative work begun with our urban design colleagues, Ombretta Romice and Sergio Porta, at the Urban Design Studies Unit, University of Strathclyde. This will be detailed in subsequent pages and focuses on one of the central structures in the development of the socially restorative urbanism concept: the transitional edge.

Our ideas about transitional edges are in essence an attempt to conceptualise a distinguishable component of urban order which could be defined in socio-spatial terms, recognising its transient nature as an intrinsic characteristic. Informed by a review of urban settlements, their physical structures and units of development, we initially saw this as a potential candidate for a new kind of urban morphology that would have definable structural qualities amenable to bringing spatial and sociological dimensions of urban order together in a more integrated way. We intended that this would provide an opportunity to better understand and address current approaches to urban design which appeared to be eroding the complexity of edge settings, restricting their capacity to encourage and support the territorial experience that was important to social sustainability.

Transitional edges, as we see them, are coherent socio-spatial domains and not simply boundaries between the architecture and the external public realm. We will describe in the forthcoming chapters how this was taken forward to achieve greater conceptual depth by building from and combining two, as yet unrelated, theoretical structures: aspects of the transition concept associated with Experiential Landscape (Thwaites and Simkins, 2007); and John Habraken's framework of *form* (structurally stable framework), *place* (processes of occupation) and *understanding* (expressions of individual and community ownership) as three inter-related influences on the structure of the ordinary built environment (Habraken, 1998). We will demonstrate how this new conceptual structure can be developed to provide an anatomy for reading different qualities of transitional edges, bringing new insight into their socio-spatial structure and relationship to human territorial activity.

One of the things this helps us to do is reveal that current approaches are often excessively 'form'-orientated, subjugating expressions of 'place' and 'understanding' in the public realm. With this morphological structure, referring to examples drawn from worldwide urban contexts we can show how social sustainability requires a better balance of 'form', 'place' and 'understanding' through optimising opportunities for territorial expression in transitional edges. Currently, we appear to design for a very limited range of transitional edge experiences and need to re-orientate ourselves to ensure the delivery of a much greater diversity of edge types. When this is achieved, and related to a more structured review of literature, a range of themes begin to emerge as significant. The property of *spatial porosity*, for example, a kind of structural catalyst for the kind of *placeleaks* envisaged earlier by Castello, is characterised by open and flexible spatial frameworks which allow

Figure 1.5: The spatial porosity of a Milan street.

diversity of territorial occupation at the human scale, and flexible, easily adaptable use. In association with other properties of *localised expression*, and *coherence and adaptability*, we will discuss in Part II how these form the cornerstones of an anatomy for transitional edges (Figure 1.5).

In many ways the idea of the transitional edge we were beginning to formulate acts as a conceptual bridge capable of linking beneficial socio-spatial characteristics of some large-scale, contemporary urban interventions to those of the, perhaps more familiar, form and fabric of traditional city streetscapes. Abdel-Hadi and Hawas relate this to the patterns of space appropriation in different socio-cultural locations in Cairo streets as a means of demonstrating such settings as places where the tangible forms of physical planning and architecture and the intangible socio-economic and cultural aspects co-exist. In quite a different context and scale to that explored by Castello, is revealed how patterns in different socio-economic levels and their associated behavioural patterns affect the flow of passage, the street façades and the socio-urban and economic sustainability of the street. Abdel-Hadi and Hawas' work shows patterns of space appropriation more obvious in arcades of older districts than in the most recent ones. Arcades and colonnade structures effectively stretch out the margin between built form and open space, creating a transitional edge which is neither one nor the other. Similar in principle to the quality of porosity outlined previously, such structural features generate pockets of territorial potential diversifying social use and patterns of occupation in intrinsically flexible and adaptable ways (Figure 1.6).

Distinguishable places of interface have also emerged as significant in research undertaken in Italian residential suburbs. Borgianni, Setola and Torricelli were able to show through complex observational and mapping methodology the nature of micro-scale relationships between spatial features of urban structure and life in the public realm. Once again, here, not only do the interfaces that embody socio-spatial relationships between public and private, residential and urban space, have their own observable and distinguishable characteristics, but consideration of these characteristics is completely absent in the design and management of building, street, open space networks, with observable detriment to their social success.

This echoes the point made earlier, that although interface or edge environments are widely acknowledged for their significance to the social life of urban areas, they have rarely received systematic attention. In Italy, this is no exception as the results of past experiences of urban regeneration show that the 'weak spots' in the success of redevelopment works are the threshold spaces between

Figure 1.6: Even makeshift colonnade structures like these in Alexandria add porosity to an edge facilitating local identity and cultural expression.

the urban sphere, the public and the most intimate private sphere, where the seemingly opposing needs of privacy and security can co-exist. Borgianni, Setola and Torricelli's observations show that there are some spaces, close to the entrances of buildings, for example, where there is a tendency for people towards domestic use of outer public and semi-public space, suggesting a relationship between the colonisation of spaces and certain spatial features. These elements encourage the social use of the space, further evidence for a close correlation between spatial organisation and encouragement of social acts.

A further, and somewhat differently focused, contribution to the 'New Age-ing Cities' symposium drew attention to another important dimension in the delivery of socio-spatial solutions beyond the capacity of spatial arrangement to encourage social acts. Robinson's experimental architecture design studios show that delivering the New Age-ing City also depends crucially on the capability of planning and design professionals to act in ways compatible with the needs and expectations of those who will eventually inhabit the consequences of their decisions. This project, involving collaboration between architecture students and a local community in the city of St Paul, Minnesota, USA, highlighted the value of collaborative processes in revealing favoured ways to approach increased density in a neighborhood. As Borgianni, Setola and Torricelli had discovered through their observational research in Italian residential areas, there are complex processes at work, especially in urban residential settings, vital to the social health of developments, which are largely unavailable to, or are ignored by, conventional development processes. These are partly spatial, highlighting aspects which can be controlled by design development processes, but they are also partly socially orientated and outside of the control of external agencies. Succeeding here not only holds significant implications for educational practices, but also for the existence and application of appropriate participative processes that can encourage, facilitate and sustain inclusive access to the decision-making processes. This will be a major theme later in the book, in Part III, where we will outline empirical research that has underpinned the development of such a process.

Our conceptual exploration of the New Age-ing City in Daegu helped to highlight that, with the increasing pace and extent of urbanisation across the world, there is growing need for agencies responsible to find ways of becoming more socially conscious in their decision-making processes. As Abdel-Hadi and Hawas demonstrate through their work in Cairo, there can be little doubt that there is a close bond of association between social processes and the physicality of where this takes place. This is a universal feature, present as much in the contemporary urban realm as the traditional, operational at all levels of scale and equally relevant to monumental architectural interventions, as Castello shows, as to the detail of our residential settings, as discussed by Robinson and Borgianni, Setola and Torricelli.

It is notable in our early search to understand the evolutionary nature of urban socio-spatial structures that it is often the interface, or 'between-ness' of things that matters most: either between inside and outside, or between human action and material form. The edges of things stand out as being especially significant to the socio-spatial anatomy of the urban habitat, yet they receive little or no special attention from professional agencies. We respond to this by trying to develop a better understanding of the morphological nature of edge environments and the necessity for them to harmonise the tangibility of physical form and spatial organisation with the intangibility of the cultural life they support. These begin to provide theoretical tools with which to continue to explore with rigour the nature of these realms, and we have begun to experiment with methodologies and educational practices that will substantiate future findings and embed important principles in the development of tomorrow's professionals. We will develop these ideas in subsequent pages, but above all, progress in this will require a holistic and cross-disciplinary mindset: an intellectual orientation capable of synthesising the acts of planning, design and management with better sociological and psychological understandings.

The nature of boundaries: professional, spatial and social

Our explorations in search of more human-orientated approaches to urban design crystallised in the experimental 'New Age-ing Cities' symposium bringing to the surface a number of recurrent themes that would help us to shape further development. These included:

- The significance of edges to the social value of urban settings.
- The nature of edges or interfaces as distinguishable components of city order, but currently without specific disciplinary attention.
- The need to understand such edges as fusions of spatial organisation and social activity – as holistic socio-spatial realms, where space, occupation and use exist in mutual interdependency, and because of this, the realisation that it is not possible to 'design' everything about an edge.
- Certain kinds of spatial organisation seem to be more conducive as attractors for social activity.
- That although socially active edges are perhaps more visible in traditional urban settings, as a consequence of their growth and adaptation through time, the essential socio-spatial characteristics appear to be equally applicable in contemporary cities and to larger-scale architectural interventions.
- As socio-spatial structures, their delivery seems to depend on the achievement of a balance of professional intervention, focused on the delivery of morphological infrastructure, and patterns of occupation and use: the latter often being more prominent in the overall visibility of urban order.

We move on from our brief exploration of the New Age-ing City to set the scene for Chapters 2 and 3, which will concentrate on the significance of the control occupants have over the determination of places they use and that of external professional agencies. This focuses attention on the boundary between the user and the professional specialist and our argument here is that professional interests and levels of control in urban place-making currently far outweigh those of occupants. Later, through reference to John Habraken's (1998) exploration of the structure of ordinary built environments, we suggest that this is leading to the delivery of excessively 'form'-orientated solutions which are rarely sufficiently conducive to encouraging necessary territorial expressions from occupants. One significant question for us here, then, is how to understand where professional interventions must begin to recede to encourage and facilitate the territorial expressions and self-organisation of occupants.

In addition to an interest in the boundaries that characterise relationships between professional agencies and occupants, we also find ourselves drawn to other related kinds of boundaries. As we will later show in Part II, there is a consistent thread of attention in the development of urban design theory given to the importance of edge environments. These are variously defined, but generally converge on what happens at the interface between the built fabric of urban settings and its adjacent open space. There is a detectable consensus that, when this interface is appropriately configured, it has a significant role to play in the social vitality and therefore social sustainability of urban realms. *Active edges* is a term well established in the lexicon of urbanist thinking, highlighting that one of the keystones of successful urban design should be planning and design decisions that can encourage social action at these edges. The most pronounced example of this would be a busy and varied city streetfront, characterised by a variety of retail and leisure outlets which are attractive to people and which to greater or lesser extent project across the interior/exterior threshold. Equally, on a more domestic scale, such active edges can be found in the form of the marginal zones at the front of residential buildings which act to blur the abrupt interface between private and public. Many commentators and researchers, from Jacobs (1961) to Hillier and Hanson (1984) and Gehl (2010), have drawn attention to the value of these transitional strips to increase the likelihood of passive surveillance, social encounter, territorial identity, and so forth, and the significance this has for the social value of the urban environment.

What is fascinating about these kinds of edges, widely and enduringly recognised for their importance to the social value of urban settings, is that they are the very places that tend to receive little or no direct professional attention: they more often than not simply define the end of one kind of professional attention and the

Figure 1.7: 'Loose' acts of occupational expression and management through laundry and food preparation, Delhi, India.

start of another. Franck and Stevens (2007) have called these 'loose spaces': places where 'design intention' is absent, or at least ambiguous, where its appearance as part of the urban landscape is given by acts of occupant appropriation, which may be enduring or fleeting (Figure 1.7). Again, obvious examples include, the way that shops and food outlets will manage their shop–street interface to optimise commercial exposure, or how home owners may demonstrate their individuality, social conformity or status, by the arrangement and maintenance of space immediately adjacent to the dwelling.

These are acts of occupational expression and management, rather than acts of professional design decision-making. At the human scale of ordinary routine experience of the urban realm, they are perhaps the most prominent influence on the way that towns and cities are perceived and experienced, and they tend to occur where pronounced professional determinism begins to recede, leaving places which fall between professional disciplinary focus. Here, what we see and interact with has more to do with expressions of occupancy and use than external professional decision-making and this highlights another kind of boundary between what is materially constructed and what is socially constructed. Again, there is detectable consensus in the literature highlighting such edge environments as elements of urban form that cannot be fully understood as either material or social entities, but exist in some kind of holistic relationship of the two. Furthermore, they tend to be recognised as indeterminate: places of 'becoming' as Kim Dovey (2010) suggests, where processes of appropriation and use continually maintain a steady state of flux and fluidity.

If, then, we accept the significance of such edge environments to the achievement of urban social sustainability, we must also accept that they require specific attention in approaches we adopt in urban place-making. This means understanding something of their form and the processes of their generation: how much can be designed and how much must be left to self-organisation through occupation and use? Because they appear to currently fall between established professional disciplines and because they appear to require understanding as fusions of material fabric and social processes, this presents a challenging prospect with implications for professional boundaries, the boundaries of professional services and user occupancy, and boundaries of the material, spatial and social environment.

In the exploration that follows in this book we will suggest that progress may require a shift of thinking, away from a prevailing emphasis on inwardly focused, largely self-referential professional processes and disciplinary categories, which currently define and more importantly here, divide, what is understood as architecture, landscape architecture, urban design, sociology, psychology, etc., towards a focus of attention on the boundaries between them. We hope that in doing so we might be able to bring into clearer focus the nature of the relationship between these, where they converge rather than diverge, and how this may help us to develop a better understanding of how to deliver the kinds of edge settings that are widely associated with social value in urban realms.

In relation to these settings, for example, what we mean by this is that their nature is not at all easy to categorise: they seem to be defined in terms of what they are 'inbetween', rather than what they 'are'. As we hope to be able to show later in the book, if any form of consensus about their nature is detectable, it is that they are intrinsically transitional, neither entirely interior or exterior, private or public, material or social. As such, they do not fall neatly into the realm of any particular professional group, but fall between professional interests, being partly architectural, interior design, urban design, landscape architectural, and in relation to their human dimensions, neither entirely sociological, anthropological or psychological. Our assertion here is that, because they cannot be entirely captured within the territory of any specific professional or disciplinary category, they have never been fully addressed at all. We simply do not have a specific professional body, or academic discipline, equipped to deal with anything other than specialist parts of what they are in entirety. Even if we did, so much of the form and function of these marginal settings depends on indeterminate patterns of appropriation, occupation and use, which change and adapt across time and space according to prevailing circumstances, that even if there were a specific profession of 'the edge', it could do only so much to influence how the object of its attention would appear.

We feel that we are dealing here, therefore, with something that has to be understood, not only as holistic integration of the material, spatial and social, but also something which puts limitations on the role of any kind of professional intervention in its manifestation. Professional and occupant influences must then become inclusive and mutually informative, and structural and design decision-making must cross the boundaries between material, spatial, social and psychological considerations.

Addressing boundaries: some thoughts on material, spatial and social integration

Similar demands have, in fact, characterised the development of urban design thought in the West for almost half a century, beginning perhaps with Jane Jacobs' observations of city street life. Jacobs' *The Death and Life of Great American Cities* (1961) to this day remains a seminal statement about the social sustainability of cities and highlights two things central to our discussion here. One of these is that, if we are to deliver successful cities for people, then planning and design decisions must be led by understanding of the social processes that keep cities alive. The second is that this often comes to focus on the quality of the interface between building and street, particularly the capacity of streets to encourage and support the occupation and appropriation of space on them. Both these issues point emphatically for Jacobs to a view of the 'life' of a city being dependent on understanding the city as intrinsically social where material fabric and spatial organisation must reflect and accommodate the social nature of urban order. Urban morphology and social aspects simply cannot be meaningfully decoupled and this has to become a fundamental cornerstone of our efforts towards better forms of urban social sustainability.

We can find numerous instances throughout the development of urban design theory of attempts to try to do this in various ways. By way of example, a few notable contributors are highlighted here. Among the first to understand the anatomy of cities from a human perspective, and thereby begin to find ways to integrate human psychological functioning with spatial organisation and form, is Kevin Lynch's seminal work *The Image of the City* (1960). Here, the concept of imageability is attributed to visual messages given by aspects of a city's spatial and physical arrangement that help people orientate. After Lynch it became more possible, and plausible, to understand city form in relation to human psychological functioning rather than just as assemblages of buildings and spaces.

This became something of a cornerstone in the work of some architectural theorists during the 1970s as conceptions about the psychology of place began to be better understood (Maslow, 1968; Canter, 1977; Tuan, 1980). Notable and enduring contributions, for example, can be found in the work of Christian Norberg-Schulz (1971) and Christopher Alexander (Alexander *et al.*, 1977; Alexander, 1979) in particular. Norberg-Schulz's phenomenological interpretation of human–environment relations proposes an approach to place-making based on a holistic relationship between human functioning and the locations where this takes place. This was a more complex level of integration between people and their surroundings than Lynch had envisaged, suggesting that there are spatial dimensions to human existence which are just as significant as the psychological, cultural and social dimensions, for example. If these spatial dimensions could be identified and understood, then the task for professional place-making agencies was to see to it that they were incorporated into planning and design decisions so as to harmonise human functioning with its spatial settings more closely.

A focus on the 'fit' between human functioning and space is the embodiment of Christopher Alexander's exhaustive exploration of the holistic relationship between people and their spatial settings (Alexander *et al.*, 1977; Alexander, 1979). Alexander's biographer, Steven Grabow (1983), acknowledges a common ground of understanding between Norberg-Schulz's view of human–environment relations and that of Alexander, whose essential contribution is to move away from focus on features and objects, or buildings and spaces, altogether and concentrate instead entirely on the relationships between them and the people who interact with them. An important aspect to this understanding, developed by Chermeyeff and Alexander (1963) in the early 1960s, is the concept of spatial hierarchy, suggesting that it is important for people to be able to distinguish in their surroundings degrees of public-ness and private-ness, because this has an important bearing on the way people behave. In many ways this is an architectural expression of the ideas of anthropologist Edward Hall (1959, 1963, 1966) who elaborates details of the way people occupy and relate to territory suggesting that territories can be likened to a series of expanding and contracting fields of space that people continuously carry around with them. He considers that humans have situational personalities related to spatial distances and in so doing makes a significant contribution to defining the nature of the disciplinary boundary between anthropology and spatial planning and design.

By relating human psychological functioning to spatial principles and then arguing that these concerns lie at the heart of successful human occupation and use of urban settings, such contributions lay the foundations for what is increasingly understood as urban social sustainability, beginning to provide criteria with which it might be captured and evaluated qualitatively and quantitatively. Particularly influential in this respect is the work of Jan Gehl and Lars Gemzoe (Gehl, 1996; Gehl and Gemzoe, 2000, 2004) who have identified a range of simple human needs, the presence or absence of which gives a qualitative indication of sense of place. In relation to the influence of space on social activity, the empirical work of Hillier and Hanson (1984) presents comprehensive evidence that a high density of linked spatial enclosures, defined in terms of their convex geometrical characteristics, is directly related to a neighbourhood's potential for social inter-action. Like Norberg-Schulz, Hillier and Hanson conclude that there are spatial dimensions, as well as personal and cultural ones, to the sociability of urban settings. Another attempt to quantify the social sustainability of urban environ-ments can be found in the streetscape indicators framework developed by Sergio Porta and John Renne (2005). From research carried out in Western Australia, eight indicators are proposed that they associate with the social sustainability of streets. Taken generally, the indicators seem to suggest that the socially sustainable street is one that has an overall sense of visual coherence and continuity, but at the same time has a fine grain of localised variation, perhaps given by visual variety in building façade detail, street furniture and paving surfaces, for example.

The purpose of this, inevitably highly selective, account of contributors to theory and practice is to highlight that there is a strong and enduring humanistic aspiration in the background of urbanist thinking. There is evidence to support that the essence of ideas to emerge from these and other[1] examples of research and intellectual development, particularly that quality of place must include explicit human psychological and behavioural dimensions, has been translated to greater or lesser degrees in recent UK political drives towards urban regeneration. Initially embodied in the Urban Task Force's (1999) call for an urban renaissance, principles of human value rather than economic growth were meant to provide a stimulant for the repopulation of cities.

The challenges of achieving this in ways that can influence practice have proved, however, to be considerable and a recent review of the current state of urban design theory in the West would suggest that, for some at least, progress made to date remains far from adequate (Cuthbert, 2007; Punter, 2011). There is clearly scope for considerable further development, and it is with this in mind that we intend to try in this book to look at what can be done through focusing on ways in which urban morphology and social issues can be brought into a unified conceptual framework. In highlighting the significance of boundaries here, between professional agencies and occupants, between the social and material dimensions of urban order, between interior and exterior realms, for example, we seek not so much to break these boundaries, but rather to recognise that it may be the intrinsic nature of the boundaries themselves that requires our attention.

In so doing, we are trying to imagine a different kind of professional agency which can recognise progress towards the delivery of socially sustainable solutions, beginning with an understanding of urban order from a uniquely socio-spatial perspective, in which morphological and social dimensions are complementary expressions of the same whole. If such a thing can be experienced, we believe that its development will require a focus on urban edge environments as the most prominent expression of that socio-spatial realm, and for those environments to be understood as emergent and becoming where their material and spatial structure, and their occupation and use, are delivered in much more integrated ways than is often the case at present. We will show in what follows how we believe this can be achieved in principle through the development of an anatomy of edges, which we will call *transitional edges*, and through a unique process of participative practice, called *Experiemics*.

Chapter Two

Balance of control at the margins

Introduction

In this chapter, in order to begin to respond to the issues of boundaries discussed earlier, we will discuss John Habraken's (1998) analysis of the structure of the ordinary built environment and the role of people in its development. Habraken sees the structure of the ordinary as the interplay of different levels of control which he calls form, place and understanding. As the foundation for our search for a way to explore the socio-spatial dimensions of the urban realm, Habraken's conception of form, place and understanding provides a framework that relates physical structure and spatial organisation directly to patterns of human behaviour. It provides us with a place to begin to formulate a socially orientated approach to urban morphology, which we will call *transitional edges*, directly related to territorial activity through occupation and the expression of that occupation in the material world.

Habraken provides a conceptual structure from which to develop bridges between the social and physical dimensions of urban realms, highlighting that territorial issues at the margins of the social and material world are especially important. It enables us to show that we often currently deliver excessively form-driven solutions which may subjugate expressions of place and understanding. Place and understanding are essentially concepts that can be related to human well-being, via issues of territorial expression, development of self-esteem and the experience of belonging, yet we find that these important human–environment interactions can be restricted by prevailing approaches to urban design and development. Our aim in what follows is to try to find ways in which we may be able to restore a better balance of form, place and understanding in our urban place-making; to emphasise that there are implications for human well-being in this balance and that such balance may be especially visible at the edges where human activity and material form interact. Important in this respect is the principle of participation and how this relates to processes of self-organisation which must begin to recognise and value the delivery of social as well as material gains. This will be discussed in detail at the beginning of Part III, setting the scene for our development of the Experiemic Process which we propose as a practical way forward to rebalance form, place and understanding which is relevant in particular to the UK localism agenda.

Evolutionary urban morphology and socially sustainable urban design

> This order is all composed of movement and change, and although it is life, not art, we may fancifully call it the art form of the city and liken it to the dance – not to a simple-minded precision dance with everyone kicking up at the same time, twirling in unison and bowing off en-masse, but to an intricate ballet in which the individual dancers and ensembles all have distinctive parts which miraculously reinforce each other and compose an orderly whole.
>
> (Jacobs, 1961, p. 50)

John Habraken's socially orientated perspective has a lot in common with Jane Jacobs, at least to the extent of recognising that social action plays a pivotal role in how some aspects of the urban fabric are formed. Like Habraken, Jacobs' vision of urban order is not only social in nature but also intrinsically dynamic, characterised by the continuous movement and change of people's daily interactions with one another and their surroundings. As this happens, people change and adapt themselves, others in their community and their structural fabric continuously, yet somehow manage to retain a recognisable and enduring sense of order. Once again in common with Habraken, Jacobs identified life at the interface of building frontages and their adjacent public realm as particularly significant to the generation of necessary diversity and mixed use. Despite the considerable reach of Jacobs' influence on the development of urbanist thought over much of the last half century, concern is expressed that there seems little to show for it in the fabric of urban renaissance in Britain today (Punter, 2011).

Figure 2.1: An intricate ballet of movement and change. Urban theatre in Chester, UK.

In response to this, we will focus on edge environments which constitute the socio–spatial margins between built form and adjacent public realm, emphasising how their social value can be enhanced by adopting a different approach drawn from a better understanding of and use of principles of urban morphology. Our assertion is that by increasing our attention on such edge environments, especially by developing an understanding of their form and the way social processes can become active there, we can begin to make frameworks to help deliver more socially sustainable urban design solutions. Additionally, we emphasise that 'designing' without sufficient awareness of societal consequences is likely to remain a significant obstacle to the delivery of socially sustainable solutions. The act of design, in the relatively recent history of town and city development, seems to have become progressively detached from some of the social processes regarded as important to the well-being of urban inhabitants (Alexander, 1979; Habraken, 1998; Cuthbert, 2007).

In what follows, we will begin to develop some ideas which we hope may contribute to the further development of interest in the social value of edge environments by building a conceptual framework in which the built form, open space and social dimensions in urban settings can be brought together as an integrated system. We will explain how this concept brings into sharper focus the importance of a socio-spatial component of the urban environment we will call transitional edges. In building this conceptual framework, we see particular relevance for application in the kind of mixed-use, compact urban development increasingly associated with the delivery of urban social sustainability (Rudlin and Falk, 1999; Urban Task Force, 1999; Gehl, 2010) (Figure 2.2).

We suggest, first, that transitional edges need to be thought of as coherent domains in their own right and not simply as the boundary between the architecture and the external public realm. In using the term *transitional edges* we wish to highlight their complex and intrinsic transformational nature: not just as realms of transition from one place to another, but as places formed and transformed as much by patterns of occupation and use as their spatial and structural properties. Central here is the effect of transitional edges on people's behaviour. Their intrinsic fluidity, which does not restrict or exclude a certain type of use or

Figure 2.2: Overlapping dwelling, work and leisure opportunities in Manchester's Castlefields development (left) and some earlier phases of regeneration in the Calls and Riverside, Leeds, for example, Victoria Quays (right), have some enduring hallmarks of sustainable compact urban development.

user, has potential to create a positive sense of belonging and ownership, unlike other more rigidly and prescriptively designed spaces. This has particular relevance in relation to the wider aim of inclusive design, an approach to disability studies which does not target disabled people as its audience, but foresees inclusion as an 'equity and quality (of life) issue for everyone' (Imrie and Hall, 2001, p. 18). We will discuss research we have undertaken with learning disability communities in Part III, highlighting the importance of inclusive settings to the integration and empowerment of these communities into society, and the pro-active part they can play in contributing to the delivery of inclusive settings for all. Such holistic interplay of the social and spatial therefore highlights a particular characteristic of our developing concept of transitional edges which may be especially important to the wider social sustainability of urban environments. Current approaches to urban design often act to erode the complexity of these edges, restricting their capacity to encourage and support territorial experience important to social sustainability (Figure 2.3). Gehl illustrates this as a process: 'The human dimension – overlooked, neglected, phased out' (2010, p. 2).

Second, we assert that by de-scaling the way that transitional edges are generated, emphasising the plot rather than the block as the fundamental unit of urban form, particularly at ground level, we can begin to examine more clearly the social relevance of the relationship of plot to streetscape and how this can support a wide diversity of experiential and functional opportunity. The interface of plot to public realm is manageable in this respect because it is more conducive to an informal interaction scale which larger units overshadow, inhibit or simply do not encourage in humans because they do not afford sufficient variety. This should not be understood as a call for a return to the traditional urban layouts usually associated with historic towns and cities. As Lineu Castello shows, in relation to the discussion of New Age-ing Cities in Chapter 1, awareness of the social significance of transitional edges does not necessarily prohibit large-scale architectural interventions commonly associated with contemporary cities, nor is it necessarily in conflict with the economic and political circumstances that underpin their development. The application of such awareness is, however, less likely to lead to the delivery at ground level of lengthy, disengaging and socially sterile façades which can become ubiquitous in many urban areas and which are especially vulnerable to changing economic conditions (Figure 2.4).

Third, in order to address concerns about a lack of societal awareness in urban design theory, the transitional edge framework can be given a specifically

Figure 2.3: 'The human dimension – overlooked, neglected, phased out'. The tiny speck of a person to the left of the boat serves to highlight the sheer scale of the injustice. Lincoln waterfront.

sociological interpretation by relating it to human territorial activity. We will discuss how achieving and sustaining a sense of self-worth and self-esteem are intimately related to the opportunities people have to express territoriality in places they use, how this is restricted by some aspects of the prevailing approach and how this can be restored by adopting alternatives (Figure 2.5). By this means we argue that certain types of urban spatial organisation may be more conducive to sustaining the social well-being of urban populations, and that achieving this requires greater levels of active participation than current approaches often allow.

Control, territoriality and the balance of form, place and understanding

John Habraken's (1998) perspective on the fabric of the ordinary built environment is that it is more about the levels of control that can be exercised by people who

Figure 2.4: The scars of changing economic conditions on the urban landscape become profoundly explicit when they impact on lengthy sterile and socially disengaging façades.

use it than it is about the 'design' of physical structures. What Habraken means by 'ordinary' in this context is the wide fabric of the built environment of human habitation, where the routine of daily life occurs, which until relatively recently managed to evolve and be sustained without the sort of professional attention it receives today:

> For thousands of years, built environments of great richness and complexity arose informally and endured. Knowledge about how to make ordinary environment was ubiquitous, innately manifest in the everyday interactions of builders, patrons and users. Built environment arose from implicit structures based on common understanding.
>
> (Habraken, 1998, p. 2)

Figure 2.5: Some territorial gestures may be fleeting and theatrical, as in Manchester's Exchange Square (left), or may be more enduring expressions signalling occupation and personality, as in the Greek town of Parga (right). Urban structure needs to be configured to encourage and accommodate territorial behaviours of all kinds to give texture and life to urban order.

Habraken points to an expansion of architectural influence during the modern era that now sees almost every part of the built environment as a design problem to be solved: 'Ordinary growth processes that had been innate and self-sustaining, shared throughout society, have been recast as problems requiring professional solution' (ibid., p. 3).

Resonant with Jacobs, Habraken sees the ordinary built environment as something evolutionary in character: that which occurs where human habitation and material form interact. It is the nature of the interaction that generates the form and, for this reason, Habraken says, environment cannot be invented, in the sense that it can be predetermined in all its parts and then made. Habraken describes how urban order evolves out of an inter-relationship of three levels of control he calls form, place and understanding (Figure 2.6). Form is what establishes an organising, structurally stable infrastructure that can then be occupied. Particular spaces within infrastructures become controlled as occupants determine what and who comes in and stays out. In Habraken's view, occupation transforms space into place and therefore has an explicitly territorial meaning related to the human impulse to control our surroundings by identifying and defining territory. Habraken's third level of control is that of understanding. This means the general desire in humans to relate to one another via common structures or

Figure 2.6: Harmonious balance of form, place and understanding in the Croatian city of Dubrovnik. The heavily perforated *form* of the old town walls (left) absorbs a network of occupation (centre). As space become *place* through occupation, sense of neighbourhood belonging is sustained through common *understanding* about use of shared areas (right).

shared meanings, for example, cultural, ideological, aesthetic, and so on. If place is driven by territorial factors, understanding is essentially social in nature. What appears visible results from the resolution of tensions between the biological need for people to assert their individuality through territorial expression and the wider need for personal assertions to remain within commonly accepted norms.

Habraken argues that the structure of the ordinary is essentially a visible manifestation of the way people act as social beings in exercising control in the built environment. The overlapping relationships between levels of control create active and continuously shifting patterns of occupation and expression, creating a kind of margin at an indeterminable boundary where the control neces-sarily exerted by specialists gradually gives way to the social forces of occupants. Although such margins retain a form of stability and coherence over time, they may in fact be in continual change as the patterns of occupation and control ebb and flow with objects placed for short or longer periods, according to local custom, practicality and negotiation between neighbours.

Something of the balance of form, place and understanding in terms of terri-torial behaviour can be observed in beach etiquette, the unwritten and largely subconscious way in which sun worshippers the world over organise themselves and their belongings in modifications to temporary territories according to their personal needs and comforts (Figure 2.7). At the start of each day the *form* of plots is given by the beach keeper through the formal arrangement of umbrellas and sun beds. Plots gradually become territorialised as occupiers take control,

Figure 2.7: Balance of form, place and understanding as the 'ordinariness' of beach culture plays out throughout the day.

making minor modifications to the original arrangement, personalising their chosen plot and thereby making their *place*. Thousands of tiny adaptations change the 'settlement' throughout the day in continuous evolution, as the sun position moves and the occupants come and go. The sense of an orderly, coherent and recognisable whole is retained throughout the performance through unwritten, yet acknowledged, common *understanding* that determines the limits of acceptable modification and maintains mutually acceptable boundaries between plots. Beach culture is settlement evolution compressed into the timescale of one day. It is in continuous flux, adaptation and change, providing for personal needs and preferences while maintaining the harmony of the whole. It is a balance of form, place and understanding that sustains for the most part without need for formal language, explicit rules or external controls.

The accumulation of many such small adaptations over time makes these marginal areas highly dynamic, places where territory may be implied by the physical fabric of buildings, but may actually move about in response to ongoing acts of occupation. Habraken is clear that special professional know-how is necessary to make gravity-resistant structures, especially at large scales, but says such know-how has to include a realisation that space and time must be left for innate territorial and social processes to find their own expression. Urban regeneration based on large-scale spatial interventions and compressed timescales squeezes such opportunities.

Habraken's analysis is primarily based on how different levels of control influence the structure of the built environment, and significant within this is the concept of territoriality, particularly sociological understandings, and how this is

Figure 2.8: Thriving shop windows, like this delicatessen-café in Milan (left), blend interior and exterior realms becoming part of the life and theatricality of the street. Unused shop fronts have the opposite effect, deadening the street, and if the block is large enough, like this one in Chester (right), the impact is greater.

achieved and sustained through communication. Anthropological studies suggest that processes of communication sustain a sense of territorial awareness so that, as well as being rooted in individuals, territories are stabilised by groups through shared activities and common language: 'City people are constantly making and unmaking places by talking about them. A network of gossip can elevate one shop to prominence and consign another to oblivion ... in a sense a place is its reputation' (Tuan, 1980) (Figure 2.8).

Territorial associations can be powerful influences on people's place attachment and apply in both private and public realms. Altman (1975), in particular, has provided a categorisation of territorial experience which shows a complex inter-relationship of individual and collective processes behind the development of territorial awareness and behaviour according to the intensity of psychological centrality a space holds (Bonnes and Secchiaroli, 1995). Primary territory, for example, implies relatively high levels of psychological centrality and tends to focus on the individual or intimate group, where territoriality is often expressed through acts of personalisation and lengthy periods of sustained occupation: the dwelling place and immediate vicinity, for example. Conversely is public territory: a favoured table in a street café, or routinely used seat on a bus, for example.

Figure 2.9: Reading corner, Stockholm, Sweden. Duration of occupation may be short but the sense of territorial attachment develops with frequency of use and association with particular activities.

Here, the strength of psychological centrality diminishes due to the increased awareness of a wider and openly accessible public context. Although duration of occupation here tends to be short, the sense of territorial attachment develops with frequency of use (Figure 2.9). Primary and public forms of territoriality lean mainly towards the capability of individuals to control the circumstances of their occupation, albeit within some temporal and social parameters. Between primary and public, however, is the concept of secondary territory, which is much more subject to controls at the level of community. A typical example here would be a social club or society where an individual may feel territorial association, or a sense of belonging, but within which territorial expressions, such as freedom of access, duration of stay, degrees of personalisation, for example, are dependent, not on individuals, but on communities that have control over these territories through possession (ibid.).

Relevant here is how this understanding of territorial experience points to a complex and innately experienced phenomena that binds together social and spatial dimensions of human existence with their individual and community implications. This kind of territorial awareness can be related to human psychological health in terms of the need to achieve self-esteem and affirmation. Through their mental and physical actions, individuals make their ideas into something permanent and thereby become aware that they have a mind of their own. When actions receive positive recognition from others, individuals can enjoy self-esteem, a crucial component in the development of self-identity (Honneth, 1995). Honneth identifies recognition as a vital human need and this requires a mutually supporting community where individuals experience themselves as having status either as a focus of concern, a responsible agent, or as a valued contributor in a shared project. The fulfilment of these higher-order needs (Maslow, 1968) in contemporary society is the catalyst for the satisfaction of other related higher-order needs: a positive process of individual and collective growth which requires an infrastructure to develop. This infrastructure has to do with social as well as spatial relationships and the possibility of exerting a degree of independent control over the spaces used. This resonates with the overlapping relationship between Habraken's second and third levels of control: people act to control territory and make *place*, while the need to belong tends to control extremes of territorial expression through awareness and recognition of a common *understanding*. The framework of common understanding is what, for Honneth, provides the context of recognition that is central to the achievement of self-esteem (Figure 2.10). Another way to talk about Habraken's concept of common understanding, effectively Honneth's context of recognition, is to relate it to the experience of a sense of 'ours', or the sensation of belonging. We will discuss how this can be developed as an essentially territorial and inclusive linguistic approach in Chapter 3.

Figure 2.10: 'Ours': belonging to the river's edge community of Uppsala, Sweden.

Chapter Three

The socially restorative urban environment

Introduction

In Chapter 2, we discussed issues relating to control balance in the creation of socially sustainable urban development, suggesting that a redress of balance might be needed that can facilitate greater levels of meaningful user participation. At the beginning of Part III, we will discuss how this is beginning to be seen as consistent with a developing political and social emphasis on localism and the ways in which policy and practice agencies are responding with the development of operational strategies. In this chapter we will develop ideas relevant to this by referring to the restorative capacity of the environment. The ability of environments to provide restorative experiences has to be one of the most potent social benefits possible. It raises the possibility of significant gains to public health and well-being, as well as community cohesion and the delivery of social capital, by means of particular arrangements in the content and organisation of the environmental settings that people routinely use.

We begin here by outlining that environment has long been understood to have restorative capability and this awareness can be seen reflected in the arrangement of built form throughout history, underpinning an expanding interest in restorative environments research within the discipline of environmental psychology in present times. Here, we will build from this with a particular focus on speculation about the spatial implications of environmental restoration in an attempt to expand the concept of the restorative environment to embrace a wider range of issues relating in particular to the urban environment. We discuss, in particular, the significance of this to a move in the direction of a more localist agenda, suggesting that this involves a shift of thinking towards delivery of social as well as material and economic gains. This again relates to the fundamental requirement for people to experience a sense of belonging as a vital human need, central, as Honneth (1995) demonstrates, to sustaining self-identity and self-esteem. Two aspects here are especially significant. One is the need for spatial arrangements capable of generating opportunities for belonging, associated with social absorbency and the particular significance of edge settings in this respect, which will be developed in more detail in Part II. The second, discussed here, is the importance of inclusive language. We will articulate this in terms of a framework of fundamental human experience centred on how we become aware of what is *mine, theirs, ours* and *yours* (MTOY). We will show how the framework of MTOY as an inclusive communicative approach in the context of Habraken's concept of control provides an intellectual and practical bridge between social and spatial dimensions of the urban realm.

Developing the socially restorative environment

Restorative environments research has its formative roots in environmental psychology and is concerned with developing an understanding of environments that promote the restoration of depleted psychological, physiological and social resources. Stephen and Rachel Kaplan (1989), and others (Ulrich, 1979, 1984; Hartig *et al.*, 1991; Hartig, 2004), show that people, particularly in urban environments, can suffer mental fatigue and decreased attention span as a consequence of the stresses associated with the continuous stimulation and decision-making that urban living often demands. Escape from urban stress has been a principal factor in encouraging people to migrate from cities to peaceful green suburbs as soon as their economic and social mobility allows. Making city places that can, in some way, 'restore' must be an important part of encouraging people to return to city living and, perhaps importantly, to stay and raise families there.

Contributors like the Kaplans, Roger Ulrich and Terry Hartig show that people experience tangible benefits to physical and mental well-being through contact with certain kinds of open space. Their research contributes to growing evidence that contact with, or even simply awareness of, natural elements such as water and vegetation can deliver restorative experiences. Important though this is in helping to shape public parks and gardens (Kaplan *et al.*, 1998) and in highlighting the importance of informal natural settings in urban environments (Jorgenson and Keenan, 2008), it tells us relatively little about the ordinary streetscapes and built-up places where we live and work every day. As Gehl (1996), Jacobs (1961), Whyte (1980) and others show, people gravitate to places where there are people and seem intuitively to recognise that urban settings can offer benefits regardless of predominance or even necessarily the presence of natural elements. May there be, then, other dimensions to human restorative experience particularly relevant in urban settings that warrant inquiry?

We advance here that there may well be and suggest that it is important for this to receive more systematic research than has perhaps taken place to date, to develop further our understanding of these potential dimensions of urban restorative capability. Our assertion in this respect is that fruitful avenues of research might be focused on spatial organisation and particularly the capacity of urban streetscapes to act as networks of linked spaces associated with a wide diversity of functional and experiential opportunities. In Part II, we will further develop our hypothesis on this by describing a potential candidate in the form of a morphological structure called the transitional edge. Transitional edges are proposed as socio-spatial components of the urban realm which, we suggest, when combined with the participative processes that we develop in Part III, offer the potential to achieve a more socially optimal balance of form, place and understanding, as discussed in Chapter 2. We suggest that, if indeed it can be demonstrated that there is an intrinsic social dimension to urban restorative experience, then this approach to urban morphology is particularly compatible owing to the way in which social processes, spatial organisation and material form are integrated. In order to provide foundations for this, however, we will first briefly outline a background to the development of restorative understandings of environment.

That landscape settings have the capacity to benefit human health and well-being has been well established by research, particularly in the field of environmental psychology (Ulrich, 1984; Kaplan and Kaplan, 1989). At the start of the twenty-first century, however, in the midst of a renaissance in urban regeneration that calls for liveable towns and cities capable of accommodating and sustaining contemporary urban lifestyles, urban open spaces that have restorative potential are perhaps more necessary than ever before. The World Health Organization states that health is not the mere absence of illness, but means physical, social and mental well-being (Mercer, 1975). In this context, then, the term *restorative* is used in this general sense to explore the potential of outdoor settings in towns and cities to provide a general sensation of revival or renewal, mitigating the stress and mental fatigue which can arise from prolonged exposure to some aspects of urban environments (Figure 3.1).

Harnessing the landscape and natural elements to induce reflective and contemplative states of mind for restorative benefit has its roots in antiquity, particularly in the institutional health care facilities of the Greeks and Romans and in the more spiritually orientated Islamic paradise gardens. Spatial considerations, such as the Greek *asklepieia*, which aided patient recovery with wards that had southern orientation, and the Roman *valetudinarium* hospitals with central courtyards to allow patients access to fresh air and ambulation, appear to have been regarded as significant health-inducing features (Westphal, 2000). Again with a strong emphasis on spatial organisation, Islamic paradise gardens provided ordered oases in otherwise hostile environments, representing the heavenly paradise described in the Quran. British monastic cloister gardens were designed with patients' cells facing an

Figure 3.1: Natural elements inducing reflective and contemplative states of mind in a Venice park.

arcaded courtyard offering sunlight, shade, seasonal plants and places to walk and sit. These gardens were also intended to induce a spiritually reflective mood by providing access to nature in a safe and ordered environment (Gerlach-Spriggs *et al.*, 1998). In the seventeenth and eighteenth centuries, the dual emergence of scientific medicine and the broad cultural movement of Romanticism combined to encourage the re-emergence of usable gardens for hospital patients (Cooper-Marcus and Barnes, 1995). Romanticism promoted the role of nature in bodily and spiritual restoration and these green spaces were sometimes intentionally arranged to form park-like spaces for convalescents, hospital staff and visitors alike (Gerlach-Spriggs *et al.*, 1998, p. 22).

Twentieth-century advances in medical science combined with technical advances in high-rise construction, along with increasing demand for cost-effective efficiency, brought about more compact multi-storey medical complexes. If it was present at all, landscape became largely cosmetic and bore no relation to historic ideas that natural areas could have a bearing on the healing process. Experiments like Roger Ulrich's influential study of surgical patients in 1984, in which he showed patients with a view of 'nature' recovered more quickly and took fewer drugs than a control group, have perhaps contributed to a resurgent interest in the restorative potential of natural elements in particular (Ulrich, 1984). Ulrich's work along with the Kaplans' empirical work in wilderness settings provides some of the key foundations for what has developed into modern restorative environments research (Hartig, 2004).

Today there is a rapidly growing and internationally influential community involved in restorative environments research providing what is now commonly regarded as irrefutable evidence for the restorative effects of exposure to natural settings and features. Yet, despite this achievement, its impact on design decision-making seems to remain tenuous. Interestingly consistent with our discussion in Chapter 2 about the potentially obstructive influence of disciplinary boundaries, the Kaplans and their colleagues have suggested that a general inertia in the application of restorative environments research in design decision-making might relate to difficulties in the language of research translating into design practice (Kaplan *et al.*, 1998). Although the Kaplans' findings derive from a research programme in wilderness settings, an interesting parallel can be drawn with urban lifestyles through their association of restorative potential with the mitigation of mental fatigue that can arise through long periods of concentration. They argue that this is a special kind of tiredness that does not preclude engagement with certain types of activity that can assist recovery from mental fatigue. In general, this is based on the relationship that exists between the mental world that can be imagined and the physical surroundings. Their work conceptualises four characteristics of settings (being away, extent, fascination and compatibility) that, when combined, can facilitate this kind of restorative benefit (ibid.):

- *Being away* refers to the capacity of the mind to wander and induce a sensation of being in another, desirable, location that is different from the one causing the fatigue, perhaps stimulated by a view through a window, for example.
- *Extent* is a characteristic of settings that offer the opportunity to contemplate breadth of scope and possibility. Places that may be relatively small but where boundaries are not easily discernible might offer such potential.
- *Fascination* refers to properties of places or things that engage and hold the attention by stimulating a sensation of wondering and mental challenge.
- Finally there is the requirement for a setting to be *compatible* with expectations and inclinations.

Figure 3.2: The generous naturalistic margins that characterize the landscape of Hammerby Sjostad, Stockholm demonstrate how the greening of edges can provide restorative opportunities for residents and visitors, as well as enhancing habitat creation and the delivery of other ecosystem services.

Many, including the Kaplans themselves, interpret this restorative environments framework as evidence in support of settings with a predominance of vegetation and other natural elements as the ones most conducive to its delivery (Figure 3.2). While the growing weight of empirical research in this field does indeed provide ample support for the benefits of natural settings in this respect, there is no obvious reason to assume that the combined experiences of being away, extent, fascination and compatibility are to be found exclusively in such places. At the root of these lie implications for certain kinds of spatial arrangement, capable of inducing the sense of being away and extent, for example, combined with socially orientated experiences related to psychological (fascination) and participative (compatibility) engagement. It is logical, in principle, that urban environments, regardless of their vegetative content, can deliver these experiences if they are configured in their material elements and spatial configurations to draw together the physical and mental worlds, stimulating the mind to wander, to contemplate and wonder, and to find satisfaction in the realisation of expectations. Scopelliti and Giuliani (2004) are notable among very few researchers to have tried to address this, highlighting in particular the potential of historic buildings in restorative processes (Figure 3.3).

We suggest here that further work in the field of restorative environments research might focus more on the urban realm and in particular on the possibility that social dimensions of urban life can contribute to human restorative experience, but in different ways. Restorative environments have been understood as those that have non-demanding content: generally, features that engage the mind without the need for directed concentration. Rooted in 'Attention Restoration Theory' (Kaplan and Kaplan, 1989), the central premise is that people can be restored to better levels of concentration when they spend time within and also looking at natural places that offer opportunities for effortless attention. This instinctively seems the antithesis of what most built environments deliver, yet increasingly people choose certain kinds of urban settings for leisure and recreation, social interaction and dwelling, and from this they derive experiences that contribute positively to their quality of life.

While these benefits may not necessarily be restorative in the sense understood in the mainstream of restorative environments research, it might be argued that a person's sense of self-worth and self-esteem could be regularly restored through opportunities that urban life may offer: experiencing social acceptance, making choices and mastering challenges, for example. These positive effects on

Figure 3.3: The architectural heritage of cities like Rome may hold clues to the restorative potential of urban environments, although we believe care must be taken to avoid the implication that it is only the historic that is providing the restorative 'active ingredient'.

well-being may not be delivered by non-demanding settings but may instead require contact with more dynamic environments offering social interaction and challenge. It could be hypothesised that human restoration, especially in the urban realm, may have two sides. One side relates to recovery from mental fatigue, currently well established and pointing towards natural, non-demanding environments. The other relates to achieving and sustaining self-worth and self-esteem, pointing towards much more active participation within dynamic and socially orientated environments. In support, there is now a growing interest in expanding the exploration of restorative environments to include the spatial, aesthetic and physical attributes of urban spaces (Hagerhall *et al.*, 2006; Nenci *et al.*, 2006; Tenngart and Hagerhall, 2008), and social and experiential dimensions (Thwaites and Simkins, 2007).

Relevant is increasing evidence that social activity not only has spatial implications (Hillier and Hanson, 1984; Alexander, 2002; Day, 2004), but also implications for the balance of control between what specialist practitioners provide and the empowerment of people to influence the environment they use (Habraken, 1998; Thwaites *et al.*, 2007). Perhaps, because of a gradual over-professionalisation of urban place-making in certain instances, people may have become effectively shorn of participative opportunities, having found their control over the form of places they use significantly restricted. This exposes a fundamental philosophical obstacle underpinning an assumption of people as recipients of, rather than participants in, the development of places they use. We suggest that a shift in mental orientation towards more phenomenological perspectives on human–environment relations may offer a way forward moving from a predominant focus on the content of the built environment to one on social value, and how such social value may relate to spatial organisation and participative action.

Social restoration: issues of social exclusion and participation

One of the main implications for such a shift in mental orientation lies with issues of communication and the extent to which this can either encourage or hinder the capability of non-professional people to influence change in places they use. As we have discussed earlier, it seems that methods of public consultation are insufficient, because they place people on the receiving end of decisions made by external agents. Even practices which genuinely seek to be more actively participative are open to criticism that what people participate in is what professional agencies decide they can and in ways they can. We have tried to show through our discussions about the importance of territorial behaviour and how this is intimately related to the opportunities people have to develop self-worth and self-esteem, that more equitable kinds of participation are needed, where all stakeholders in decision-making experience themselves as having value within the process and, moreover, an element of control, especially when it comes to the occupation of places and the expression of that occupation. Delivering socially restorative urbanism is, then, as much about effective communication as anything else.

People are routinely excluded, in various degrees, from the processes of decision-making about places they use. If we are to effectively move towards a more empowered and pro-active community decision-making approach, as envisaged in the current localism agenda, then ways will need to be found, not only to overcome communication boundaries of many kinds, but must do so in ways that can build empowerment and environmental competence. Only then will we begin to see a reduction of dependency on professional services in favour of more independent and pro-active local decision-making and this will require the inclusion of all in society, not just the vocal and motivated minority.

In trying to develop a practical response to this, we were fortunate to be able to work with members of the learning disability community in Sheffield and elsewhere in the UK on the development of their effective participation in decision-making processes relating to environmental experiences. People with learning disabilities are often among the most voiceless of the voiceless in society, sometimes disenfranchised to the point of dehumanisation. We will go into more detail about this in Part III, but relevant here is the way our partnerships with this community helped us to understand and recognise the importance of inclusive communication and indeed, how difficult this is to achieve within a predominant culture of professionalism. It also helped to bring into sharp focus what it means to recognise the value of social benefits and development of social capital through processes of environmental improvement. It also shows, as we will describe later, that significant social gain often requires relatively little material change and this may be especially significant to the delivery of a genuinely empowered localism agenda.

Mine, theirs, ours, yours: a framework for universally inclusive communication

Traditionally, academic discussion on public participation has focused upon the compatibility of community opinion and professional interpretation and execution. When examined in these terms, we see an immediate segregation of views and desired outcomes between the two parties. In order to understand why these two factions continue to be so removed, we need to acknowledge the following influences: control, territoriality and the legacy of professionalism. The impulses that drive an individual to evoke change in his or her neighbourhood are very different from the practical and technical briefs that professionals must respond to. Yet, polarised as these positions first appear, an alternative perspective exists which unifies these conflicting views: the language of mine, yours, theirs and ours.

This language explains the inter-relations which occur between individuals in any environment, at any scale and at all times. As a consequence, labels such as *professional* and *community* become redundant as we comprehend their connections and not their discipline-specific categorisation. The first three perspectives (*mine, yours, theirs*) illustrate the constructed territoriality more commonly present in our public spaces. On the whole, environments that display these characteristics are designed by professionals and on occasion modified through incremental additions by individuals. However, as professionals increasingly subsume what was previously in the realm of the local population, the opportunity for individuals to take ownership over their environment diminishes. Professionals currently design buildings and spaces that remain rigid in their utility and inflexible in their humanity. Through the professional dictation of our behaviour and the creation of set physical form, today's urban environments are littered with a legacy of alienation and abandonment; ultimately resulting in rejection by the masses of much modern urban form. The following example illustrates the interaction of mine, yours, theirs and ours through an ordinary environmental experience, one familiar to most of us: waiting at a bus stop (Figure 3.4).

1. MINE: The *mine* in an environment is experienced from everyone's first-hand perspective. For example, when waiting in a bus queue, each individual has

Figure 3.4: This bus stop in the city of Sheffield featured in a research project carried out with some of our learning disability partners called 'What's the Fuss, We Want the Bus!'. A detailed account of how this work helped in the development of the Experiemic Process is given in Part III.

Figure 3.5: 'Mine', ownership over personally occupied space.

ownership over the space which they occupy, either by sitting or standing. The extent of this ownership, or *mine-ness*, is determined by how comfortable and confident each individual is in the environment at any given time. This provides the first level of territory, one which we all experience most acutely (Figure 3.5).

2. YOURS: *Yours* refers to the space, object or form appropriated by someone close to you (physically and/or in terms of familiarity). For example, once another individual joins the bus queue, a separate territory is created. Again this territory is *mine* to the individual, but *yours* to the original bus queue member. Ownership over this territorial *yours* is also distinct, but less concentrated or dense when not experienced from a first-hand perspective. This therefore creates a second level of territory in the environment, extending beyond the remit of the original bus queue member (Figure 3.6).

Figure 3.6: 'Yours', a separately occupied nearby space which enables mine to be differentiated from yours.

3. THEIRS: The third level of territorial scale is *theirs*. This describes a removed relationship to others with whom we share a space. Here there may be a distant physical connection (through sight, sound, etc.), however, there is less behavioural contact. There may be awareness that others are present, yet they do not enter into a close enough personal sphere to be associated with ourselves. In the case of the bus stop, this could be a passing pedestrian or a nearby driver stuck in traffic (Figure 3.7).

Figure 3.7: 'Theirs', presence of territorial occupations that we are not a part of, yet we are aware they are there.

4. OURS: *Ours* is the territorial scale that envelops individuals and connects them, functioning at any physical or social scale. Few public realms successfully cater for a sense of *ours*. At the hypothetical bus stop, physical form may only encourage the notion of *ours* if individuals are incidentally exposed to negative elements such as anti-social behaviour or adverse weather conditions. We can therefore view the sense of *our-ness* as an aspiration for the design of all urban form (Figure 3.8).

Figure 3.8: 'Ours', the sense of belonging in common purpose and experience.

When we experience 'ours', we are subconsciously acknowledging a sense of belonging to something, or somewhere, to which others may also feel the same. A sense of ours also helps us to define what is mine and what is not. A sense of mine is an important component of self-identity and integral to the recognition that others have 'their' identity too. The sense of 'ours' is vital to overcome extremes of possessiveness and self-centred introspection by providing a territorial (mental and physical) realm that encourages communication, negotiation and reconciliation of differences. The concept of ours understood here is highly resonant of Habraken's control level called understanding. Ours and understanding share common ground as a kind of psychological realm which binds us together with others in mutually supporting groups, enabling and indeed encouraging independent expression to project a sense of individual identity within the group, while recognising the presence of boundaries beyond which our sustained acceptance within the group might be jeopardised. It is also the realm that delivers us with choices: we can choose either to embrace and express our sense of belonging, through social contacts, for example, or we can preserve our privacy without the risk of permanent isolation.

Something like this can be illustrated in a built environment context with Michael Martin's discussion about the potential of the back alley as a community landscape (Martin, 1997). Martin discusses the way different configurations of boundary treatment affect social potential in American residential development. When boundaries are configured to achieve a balance of what Martin describes as 'hidden-ness' and 'revealing-ness', the back alleys can be transformed from being merely functional conduits into settings rich in social potential, capable of encouraging and sustaining neighbourly behaviour in residents. Hidden-ness and revealing-ness reflect that people, depending on mood and circumstance, sometimes wish to preserve privacy while at other times choose to be more openly available to contact with neighbours. Martin links the development of community spirit in residential settings with the extent to which the built environment allows individuals to control when they wish to hide or reveal themselves as they move about in daily life. Boundaries of different heights and degrees of transparency, gate orientation, location of outbuildings and bin storage, places for car maintenance, children's play, and so on, can become strategically arranged to optimise such control, allowing inhabitants to position themselves according to how sociable or otherwise they may feel. Again, there is a question of balance. Infrastructures that facilitate too much hidden-ness may obstruct the sort of spontaneous social encounters from which good neighbourly relations often develop, while infra-structures that are too revealing can lead people to feel themselves oppressively overlooked (Figure 3.9).

The kind of back alley community landscape that Martin advocates represents the 'ours' of that specific community of people. What is right for them in how they come to sort out levels of overlap between their 'ours' and their 'mines' may not be right elsewhere. Consequently, it is hard to imagine that this sort of fine-grained tuning of features to achieve just the right balance of hide and reveal for the inhabitants of a particular neighbourhood could ever be successfully

Figure 3.9: Open boundaries in the Vastra Hamnen development, Malmö, Sweden, have the effect of integrating private and public space. Different boundary treatments, heights and degree of open-ness and enclosure enable personal control of hide and reveal.

specified by an outside specialist. The correct configuration of objects seems to be so intimately woven into the personal life-patterns of individuals that to get it right 'by design' would require super-human insight from even the most socially sensitive professional.

As we will discuss later in Part III, the main aim of the development of the Experiemic Process was to find ways in which different individuals and stakeholder groups can collectively expose and then explore issues of mutual concern about the nature of their relationship with the environments they use. Referring back to Honneth's ideas about the importance of recognition as a vital human need, the identification and exposure of issues of mutual concern is what sets the background against which a community of mutual support can then begin to develop around those issues. The various stages of the process of participative activity are then designed to allow participants to become aware of themselves as having particular individual and group self-interests within the project. This brings to the surface the 'mines' and 'theirs' and the Experiemic Process is designed to recognise this awareness as important in the development of self-identity and self-worth. This form of social awareness is especially heightened in importance for the learning disability partners with whom we worked and for whom opportunities to experience this kind of self-affirmation can often be very limited. But it is equally necessary for any individual or group in society to be able to understand and then to experience some control over environmental circumstances that affect the quality of their lives.

As Honneth argues, however, awareness of self-interest and the ability to act in ways that afford control of that self-interest, and thus establish self-identity, are not entirely what leads us to develop self-esteem. It is the recognition and value of our self-identity which are the cornerstone of self-esteem and this requires us to be able to experience being a part of a community with whom we share some common interests, even if those common interests do not always mean agreement. So, in addition to raising awareness of self-interest, the Experiemic Process is designed to balance this with ways in which the arena of common interest can be brought to the surface, providing the sense of belonging, or 'ours'. This acts to restrain expressions of self-interest within communally established boundaries, but also allows the self-identity of individuals to find recognition in some way or another within it. An internal balance is thus achieved, preserving the important sense of 'mine' as distinct from 'theirs' and 'yours', but simultaneously recognising that such a sense of 'mine' can only be preserved in a positive way through the sustainability of the sense of belonging, or 'ours'.

We will develop this in more detail in Part III, but before doing so we will move on by suggesting that the achievement of this kind of sociological balance, essentially a balance of territorial tensions relating to the mutually dependent integration of self and community, can be related to particular spatial circum-stances. As Martin's exploration of American back alleys helps to highlight, however, this is not simply a case of providing optimal spatial arrangements in entirety 'by design'. It requires a more integrated and holistic mind-set capable of understanding spatial organisation and social organisation as mutually generative systems. Isaiah Berlin captures the essence of this in his interpretation of the work of German philosopher Herder: 'Men, according to Herder, truly flourish only in congenial circumstances, that is, where the group to which they belong has achieved a fruitful relationship with the environment by which it is shaped and which in turn it shapes' (Berlin, 1965, p. 95).

PART II

IN SEARCH OF THE EDGE

Introduction

We concluded Part I by alluding to an important underpinning principle of our developing concept of socially restorative urbanism. This is to recognise that, through routine environmental contact, people, as individuals and communities, develop aspects of themselves as they make and experience changes and adaptations to their surroundings. The opportunity to do so is important to the establishment and sustaining of self-esteem and, by extension, the quality of life. We have suggested that, following Habraken (1998) and others (Cullen, 1971; Alexander, 1979; Tibbalds, 1992; Gehl, 2010), there are certain arrangements of urban form that can either hinder or encourage this process. From this point of view, we advance the argument that spatial organisation and social organisation are consequently integrated at some fundamental level and that we need to take this into account in the way that we approach urban planning and design if the consequences of our decision-making processes are to be socially sustainable. This is not a simple case of designing and then delivering the 'right' urban form as if it were a stage set upon which some subsequent performance will later be played out: this approach fails to acknowledge the importance of control that the 'players' must have in the determination of the environments they interact with. Instead we have to recognise a mutually reciprocal generative relationship between aspects of social development and the places where this takes place. As Arnold Berleant (1997) has pointed out in his book *Living in the Landscape: Towards an Aesthetic of Environment,*

'What we need now is to reconceptualise our world in a way that comes to terms with this, for what we do in environment we do to ourselves' (1997, p. 121).

In Part I, we sought to discuss how this mutual reciprocity between people and their routinely used environments has become gradually eroded in current urban design processes, as the pace and scale of urban redevelopment have advanced in response to economic pressures and political aspiration. We have in many cases succeeded in making significant and beneficial changes to our urban settings, but in the process have often decoupled this from its social relevance. We have shown with reference to Habraken's analysis of the structure of ordinary built environments that this can usefully be understood in terms of form-dominant solutions which do not provide sufficient opportunity for the necessary socially orientated processes of occupation (place) and individual and community expression of occupation (understanding) to become embedded. Redressing the balance, we have argued, has implications for the professionalisation of urban place-making, an essentially top-down matter, and for how we understand the role of participative action in this, an essentially bottom-up matter. Our discussion underpins the central assertion of this book: that it is not a case of either/or, but of arriving at an appropriate balance of the two.

In other words, where should form-orientated professional interventions begin to recede to make way for greater levels of occupant control in decision-making? Our response in the development of socially restorative urbanism is to highlight that such balance can frequently be seen to be most active at the interface of material form and human habitation: the edge realms where the dynamic and evolutionary nature of human social activity blends with the spatial and physical settings. We see potential opportunities to develop better understanding of this in urban design decision-making through an approach to research and professional practice which can operate on such edges, not simply as boundaries, but as coherent realms in their own right, through bringing together new morphological understandings together with participative processes. This requires holistic socio-spatial thinking which can relate space to social processes more explicitly and an approach to practice that can deliver material settings likely to encourage the evolution of form in edges at least as much through occupation and use as through design.

Part III of the book will detail our approach to participative processes by discussing the development of thinking and research behind a new process called

Experiemics, providing examples of its application. Here, however, in Part II, we will concentrate on the development of ideas for an urban morphology which we hope may provide a structural basis from which to understand the socio-spatial nature of edges in ways relevant to design decision-making agencies. This Part, then, concentrates on developing an anatomy for edge environments. It does this by taking the essence of Habraken's focus on the importance of margins and extends this through an expansion of the Experiential Landscape principle of transition (Thwaites and Simkins, 2007), ultimately developing one of the two main concepts underpinning socially restorative urbanism: transitional edges.

As we will discuss later, attention to the social relevance of edges in the built environment is not new. Jane Jacobs was probably one of the first to highlight the importance of well-integrated street fronts and the adjacent public realm to the social vitality of cities: many others have followed since. Yet over fifty years on from Jacobs' seminal work *The Death and Life of Great American Cities* (1961), there is still no fully coherent and effective approach capable of delivering the kind of urban realm she eloquently advocated. The transitional edges we develop here, therefore, form part of a new conceptual framework for urban spatial structure in which we believe urban form and space can be more easily reconnected to social organisation and experience. We propose in Chapter 4 that this provides an important conceptual thread, crucially relevant to contemporary urban development concerns, that is capable of drawing together hitherto unconnected social and spatial dimensions of urban form.

Part II concludes with Chapter 5, a summary of properties and characteristics associated with transitional edges illustrated with built environment examples. This is intended to give an indication of the kind of environmental qualities that might be expected to arise from the application of the transitional edge concept, along with the social benefits they may bring. These work towards delivery of a better balance of MTOY relationships, discussed in Chapter 3, which can mitigate the tendency towards form-dominant solutions, which in Habraken's terms would equate with achieving better balance between form, place and understanding. This will then be related in Part III to the Experiemic Process which collectively begins to pave the way for a new approach to the education of environmental design professionals, which takes an explicitly humanistic stance to the identification, exploration and delivery of transitional edges as key components in the socio-spatial order of the urban habitat.

Chapter Four

The edge as socio-spatial concept

Introduction

In this chapter we will develop the anatomy of one of the principal structures underpinning the concept of socially restorative urbanism: the transitional edge. We will show how this emerges from the vocabulary of Experiential Landscape (Thwaites and Simkins, 2007), highlighting in particular the significance of different types of segments, a particular type of transition, as the fundamental socio-spatial building blocks of transitional edges. Later, in Part III, we will explain how these provide a basis for the de-scaling of urban form to a more human level which we suggest is likely to be more amenable to the participative processes that are a necessary part of their realisation. Before developing the details of this, we want to set the idea of transitional edges in the context of existing understandings of urban edge settings and the social potential associated with them (Figure 4.1).

This is important for two reasons. First, it helps to underpin how much significance has been given to the social importance of edge settings over the course of the development of urban design theory. This brings a wide range of sources together from which we can summarise ten categories distinguishing different aspects of their social relevance. Second, is that although this serves to emphasise the social significance of urban edge settings, it does not really help with design decision-making processes because, except implicitly, there is no fully coherent framework of design guidance that can be made operational within urban design practice. In response to this, in the context of the socially restorative urbanism concept, we want to see if it is possible to distil the essence from this knowledge and develop structural characteristics that might address urban design decision-making more

Figure 4.1: What not to do with edges! Breathtaking insensitivity applied to the treatment of edges along Lincoln's waterfront has transformed a prime urban open space into a joyless socially barren scar across the city's central retail district.

directly. We have tried to achieve this by drawing on Habraken's focus on margins, as transitional realms with both spatial and social dimensions, and then looking to see how experiential landscape transitional concepts could be expanded to develop an anatomy for transitional edges. In Chapter 5 we will draw these theoretical and morphological developments together to reveal particular qualities that we believe transitional edges should possess in order to deliver socially sustainable outcomes, and that professional and community agencies involved in their realisation should aim to achieve.

The phenomenological nature of transitional edges

Following Habraken's lead, we have interpreted human habitation in terms of territorial experiences relating to the way people occupy space and then express the nature of their occupation through their uses and adaptations. We have suggested that one way to understand these social processes in an inclusive and jargon-free manner is through consideration of the balance in our awareness of MTOY. Our central assertion is that the necessary sense of 'ours' is often difficult to achieve within many of the built environments delivered by currently prevailing approaches, and that there are consequences here for the quality of human life.

We propose that the transitional edge structure we develop here can provide a morphological basis from which to begin to deliver a response to this limitation, and, as such, we suggest that design activity might beneficially be guided by its principles. We are not suggesting, however, that transitional edges can be 'designed' in the prescriptive way that this is often understood in the current professional culture. As Habraken points out, these interface environments are tangible and often highly visible components of urban order, yet they are indeterminate, by which he means that they are realms which are subject to continuous change and adaptation in response to how they are used and experienced. Their tangibility is given by their dynamic and adaptable nature and not imposed by external design decisions entirely. Transitional edges have to be understood, then, as mutually inter-dependent holistic realms within which spatial organisation and social organisation are integrated at some fundamental level. Space shapes social activity, which then in turn shapes space, and so on in infinite mutual generation and regeneration. Transitional edges are therefore evolutionary in their development and essentially expressive in their nature: the growth and development of their form come from the expressions of territorial occupation and use that are established there and this requires a shift in mind-set to accommodate a more holistic understanding of the interdependent relationship of the social and spatial dimensions of the urban environment.

Kim Dovey, Professor of Architecture and Urban Design at the University of Melbourne, Australia, has contributed much in recent times to our understanding of the mutually defining relationship of social processes and urban order (Dovey, 1993, 2005, 2010). Dovey takes an explicitly phenomenological perspective to the analysis of sense of place as socio-spatial assemblage in order to demonstrate the wide diversity of ways in which '[s]ocial space tends to be translated, with more or less distortion, into physical space' (Dovey, 2005, p. 285). Particularly relevant to our developing idea of transitional edges here is Dovey's conception of place identity as being in a continuous state of becoming (Dovey, 2010). Becoming is, by definition, a transitional experience and therefore especially relevant to how we want transitional edges to be understood: as components of urban order where interior becomes exterior, enclosed becomes open, social becomes spatial, public becomes private.

The idea of places defined by their becoming or in between-ness is a phenom-enological view of human–environment relations where human experience and its spatial context are integrated. That human experience can be thought to have spatial dimensions has philosophical roots in the work of phenomenologist Maurice Merleau-Ponty, who drew conclusions about the inter-related nature of human existence and the spaces within which it is played out: 'We have said that space is existential; we might just as well have said that existence is spatial' (Merleau-Ponty, 1962, p. 293). Merleau-Ponty points to a spatial dimension at the heart of what it is to be human, which has profound implications for the way that space is understood: 'Space is not the setting (real or logical) in which things are arranged, but the means whereby the positing of things becomes possible' (ibid., p. 243). This implies that people and their settings create a kind of totality where different contexts activate different habits and thus become a part of the way those habits are expressed. For Merleau-Ponty, this kind of fit between bodily action and its environment is crucial to our ability to make sense of our actions and the world around us. From a phenomenological perspective, our surroundings are experienced as a projection of our sense of self: its condition is our condition. This brings about a substantial shift of awareness from geometric space as a finite, static container, to a lived space as a more elastic phenomenon: a pliable and dynamic entity that bends, stretches and moulds at different scales in response to action (Dovey, 1993, 2010).

This conception of lived space may seem challenging from within the mainstream planning and design fraternity, yet it has strong foundations in other discipline areas, especially anthropology. Concepts developed by Edward Hall in the 1960s (1959, 1966), for example, give rigorous intellectual foundations to an idea of space as an entity capable of growing, changing and declining along with the way people give different meanings to it or choose to ignore it (Tuan, 1977, 1980; Proshansky *et al.*, 1983). A phenomenological perspective not only embraces human functioning in its view of the environment, it actually requires it to bring a full definition. An understanding of urban order as something intimately connected to human lived experience, rather than something rationally generated from specialist professional practices, also resonates in Jane Jacobs' (1961) appraisal of the social vitality of streets. Streets and streetfronts require diversity and adaptability to support urban life and this is essentially what Jacobs meant in highlighting the kind of problem a city presents (Jacobs, 1961, p. 14): a product of collective formation in time rather than the outcome of one single process stated and delivered once and for all.

If we are to incorporate more time-conscious and adaptive processes into the way we develop our urban environments, then we suggest here that the structure of urban form has to be conducive to small-scale adaptation. The development of plot-based urbanism provides a place to begin in this respect by defining urban development more as a process than a product, but a process that can only partially be designed (Porta and Romice, 2010). Plot-based urbanism is an ongoing research agenda of the Urban Design Studies Unit at the University of Strathclyde, UK, developed from evidence-based research into the structural characteristics of urban settlements worldwide (Figure 4.2). Here, plots are conceived as elements of urban form variable in function and control so that, in combination, they deliver complexity rather than uniformity in the form of the street fronts they define. Individuals and small groups are more likely to be able to express their occupation and use of small-scale plots, over which they have a degree of autonomous control, than they are within large-scale blocks which offer little encouragement or opportunity for such acts of self-organisation. In this respect especially, plot-based urbanism directly reflects the type of urban structure that Jacobs argued for. From

Figure 4.2: The plot-based urban form of the island of Burano in the northern Venetian lagoon.

this position it is possible to conceptualise *transitional edges* as coherent holistic socio-spatial realms integrating spatial and social dimensions of urban form. The social dimension of transitional edges derives from interactions which generate engagement, action and change (Newman and Kenworthy, 1999).

The importance of plot-based urbanism in this context is that it enables us, by virtue of its focus on relationships of plots and street fronts, to conceive of a unified realm which is neither entirely internal or external, nor entirely spatial or social. As a process-orientated approach to urban design, plot-based urbanism provides for the generation of transitional edges by de-scaling the unit of urban structure to levels more amenable to control by occupants. Returning to Habraken, the exercise of such control delivers *place* through processes of occupation and *understanding* through the territorial expression of individuals and groups within frameworks of common understanding. Transitional edges thus become the visible socio-spatial *form* of built environments: that which gives meaning through use, character and identity through territorial expression, and sustainability through adaptation.

The social significance of the edge

With this phenomenological conception in mind, we want now to move forward to explore how this corresponds with the social relevance that others have associated with similar edge settings, to see what can be learned about their properties and characteristics by drawing themes together in a common framework. The following review develops from work carried out by John Edwards during the course of his research for the degree of Master in Landscape Architecture at the University of Sheffield, 2011. By researching and evaluating commonalities and differences from a wide range of sources which, to a greater or lesser extent, discuss various aspects of social association with these components of the urban realm, Edwards' work helps to underpin a framework identifying particular properties and characteristics of edges associated with integrating social and spatial issues. Reflecting the human-scale issues at the centre of our interests here, Edwards' review is focused on edges at the scale of the street, and especially the plot–street relationship. What we learn from this work is that common issues can be grouped around ten broadly related yet distinguishable themes which collectively help to provide useful insight into the socio-spatial properties relevant to transitional edges. These are then taken forward with the anatomy of transitional edges to ultimately distil a tripartite framework that can be applied to the exploration of real-world examples.

The ten themes are:

1. Social activity
2. Social interaction
3. Public–private gradient
4. Hide and reveal
5. Spatial expansion
6. Enclosure
7. Permeability
8. Transparency
9. Territoriality
10. Looseness

1 Social activity

Figure 4.3: The social attraction of a Copenhagen water's edge.

If the edge fails, then the space never becomes lively.

(Alexander *et al.*, 1977, p. 600)

The sociologist Derk de Jonge (1967) first observed the social phenomenon that people tended to gravitate towards edges in the public spaces of coastlands, forests and even restaurants. De Jonge noticed that humans would fill up the spaces closest to the edge before the more exposed places. Appleton's later prospect and refuge theory offers an explanation for this based on human behavioural ancestry, postulating that these edge spaces are aesthetically and spatially favourable to human biological needs of habitation because they provide 'the ability to see without being seen' (Appleton, 1996, p. 66). This is also noted by Gehl (1996, 2010), Franck and Stevens (2007) and Dee (2001) and seems to emphasise that people are drawn to the edges of spaces because they are prime spots for sitting or standing to survey the open space while also having one's back protected. It seems these spaces attract social activity because they allow an individual to protect their back, hide within the nearby shadows and view the scene in front of them.

This seemingly innate social phenomenon is one of the keys to the socially sustainable city advocated, in particular, by Jan Gehl. Gehl famously said that people attract people and that a benchmark for decision-making in city development should therefore be to populate with people. One of the principal city structures that can support this are the edges where 'the city and building meet' (Gehl, 2010, p. 79). Distinguishing between 'soft' and 'hard' edges, the former characterised by façades generally engaging to passers-by because of windows, openings, displays, etc., and the latter generally disengaging because of a lack of such opportunities, Gehl observes from research in Copenhagen that there is often seven times more city life in front of an active façade, or soft edge. Such 'soft' edges are variously described in other literature, but the so-called edge effect (ibid.), the observation that individuals gravitate to the edges of spaces, has been well documented by authors connected to the social aspects of urban design (de Jonge, 1967; Alexander *et al.*, 1977; Gehl, 1977, 1986, 1996, 2010; Whyte, 1980; Appleton, 1996; Chalfont, 2005; Franck and Stevens, 2007; Bosselmann, 2008; Dee, 2001).

Edge settings which appear socially attractive because of either their intrinsically engaging qualities or their capacity to combine security with vantage are often associated with an intrinsic transitional quality, defining a zone between two distinguishable realms. Bosselmann (2008) and Gehl (1977, 1986, 1996), for example, both highlight the importance of the transitional zone in increasing overall levels of activity within a street, highlighting that incidences of static occupation increase in locations where this transitional quality occurs. Gehl (1996) offers an explanation for this, suggesting that levels of social activity increase in and around these areas if: they have easy access in and out; if there are good staying areas available; and if there is something to do.

Soft, active or engaging edges are commonly associated with social activity, usually generated by their capacity to hold the attention of passers-by. Such edges are also associated with having transitional qualities defining an overlap of adjacent realms, their social activity related to accessibility across it and opportunities to be stationary coupled with things that can hold attention.

2 Social interaction

Figure 4.4: Social interaction in the semi-public streets of Delhi.

> A transitional zone between the semi-public and private space ... invites residents to spend more time outside the private space and thus offers better opportunities for spontaneous encounters with neighbours.
>
> (Hoogland, 2000, p. 61)

The association of edges with social activity discussed above relates mainly to their capacity to attract and then hold the attention of people. One of the most significant outcomes of this capacity is therefore their value as settings for social interaction. Short or longer stationary activities bring people into close proximity and this brings with it the opportunity for encounter, whether fleeting and temporary, or more enduring interactions which may contribute to greater social cohesion and the development of community. Gehl, for example, shows a correlation between the social activity, occurring at residential 'soft edges', and the level of social interaction: 'The more people used the front yards and the streets and the more time they spent on the public side of the house, the more frequently they had contact with their neighbours and passers-by' (1977, p. 7).

Gehl's study was undertaken in residential streets but the principle also applies in more public spaces and is associated here with the concept of triangulation (Whyte, 1988). Triangulation is the observation that two strangers are more likely to strike up conversation if there is an object or event close by that they can talk about. This has been shown to be more likely to occur in transitional spaces (Franck and Stevens, 2007): 'Triangulation is also more likely at the edge of public space because the attention of people watching from the edge is almost always focused in just one direction' (ibid., p. 118). Here, individuals can interact over a focal topic presented to them in the public space.

One of the main values of social interaction is that it can improve and promote a sense of place and feelings of community. Peter Bosselmann (2008) has shown, for example, that the transitional zone created both a sense of place and a perception of greater intimacy between neighbours, a point echoed also by Hoogland whose research confirms that 'among residents living in a settlement equipped with a semi-private zone, stronger social cohesion can be observed than among residents living in a settlement where such a zone is not provided' (2000, p. 28).

The transitional nature of edges is associated with social interactions because of qualities they possess which support stationary activities. It appears, therefore, that transitional edges, as elements of urban form, have a significant role to play in encouraging and sustaining the social dynamic of the urban realm.

3 Public–private gradient

To develop both privacy and the true advantages of living in a community, an entirely new anatomy of urbanism is needed, built of many hierarchies of clearly anticipated domains.

(Chermeyeff and Alexander, 1963, p. 37)

Figure 4.5: Open spatial structure simultaneously differentiating and integrating semi-public, semi-private and private space in a Lisbon courtyard.

One of the most notable characteristics associated with transitional edges is that they tend to overcome abrupt divisions of private and public spaces with more of a smooth public–private continuum which flows from privacy though to the public realm more gradually (Altman, 1975; Alexander *et al.*, 1977; Madanipour, 2003; Franck and Stevens, 2007; Rajala, 2009; Carmona *et al,*, 2010; Gehl, 2010). The public–private gradient has been prominently championed by Christopher Alexander, highlighting the need for buildings to have a 'gradient of settings, which have different degrees of intimacy' (Alexander *et al.*, 1977, p. 610). Here, in this gradient of settings, one can choose the desired level of intimacy by positioning oneself in the appropriate degree of public or private exposure. Furthermore, having the choice of appropriate privacy exposure is directly related to the nature of the social interaction available in the transitional zone. For example, if every space within the transitional zone were to have a similar 'degree of intimacy', it would remove all subtlety of social interaction.

Although Alexander highlights this intimacy gradient as extending mainly through the building, he also recognises its applicability to the area directly inside and outside the façade, an area that makes up the transitional zone. In this way the public–private gradient is a spatial quality that transcends the duality between the architecture and the adjacent open space. This is an idea shared and expanded upon by Ali Madanipour (2003), who maintains that this public–private gradient is not just confined to the home environment but extends right from the individual's body to the most public outdoor space. Madanipour also sees this gradient working through the transitional edge, saying that, 'In practice, public and private spaces are a continuum, where many semi-public or semi-private spaces can be identified, as the two realms meet through shades of privacy and publicity rather than clear cut separation' (ibid., p. 239). The idea of shades of private-ness and public-ness is an important concept to emphasise. In contemporary architecture some authors simply categorise these complex areas into four categories: private, semi-private, semi-public and public (Biddulph, 2007), but this has been shown to be a limited approach in which the actual definition of public-ness and privacy is entirely dependent on one's perspective and the amount of territorial depth (Habraken, 1998).

One of the key characteristics of transitional edges, directly related to subtle variations in the nature of social interaction, is a public to private gradient that works in
a continuum from private to public and vice versa. This is not an assemblage of clear
spaces but a smooth and complex gradient of subtle changes where a greater range
of spaces allows greater diversity of intimacy and social interaction. In spatial terms,
this begins to suggest that an edge's lateral dimension and qualities may have direct
bearing on its social functioning.

4 Hide and reveal

A good city street neighborhood achieves a marvel of balance between
its people's determination to have essential privacy and their simultaneous
wishes for differing degrees of contact, enjoyment, or help from people
around.

(Jacobs, 1993, p. 61)

Figure 4.6: Ingenious arrangement of produce in a Dehli flower market provides
a balance of hide and reveal and adds character to the colour, texture and social
vitality of the street scene.

As the previous section about private–public gradient suggests, edges that have this quality create opportunities for people to experience themselves as either being private or as part of a wider public environment. Whether explicitly or implicitly stated, a variety of authors indicate that the area that makes up the transitional edge displays attributes of both privacy and publicity (Sundstrom, 1977; Korosec-Serfaty, 1985; Jacobs, 1993; Martin, 1997; Hoogland, 2000; Gehl, 1996; Carmona *et al.*, 2010). Carmona *et al.*, for example, explain, 'the edge of the public space network needs to both enable interaction and protect privacy' (2010, p. 219).

As Jacobs, in the epigraph at the heading of this section, and the later work of Michael Martin (1997) demonstrate, people need to be able to exercise a measure of control over when they wish to be private and when to be sociable. The settings they occupy should therefore be configured in such a way as to enable this choice to be made readily. Martin encapsulates this in terms of a balance of hidden-ness and revealing-ness when discussing the social attributes of back alleys and their potential to either encourage or discourage community cohesion. Hidden-ness refers to the capacity of a setting to allow people to experience being private, away from the unwanted attention of neighbours, for example. Revealing-ness, in contrast, is the capacity of a setting which enables people to choose to be available, accessible and a part of their wider surroundings. The optimum situation for social well-being is for there to be a balance of both in the proximate setting so that people can decide for themselves which they wish to exercise, and when.

As Altman (1975) points out, this balance is related to human territorial behaviour and can impact on individual well-being. Too much enforced privacy, for example, can obstruct spontaneous social encounters and lead to the unwelcome effects of isolation, while too much exposure without the opportunity for retreat into private space can be equally detrimental by prolonging unwanted levels of exposure, leading people to feel themselves oppressively overlooked. The configuration of physical and spatial infrastructure clearly plays a significant role in whether the right balance of opportunities is available. But this does not appear to be a simple case of design because such a balance needs to be appropriate to the users' individual needs. Therefore, it is necessary that such spaces are created to be flexible and relatively easily adaptable to facilitate the potential for the users to be able to modify how much revealing-ness and hidden-ness is appropriate for them. As Hoogland puts it, 'provide them with the basic ingredients, instead of the microwave-meal' (2000, p. 63).

Mainly because of their tendency to spread the transition from private to public domains smoothly, transitional edges, as spatial elements, are more likely to deliver opportunities for people to experience the necessary balance of hide and reveal during daily routines. However, this balance appears to be highly personal and variable and therefore requires settings to be amenable to change and adaptation by those who use them.

5 Spatial expansion

Public and private claims visually and functionally overlap, which creates an identifiable urban space.

(Nooraddin, 2002, p. 50)

Figure 4.7: Interior and exterior realms overlap, stretching space in a Copenhagen book store across its expanded edge.

Spatial dimension is one of most recognisable features of the transitional edge. Unlike other street-edge treatments, they have clear spatial expansion formed by the overlap of the two adjoining realms. Research indicates that the extent of spatial expansion is proportional to its levels of social absorbency. There is significant evidence in the literature to support the view that spatial dimension, along with a distinguishable sense of space or place, is an important characteristic of the edge (Norberg-Schulz, 1971; Newman, 1976; Alexander *et al.*, 1977; Gehl, 1977; Hillier and Hanson, 1984; Bentley *et al.*, 1985; Habraken, 1998; Nooraddin, 2002; Lewis, 2005; Porta and Renne, 2005; Franck and Stevens, 2007). For Alexander *et al.* (1977) and Lozano (1990), for example, where the two spaces join, there should not be a linear boundary but instead a place in its own right with a certain thickness to it. It should be a realm between realms, in essence, a transitional sub-space between two larger recognisable spaces. Alexander *et al.* summarise this by saying, 'Make sure that you treat the edge of a building as a "thing", a "place", a zone with volume to it, not a line or interface which has no thickness' (1977, p. 755). Furthermore is the suggestion that the transitional zone could be composed of further recognisable sub-spaces, such as the smaller niche spaces in an articulated façade. This introduces the possibility that there are aspects of transitional edges that act 'across' their width, such as the public–private gradient discussed above, and characteristics that imply a 'linear extent' constructed from smaller spatial expansions connected together.

Other authors show how space is linked to social absorbency. For example, Habraken (1998), Bentley *et al.* (1985) and Biddulph (2007) show that personalisation requires a spatial dimension to flourish. Cooper-Marcus and Sarkissian (1986) and Gehl (1996) also outline optimum spatial dimensions for social absorbency. Cooper-Marcus and Sarkissian (1986), for example, highlight a British study where the size and shape of the front garden had an influence on its levels of use and personalisation. They show that front yards need to be in spatial balance and 'should be deep enough for privacy but not so large as to inhibit personalization' (ibid., p. 104). Gehl (1996) makes a similar discovery about social interaction. For Gehl, the space should be '[f]ar enough to ensure a certain measure of privacy for those sitting in front of the house, yet at the same time just close enough to permit contact with events occurring in it' (ibid., p. 189).

Gehl's studies show a spatial dimension between 3–4 metres is desirable, and anthropological theory suggests this may be due to the necessary levels of personal space required for successful social interaction. In Hall's seminal work *The Hidden*

Dimension (1966), he defines a number of suitable social dimensions. Social distance and public distance, for example, work from 1.3m–3.75m and >3.75m respectively. This suggests that in order for these spaces to function as socially active and inter-active spaces, they need to be of a particular distance that allows both closer social contact and also permits public distance. Such a distance would be around 3.75m and similar distances have been highlighted in other studies (Alexander *et al.*, 1977; Cooper–Marcus and Sarkissian 1986; Habraken, 1998).

> Transitional edges can be considered to have complex spatial characteristics, formed by overlapping adjacent spaces, which are related to their level of social absorbency. Research suggests that the optimum dimensions for these areas could be around 3.75m. Such a dimension would permit personalisation and territoriality but also allow social interaction, surveillance and communication.

6 Enclosure

Facades must once again live up to their dual role of not just enclosing and expressing the interior, but also of addressing and articulating external space, making outdoor rooms.

(Buchanan, 1988, p. 205)

As discussed above, edges can 'hold' space. The main boundary line encloses both interior and exterior and creates partially enclosed sub-spaces around its edge. Franck and Stevens explain that building thresholds are 'clearly enclosed on their private side' (2007, p. 9). Their observations suggest that these transitional edges have a strong sense of enclosure where the private building meets the public space. Usually, this is the building façade but it can also be formed by other continuous boundaries such as fences, hedges, walls or natural features (Habraken, 1998). In the streetscape, this edge environment is widely recognised as having an important function in framing and forming space in between the buildings (Jacobs, 1993; Moughtin, 2003) but this success is largely dependent on the feature of a continuous building line. Many authors indicate that there should be continuous building lines along the street to create strong street definition (Alexander *et al.*, 1977; Llewelyn-Davies, 2000; Porta and Renne, 2005; Department for Transport,

Figure 4.8: Fusion of interior and exterior in the enclosure of a South Korean traditional house.

2007; Rudlin and Falk, 1999; Frank, 2010). For example, the Department of Transport declares, 'Continuous building lines are preferred as they provide definition to and enclosure of the public realm' (2007, p. 57).

However, there is evidence to suggest that a continuous line may only be partly desirable. Frank (2010), for example, created two imagined streetscapes and had them compared by a group of academics and a group of users. Frank finds there 'is a discrepancy between the users and academics/professionals opinions on setbacks' (ibid., p. 111). The academics produced a streetscape with a continuous building line whereas the users produced a much more crenulated building edge, comprised of varying levels of setbacks and projections. The study suggests that although both the academic and professional perspective is that building lines should be continuous, the evidence is that users may prefer a more varied building line, as it is perceived to be more open to opportunities for social activity.

In fact, many authors showed a preference for an articulated façade because it creates a series of niches that can be appropriated (Alexander *et al.*, 1977; Cooper-Marcus and Sarkissian, 1986; Buchanan, 1988; Gehl, 1996; Cooper-Marcus and Francis, 1997; Macdonald, 2005; Dee, 2001). Such a crinkled façade creates pockets of semi-enclosed spaces that make the user feel more protected, and creates more recognisable and spatially distinct sub-spaces that are easier to identify with. Therefore, this creates a space that has higher levels of social activity, social interaction and aspects of territoriality and personalisation. For Cooper-Marcus and Sarkissian (1986), articulated façades have another territorial benefit. These authors state, 'the more articulated the façade, the more likely are residents to add their own touches to the design' (ibid., p. 68). In their opinion, an articulated façade has a more private feel as it does not all directly face the street and is therefore more likely to be personalised. The literature's contrast between the need for a continuous building line and an articulated façade suggests that a balance between the two is desirable, in essence, a varied building line that facilitates street enclosure while also providing opportunities for a transitional edge to emerge.

Spatial expansion implies recognisable levels of enclosure, which is usually created by a building façade or a strong continuous line of definition. The most successful enclosure is not a hard continuous building line, or a loose and unidentifiable juxtaposition of random setbacks and projections, but a subtle balance between the two.

7 Permeability

Public and private places cannot work independently. They are complementary, and people need access across the interface between them.

(Bentley *et al.*, 1985, p. 12)

The two adjacent realms of the edge are not independent but are mediated by it and this means that edges have intrinsic permeability in their capacity for connectivity between realms. As we have begun to demonstrate, they are complex components which have spatial expansion, enclosures and identity of their own, yet also they act to weave together adjacent realms. Permeability is usually understood in terms of physical accessibility but can also include visual, olfactory or

Figure 4.9: Permeable urban arrangement interconnects adjacent realms and invites exploration and discovery, Jakriborg, Sweden.

audible permeability; these qualities are sometimes referred to as transparency. Research indicates that permeability can have a significant influence on the level of activity in both the transitional edge and its adjacent space. Thus, it is desirable to offer as much permeability as the adjacent spaces can permit without compromising its function.

Numerous authors show that the transitional edge is a permeable interface between two larger adjacent spaces allowing physical access or transparency (Hillier and Hanson, 1984; Bentley *et al.*, 1985; Habraken, 1998; Nooraddin, 2002;

Franck and Stevens, 2007; Gehl, 2010). Gehl, for example, shows that, '[t]he edge along ground floors is also a zone in which doors and exchange points between inside and outside are located' (2010, p. 75). Similarly, Nooraddin explains, 'The wall, which divided the two spaces, served also as a mediator with entrances and window' (2002, p. 52). However, for Madanipour (2003) and Epstein (1998), this is not a straightforward process of access but is a more complex semi-permeable space due to restrictions placed on the site by the agent. Madanipour believes the separation should not be considered 'black or white' and that 'boundaries are crossed by the agreement between neighbours' (Madanipour, 2003, p. 66). Such an observation hints that this level of permeability is ambiguous and dependent on the negotiation or restrictions placed on the space by the users or agents. This is highly reminiscent of the balance of controls discussed by Habraken (1998), where place is established through occupation and then sustained through collectively accepted, or just tolerated, understandings.

Research indicates that permeability has a significant impact on the levels of activity encountered in the adjacent spaces. Observations and research conducted by Gehl (1996) and Lopez (2003) show that the level of activity within a street increases with the level of permeability between the building space and the street. As Gehl says, 'The studies clearly show that activities concentrate in places where there is high transparency (looking in windows) and where there are niches and opening and other opportunities for stopping (stationary activities)' (1996, p. 39). These observations have been highlighted in other literature, suggesting that such observations are consequences of the permeable transitional edges (Whyte, 1980, 1988; Biddulph, 2007; Franck and Stevens, 2007; Rudlin and Falk, 1999).

Transitional edges are by their nature permeable, but the extent of permeability may be locally controlled by those in occupation as they mediate who and what passes between the two adjacent spaces. Research indicates that the more permeable these transitional edges are, the greater the levels of social activity in the streetscape.

8 Transparency

> The best streets have about them a quality of transparency at their edges, where the public realm of the street and the less public, often private realm of property and buildings meet.
>
> (Jacobs, 1993, p. 285)

The properties of permeability and transparency are closely related. While permeability is generally, although not exclusively, associated with issues of physical accessibility, transparency has predominantly visual associations. It is probably most readily understood as a property of the urban environment that enables us to experience the interplay of 'here' and 'there' by means of features which allow us awareness of nearby settings other than the one we currently occupy. For Porta and

Figure 4.10: The transparency of a Milan bakery window brings the action and light of the interior into the street.

Renne, 'Transparency is a measure of the amount of window space/area that fronts onto the street, allowing viewing into and out of the building' (2005, p. 8). However, their concept of transparency focuses solely on windows and the visual sense. For Jacobs, 'There are subtle ways to achieve transparency, it needn't be all windows and doors' (1993, p. 287). This is further confirmed by the work of Franck and Stevens (2007), Whyte (1988) and Gehl (2010) whose examples of the wide-open thresholds of some stores create transparent and free flowing edges that allow sounds, smells and visual performance to seamlessly flow into the public domain.

The concept of transparency is a particular feature of Cullen's (1971) view of townscape as a sequence of visually connected realms that people pass through, articulated by the openings, gaps, landmark and framing features that are revealed in the gradually unfolding urban infrastructure: 'The practical result of articulating the town into identifiable parts is no sooner do we create a here than we admit a there, and it is precisely in the manipulation of these two spatial concepts that a large part of urban drama arises' (ibid., p. 182). In *The Concise Townscape*, Cullen highlights a series of ways this sense of 'here-ness' and 'there-ness' can occur in the urban landscape and shows this act of transparency occurring at the edges where adjacent buildings or courtyards meet the street.

The characteristic of transparency also has a series of valuable functions. The Project for Public Spaces (2011) summarises the main importance of transparency thus:

> A transparent building base provides the dual benefit of allowing pedestrians to see the activity occurring inside the building – a signal that encourages foot traffic – while providing more 'eyes on the street' where people inside the building can see out onto, and act as a security presence for, the public and semi-public zones outside.
>
> (Project for Public Spaces)

For many people, transparency is a desirable characteristic that increases both the social activity (Alexander *et al.*, 1977; Gehl, 1996; Project for Public Spaces, 2011) and the level of perceived and actual safety on the street (Newman, 1976, 1972; Jacobs, 1993; Llewelyn-Davies, 2000; Biddulph, 2007; Rudlin and Falk, 1999; Carmona *et al.*, 2010). It achieves this by increasing the level of street activity, improving visibility and encouraging natural surveillance. Visual access allows the inhabitants of the space to survey their territory from within the building while the openings, such as windows, add visual interest, which attracts the 'eyes' of the street user and suggests a human presence. In the evening, light emanates from these interior spaces, creating greater visual clarity.

Transparency works with permeability in opening up the structure of the urban realm, preventing it from being experienced as a disconnected set of sealed enclosures. Transparency is a property that enables people to be aware of places where they are not and therefore opens up future possibilities. This is an essentially transitional characteristic likely to be most vividly at work where edges between realms are punctured, either visually or physically, with openings, gaps, gateways and other transitional features.

9 Territoriality

The urban environment should be an environment that encourages people to express themselves, to become involved, to decide what they want and act on it.
(Jacobs and Appleyard, 1987, p. 523)

As an element of urban form closely associated with social activity and inter-action, edges are intrinsically territorial settings. Because they tend to be defined by a gradient from private through to more public forms of occupation and use, their territorial nature is complex and involves demarcation and personalisation as an extended form of boundary regulation. Research indicates that this charac-teristic is crucial for social contact, safety and personal well-being (Newman, 1972, 1976; Altman, 1975; Cooper-Marcus and Sarkissian, 1986; Buchanan, 1988; Habraken, 1998; Hoogland, 2000). For Altman (1975), this space is a territory that is inbetween the public and private territories – a place he calls a 'secondary territory': 'Secondary territories are the bridge, therefore, between the total and pervasive control allowed participants in primary territories and the almost-free use of public territories by all persons' (ibid., p. 114). The secondary territory is a quasi-defensible territory where 'an individual or a group has some control, ownership, and regulatory power but not to the same degree as over a primary territory' (ibid., p. 117). This secondary territory is similar to Newman's (1972, 1976) 'defensible space', which can take place inbetween the private and public

Figure 4.11: The transition from private to public often encourages territorial signalling through personalisation which then bridges private and public realms, Greenwich Village, London.

spaces as a transitional zone. Here these zones act like buffer zones, mediating certain individuals with a limited amount of access in and out.

These are spaces where territorial negotiation occurs (Habraken, 1998). However, although these spaces signify a shared space, they often exhibit territorial markers (personalisation or barriers) to signify that these spaces are under the influence of adjacent users. As Altman verifies, 'People exhibit various marking techniques to identify their places; these markers serve as interaction–control mechanisms; and people respond to one another's markers in a variety of ways, such as respect, interpretation to others, and even surrogate defense' (1975, p. 133). For Habraken (1998) and Altman (1975), territorial markers act as a way of defining these spaces as separate from the public and private realms. They may be the stalls or objects of shopkeepers (Habraken, 1998) but they are also acts of personalisation (Bentley *et al.*, 1985; Hoogland, 2000; Nooraddin, 2002; Biddulph, 2007). For Hoogland, '[this] zone is that of a kind of show-case, conveying information on lifestyle and preferences' (2000, p. 20). The literature also shows that this kind of personalisation takes place at the major threshold points of the transitional edge, such as the gates, doors and windows.(Bentley *et al.*, 1985; Cooper-Marcus and Sarkissian, 1986; Biddulph, 2007; Rajala, 2009). Such territorial acts are closely associated with human well-being. Altman, for example, relates territorial activity to the concept of self-identity: 'Territoriality may play a long-range role in the well-being of the whole species' (1975, p. 138). This may be because, as Habraken (1998) and Day (2002) have shown, territory is an innate and fundamental part of human nature, suggesting that without being able to inhabit and territorialise a geographic space, we are missing out on an important part of what makes us human.

However, it is not just personalisation that helps to distinguish the semi-private zone. Another clear way of showing the different levels of territorial depth is through demarcation with barriers or boundaries (Newman, 1972, 1976; Altman, 1975; Hoogland, 2000; Day 2002; Biddulph, 2007; Franck and Stevens, 2007). Newman shows that these barriers can be categorised into two groups, symbolic and real: '[r]eal barriers include elements like buildings, fences and walls' whereas '[s]ymbolic barriers include elements like low fences, shrubs, steps, changes in ground level, changes in paving texture, light standards, open portals and so on' (1976, pp. 108–9). For Newman (1972), symbolic barriers appear to be the most effective in creating, distinguishable transitional spaces. However, he notes that they require a series of conditions to be successful, such as the capacity of the inhabitants to maintain control of the space.

Research also indicates that a secondary territorial space is important for fostering social contact (Altman, 1975; Hoogland, 2000). As Hoogland states, 'Intensive interaction shall only develop where individuals are given the opportunity to appropriate and personalise a so-called "secondary" territory within the zone between private and public spaces' (2000, p. 20). Altman and Hoogland each show that the act of territorialisation promotes social cohesion. The acts of personalisation make the areas feel more protected and allow conversation and interaction to flourish. It appears it is not only important to have a transitional zone but that this zone must allow appropriation if it is to suitably facilitate social communication and thus foster sustainable neighbourhoods.

Edges exhibit important territorial characteristics such as occupation, appropriation and expression; and may include territorial barriers or markers such as personalisation or symbolic boundaries. This territorial characteristic is a highly significant component of urban order, which improves well-being, increases social interaction and improves safety.

10 Looseness

People create loose space through their own actions. Many urban spaces possess physical and social possibilities for looseness, but it is people, through their own initiative, who fulfill these possibilities.

(Franck and Stevens, 2007, p. 10)

Figure 4.12: Transient form created through the routine daily life of people in Borneo.

One of the most intriguing and unique properties associated with edges is a consequence of their transitional and thus transient nature: a property called looseness.
Loose space can be best understood as a realm that is free, ambiguous, accessible
and open-ended. Such space is indeterminate, embraces freedom of choice, is easily
appropriated and is both flexible and adaptable. In 'Urban Slippage', Dovey and
Polakit (2010), convey the looseness of public space in a Bangkok neighbourhood
as possessing three distinct components. They see looseness '[a]s a conjunction
of loose forms (or loose parts), loose practices (behaviours, functions) and loose
meanings' (ibid., p. 167). For Dovey and Polakit, *loose form* is linked to the flexible
loose parts which move around the neighbourhood, *loose practices* are the manner
in which the same space is used in a multiplicity of ways, and *loose meanings* are in
turn linked to loose relations between form and function.

Others have highlighted similar concepts. The loose form concept can be
seen in the work of Dovey and Raharjo (2010), Habraken (1998) and Fernando
(2007). Each author describes a highly flexible or semi-fixed item that is moveable
throughout the day, and includes items such as stalls, hawker trolleys, furniture and
vehicles. Their observations also show that these loose parts partake in a continuum
moving from the least fixed items, in the open space, to the most fixed items, in
the private space (Dovey and Polakit, 2010). Loose practices have been observed
by Franck and Stevens (2007), Habraken (1998) and Fernando (2007). Their ideas
suggest that a variety of functions and behaviours occurs in these threshold spaces
and that these can evolve and change over time. As Franck and Stevens explain,
'A threshold is a point where the boundary between inside and outside can be
opened; space loosens up' (2007, p. 73). For Franck and Stevens, the very nature
of the transitional edge is 'loose' and therefore susceptible to a multitude of actions
over time.

Finally, loose meanings are supported by the work of Madanipour (2003) and
Habraken (1998). For them, transitional edges are difficult to pinpoint because
of their indeterminate form created by loose parts and loose functions. For
Habraken (1998), this is because the edge is where the physical form determined
by the designer meets the ambiguous and emergent process of user occupation.
Madanipour states that this boundary has an 'ambiguous character' (2003,
pp. 63–4), and suggests that the play between ambiguity and clarity creates a
successful and socially active interface.

Transitional edges appear, then, to be associated with loose characteristics, which are ambiguous, flexible and evolutionary, delivering an impression of an element of urban order in a continuous state of flux and indeterminacy. This looseness can be characterised as loose parts, loose practices and loose meanings and can contribute to its levels of activity.

The segment hypothesis: a socio-spatial framework for transitional edges

This review highlights that there is evidence of consensus about the social significance of built form–public realm interface at the street scale that falls broadly into ten distinguishable, yet closely related, properties and characteristics which in various ways connect spatial and social issues. These are summarised here as:

1. *social activity*: capacity to hold and encourage stationary activity;
2. *public–private gradient*: experience of a smooth gradient from private to public realms;
3. *social interaction*: an interaction between, rather than an abrupt division of, private, semi-private, semi-public realms;
4. *hide and reveal*: localised capacity to facilitate choosing private retreat or social interaction;
5. *spatial expansion*: socially absorbent spaces formed from the overlap of adjacent realms;
6. *enclosure*: localised enclosure along generally coherent edge;
7. *permeability*: capacity for connection to other realms;
8. *transparency*: physical and sensory accessibility to adjacent realms;
9. *territoriality*: capacity for occupation, appropriation and expression;
10. *looseness*: capacity for ambiguity, flexibility and evolution.

Many of these are, of course, familiar terms and concepts within the discourse of urbanism in the Western world. However, what we focus on here is how the relationships among these concepts might allow us to synthesise an understanding of the overall character of transitional edges and in particular on the way that spatial structure relates to social issues. Three key things appear to emerge clearly which help us move forward with this. The first is that the kind of social activity associated with urban edge environments seems to focus mainly on the appropriation, occupation and use of edges. Second is that this manifests as a mutually interdependent relationship of activity and the space where this happens: a kind of indeterminate and evolving urban form arising from the expression of territorial behaviour. Third is that embedding this activity seems to depend on the presence of certain spatial arrangements that have a catalytic function in its encouragement and sustainability. Moving forward, then, we will now discuss the development of a socio-spatial framework for transitional edges that we propose as having the potential to deliver this catalytic function by providing a new morphological basis for design decision-making at edges. We propose this as a structural framework with optimal potential to deliver the socially orientated principles discussed above.

In order to do this, design action has to be recast as the generation of conditions under which transitional edges will flourish rather than the prescription of their finite form. We propose that a framework can be conceived for this by developing it from their underpinning transitional nature: an essentially experiential, rather than physical, conception. By using the denomination *transitional* we acknowledge the key phenomenological nature of transitional edges as realms characterised by change and adaptation, reflecting the interface where social and spatial dimensions of urban form come together. They are, by nature therefore, realms of transformation, or becoming: from inside to outside, mood and atmosphere, function and experience, dynamic in nature and in continuous flux as their form changes and adapts in response to the social forces at work there.

We have begun to explore spatial and experiential qualities of transition in our development of Experiential Landscape (Thwaites and Simkins, 2007, pp. 69–72). Here, the concept of transition is the component of spatial experience that deals with the ways in which we become aware of change and transformation as we move about in our routine daily life, and provides for the identification of certain kinds of spatial organisation that can signal this. In order to reflect that transitional experience is highly variable, from fleeting and abrupt changes through to more complex and gradual transformational experiences, four types of transition have been identified from observational research. These are called: (1) *threshold*; (2) *corridor*; (3) *ephemeral*; and (4) *segment* (Figure 4.13). Of these, the transition type *segment* reflects the existence of spatial situations that have transformational characteristics but which are more complex in nature than threshold and corridor. The main defining feature of a corridor is that it links spaces without having any explicit locational qualities of its own: it is a place to pass through rather than interact with.

A segment, however, recognises that sometimes the predominant sense of transition might also include sensations that bring to the surface specific locational awareness (Figure 4.14). This makes a segment into a kind of integration of transition and centre: a place through which to pass from one realm to another, but which may have a distinguishable sense of place. Segments are usually formed from the overlapping of two adjacent spaces and, as such, possess character-istics that appear as a continuity of both, making a place with its own particular qualities. Segments are associated mostly with spatial circumstances that soften hard unbroken edges, instead allowing adjacent spaces to integrate and flow into one another (Thwaites and Simkins, 2007, p. 72).

Figure 4.13: Thresholds (left) are transitions with little spatial depth which deliver a fairly abrupt cross-over between adjacent realms. Corridors (centre) have spatial extent and provide a tunnel-like but otherwise featureless transition between realms separated by the corridor. Ephemeral transitions (right) are those where the transitional experience is dependent on changing conditions, such as light and shade.

Figure 4.14: A segment delivers a transitional experience but also has locational qualities which give dual characteristics as places to pass through but also to interact with.

Inherent in this general idea of segment are qualities we wish to capture in developing transitional edges as holistic socio-spatial components of urban form. The key significance here is that segments are experiential components which are both complex and socially optimal. Their complexity arises from the way that two adjacent realms resolve where they overlap. Spatial and experiential attributes that characterise segments as complex psychologically and physically engaging places, with distinct identity and transformational significance, tend to reflect greater capacity for social absorbency than other less engaging transition types. Following this, there are two particular qualities useful in developing their definition. The first is the impact of segments on the extent to which directional sensation is emphasised or diminished. This can be related to how Cullen (1971) discusses a sense of place as awareness of 'here' and 'there'. Generally speaking, directional sensation is heightened where the predominant awareness is towards a 'there', rather than 'here', perhaps due to environmental attributes that draw attention to places and features away from where we are, or because there is little to engage attention in the proximate setting (Thwaites and Simkins, 2007; Gehl, 2010, p. 78). Segments can be classified in part, then, in relation to their capacity to decrease predominant directional sensation by emphasising awareness of 'here'. The second relates to what may be described as the social depth of the segment. Because segments occur where adjacent realms overlap, they tend to carry attributes of both realms, but also develop those uniquely their own (Figure 4.15). We suggest that this provides greater potential for social richness and complexity which, along with their impact on directionality, offer a further characteristic for classification which we develop next.

Figure 4.15: The relatively unbroken façade, canopy and tree line in this Rome street (left) combine to deliver a predominantly directional experience, while the setback in building line of this Parisian street corner (right) captures space providing greater social depth.

Segment as socio-spatial structure

As a working approximation, four types of segment have been identified from our observational research which can provide a basis for allowing us to describe the socio-spatial fabric of transitional edges as collectives of segments of different types. In its essence a segment is a transitional experience that becomes a place with its own sense of identity. It can occur at different levels of scale and can be visualised as stretching apart an abrupt threshold so it has extension that can encourage, hold and sustain 'life'. We can identify four types of segment, observable in built environments, which can be related to urban morphology: (1) low intensity; (2) moderate intensity; (3) high intensity; and (4) portal (Figure 4.16). Before looking at these in more detail, it may be helpful to consider the nature of what the segment hypothesis seeks to respond to.

Although perhaps an extreme example, Figure 4.17 (left) represents the kind of hard unbroken edge with no exchange between adjacent realms that can be found characteristic of some contemporary urban development. This represents the extreme antithesis of the transitional edge we envisage here: an environment so abruptly divisive as to offer virtually no prospect of encouraging and absorbing any kind of beneficial urban life. Social depth is, therefore, practically non–existent and the directional experience overwhelming along the building line. The outdoor public realm

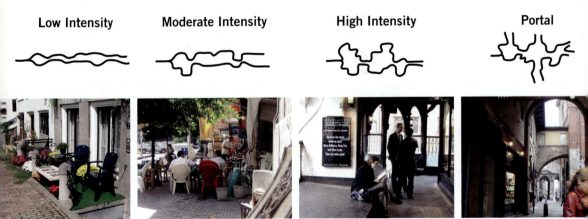

Figure 4.16: The four types of observable segment.

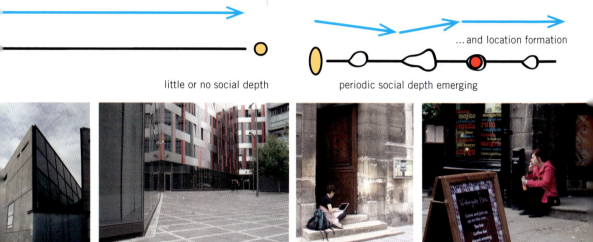

Hard unbroken edge
no exchange between adjacent realms
overwhelmingly directional

Broken edge
some exchange via doorways and windows
strongly directional

… and location formation

little or no social depth

periodic social depth emerging

Abrupt edge between architecture and public
realm with little hope of encouraging 'life'.

Abrupt edges broken by doors and windows
which begin to act as catalysts for social activity.

Figure 4.17: Unbroken and broken edges.

here is little more than that left over after building. Figure 4.17 (right) illustrates how
doorways and windows can act to begin to add social depth to an unbroken edge,
softening its abrupt division of realms by allowing exchange across its threshold. Here
the solid line begins to develop extension at intervals representing the beginning
of social depth offered by the exchange between realms at these specific locations.
Acts of urban life will tend to begin at such points, giving them a catalytic role in
the growth of socio–spatial urban form. The essential point of these two examples is
to demonstrate that where there are divisive thresholds like these, the predominant
experience tends to be directional characterised by rapid transit parallel to the
building edge, minimising engagement with the edge, either entirely, as in the first
example, or restricted to specific small spots as in the second.

In Figure 4.18(a), the edge has developed sufficient depth to encourage and allow
elements of territorial expression to occur. This edge has been able to become a place
in its own right and not just a boundary between two realms. There is beginning
to be opportunity for real fusion between exterior and interior, and because of this

there is a greater degree of engagement possible with what is happening here. This engagement begins to have the effect of slowing down the directional experience by offering perceptual, sensory and physical ways to engage with the edge. Because of this and the social depth beginning here, we identify this as a *low-intensity segment*, a transitional realm with its own emergent socio–spatial identity.

Figure 4.18(b) is an example of an edge with increasing social depth which begins to add greater complexity to its linearity by allowing more space for territorial occupation and social interactions. We will call this a *moderate-intensity segment* because, while the linearity is preserved, acting as an extended transitional realm, the increasing social depth is making the linearity more relaxed, allowing more space for locational (centre) activity to take root, thereby increasing social and spatial complexity. The directional experience here, in comparison to the previous low-intensity segment, becomes less prominent by introducing a more meandering passage encouraging exploration and engagement.

Key

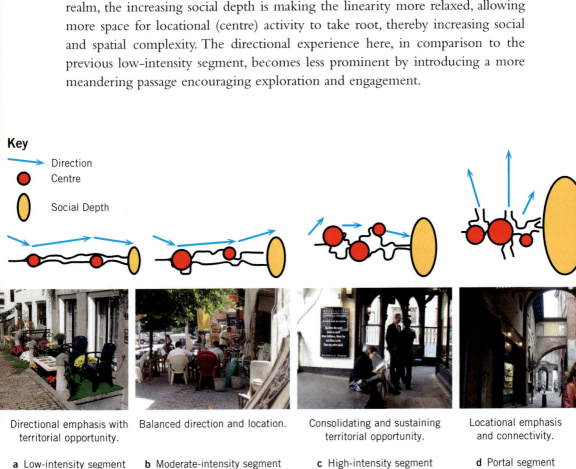

Directional emphasis with territorial opportunity.

Balanced direction and location.

Consolidating and sustaining territorial opportunity.

Locational emphasis and connectivity.

a Low-intensity segment **b** Moderate-intensity segment **c** High-intensity segment **d** Portal segment

Figure 4.18: Segments.

Figure 4.18(c) is a *high-intensity segment*, a location along a transitional edge which is stretched out to such an extent that the linearity becomes increasingly subordinate to more stable locational experience. High-intensity segments are likely to be characterised by greater degrees of spatial enclosure that can encourage higher levels of territorial occupation and sustain localised identity. At this segment level, the distinction between interior and exterior becomes less easily defined. Social depth expands, contributing to the experience of a transitional edge as a sequence of worlds within worlds. Directionality remains but is no longer the dominant experience here, replaced instead by greater awareness of location.

Low-, moderate- and high-intensity segments retain, albeit to decreasing degrees of prominence, a sensation of linearity. Observable in the built environment are components of urban form that, in addition, have a pronounced connectivity role linking together distinct regions and thereby giving permeability to the structure of the urban fabric (Figure 4.18(d)). These are the components of transitional edges that have their own sense of identity, given by their unique socio-spatial characteristics, but also allow us access to realms beyond: what in Cullen's (1971) terminology would represent the passage from a 'here' to a 'there'. These components of the transitional edge are called *portal segments* and are perhaps the most complex in that they are the confluence of connected transitional edges and also distinct socio-spatial realms in their own right.

Collectively, these four types of segment conceptualise a morphological framework with a catalytic capability to encourage the kind of human interactions that are widely acknowledged as desirable, possibly essential, elements of socially sustainable urban environments. In Part III, we will discuss the development and application of Experiemics, a participative process that can play a key role in activating the catalytic capability of transitional edges and their constituent strings of segments. Before doing so, we will try to draw together the social significance of transitional edges in a particular range of qualities they need to possess, illustrating these with examples drawn from the built environment.

Chapter Five

Transitional edge anatomy

Extent, locality and laterality

Introduction

In this chapter we move forward with the transitional edge concept, based on collectives of segments of different types, to consider some of the underlying qualities of this morphological structure to see how this may help begin to identify guidance for design decision-making. This will help to establish a bridging point between spatial considerations, an essentially design-driven issue, and processes of self-organisation, a socially orientated participative issue which we will elaborate in Part III. In order to do so, we will briefly summarise how the theoretical resources considered thus far help us to further develop the structure of segments into a more comprehensive anatomical framework for transitional edges.

Within the wider Experiential Landscape framework, segments are understood as particular categories of transitional experience: those of a more complex experiential kind which deliver a sensation of transition, yet also have locational attributes. In essence, what distinguishes a segment from other forms of transition is that segments are more psychologically engaging in their own right: they have a capacity to hold attention over and above being the mere 'threshold' between two adjacent realms. They appear when adjacent realms overlap and are stretched with spatial extent, rather than simply abutting to form an abrupt boundary.

Through investigation of this segment principle, and other experiential categories, in existing urban environments, we began to realise that segments could be further classified into distinguishable types. For example, all had transitional properties laterally, in the way that they linked adjacent realms, but varied in their predominance of directional and locational sensations. These variations appeared to reflect differences in their potential capacity to encourage and accommodate stationary activity while diminishing the sensation of direction. Using the terminology of Cullen (1971) in his articulation of townscape place experience, therefore, low-intensity segments were those that preserved a predominant sensation of 'there', while higher-intensity segments tended to replace this with a greater sense of 'here'. What this highlighted, when these variations were taken into account, was that segments tended not to appear discretely but were observable sequentially, strung out along the extent of edges formed by overlapping adjacent realms. As one progressed along the extent of such an edge, the degree to which directional or locational attributes predominated tended to change according to local conditions, reflecting the changing type of segment (Figure 5.1).

In this more holistic way, we could then imagine the anatomical structure of transitional edges as connected strings of varying segment types which collectively give particular attributes to the *extent*, *laterality* and *locational* nature of transitional edges. We found that we could usefully relate the ten characteristics described in Chapter 4 to this transitional edge anatomical structure as socio-spatial attributes

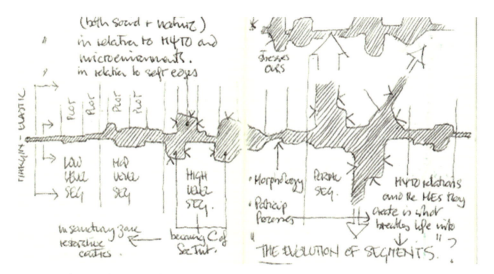

Figure 5.1: Progression along an edge, with change in directional or locational attributes.

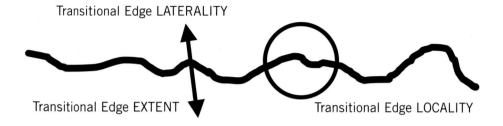

Figure 5.2: Varying segment types collectively give particular attributes to the *extent, locality* and *laterality* nature of transitional edges

that act 'along' it (in other words those with particular relevance to a transitional edge's *extent*); those which act 'across' it (those with special relevance to the *lateral* nature of a transitional edge); and those which act 'at' parts of it (those with *locational* significance at intervals within it) (Figure 5.2).

Transitional edge extent

When we do this, we can see that 'enclosure and looseness' seem to be properties that particularly relate to a transitional edge's extent. They help to develop understanding that the overall characteristic of a transitional edge's 'extent' is that there should be overall coherence but not rigid uniformity, and that this coherence should be constructed in such a way as to deliver a series of varying enclosures, perhaps visualised in terms of an informally crenulated edge. Its overall experience should be a simultaneous awareness of continuity and localised proximity and, in the context of our discussion of segments, the balance of awareness between continuity and proximity would vary according to the locally present segment type. The optimum situation would be for a balance of segment types to be available throughout the extent of the transitional edge. A degree of stability appears to be important to maintain an enduring sense of continuity across space and time, a quality that would be important in the establishment of sustaining local identity. However, this would ideally be balanced with a level of flexibility allowing localised adaptability and evolutionary change reflecting developing patterns of use, territorial negotiations, social and biological growth, etc., in other words, for there to be an inherent looseness to allow for an accumulation of human and natural adaptations to take hold, reflecting the transitory rather than static nature of the transitional edge.

Transitional edge locality

'Social activity, hide and reveal, spatial expansion, and territoriality' seem to be properties especially relevant to the locality of settings within the transitional edge. An overall emphasis here seems to be on socio-spatial factors that act to slow down the experience of continuity along the extent of a transitional edge by providing localised and stationary significance. Such stationary experience is linked to the capacity of a transitional edge for social absorbency, connected to the extent to which inhabitants can territorialise through occupation, appropriation and personalisation of spaces defined at intervals where adjacent realms overlap. Spatial expansion, therefore, appears to be necessary for locational experience to take hold, encouraging social activity of varying degrees of duration. The ability to be able to control when and how we hide and reveal, by means of localised and personalised arrangement of material boundaries, barriers and other features, enables personal control of our needs for privacy and social interaction. Research even appears to suggest an optimum dimension of about 3.75m as a spatial expansion that will bring people into sufficiently close proximity to encourage mutual acknowledgement and exchange without engendering oppressive feelings of invasiveness.

Transitional edge laterality

There are also properties which seem to focus on a transitional edge's lateral characteristics. Specifically, 'public–private gradient, permeability, and transparency' which characterise transects across the transitional edge as a smooth and seamless gradation from private territories through semi-private and semi-public ones, possibly to fully public ones and back again. The important aspect of this is not simply the capacity to deliver the gradual experience of transition from one to the other, important to allow for appropriate adjustment from 'public' behaviour gradually through to 'private', but also to optimise opportunities for social inter-actions at the merging points of these realms. It appears commonly acknowledged in the literature that a substantial amount of, particularly casual or spontaneous, social encounter occurs where private/semi-private, or semi-private/semi-public realms are allowed to become spatially integrated for an interval. Such spaces may also act as connecting points to other realms, contributing to important permeability. Another property which appears to have particular lateral significance is transparency, which, in Cullen's (1971) terms, contributes to allowing us to distinguish here from there across the adjacent realms that form the transitional edge.

Collectively, this helps us to understand the nature of transitional edges as complex components of urban form with mutually interdependent social and spatial characteristics. We have suggested that the underlying anatomy of transitional edges can be conceptualised in terms of connected strings of segments of different types, which in different but complementary ways provide the socio-spatial infrastructure of the transitional edge. This provides optimal conditions for supporting a range of important socially orientated experiences which have particular implications for the nature of the transitional edge's extent and for its local and lateral properties. Different segment types, therefore, through their connectivity and collective socio-spatial characterisation help to underpin that if the principal purpose of transitional edges is to optimise social absorbency, then this is most likely to be achieved when their intrinsic transitional nature is complemented by the capacity for the following (Figure 5.3):

- *spatial porosity*, to encourage and accommodate stationary as well as movement-related activity;
- *localised expression*, enabling such activity to become a significant factor in determining local identity;
- *coherence and adaptability*, to exhibit an enduring sense of overall coordination while remaining flexible to localised acts of change.

This tripartite framework provides a basis from which to explore how such qualities might appear in urban environments. In order to do this, we have selected a range of examples explored in detail during the development of observational criteria for transitional edges. These examples are not intended to provide a blueprint for transitional edges, but simply to begin to illustrate some aspects of material and spatial form that can be associated with the concepts we discuss here.

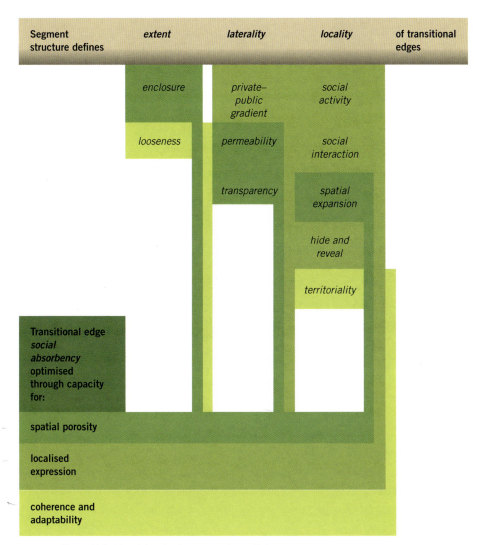

Figure 5.3: Transitional edges: a socio-spatial anatomy.

Spatial porosity

Defying any clear demarcation, spaces are separated and simultaneously connected by porous boundaries, through which everyday life takes form in mutually dependent public performances.

(Stravides, 2007, p. 175)

Figure 5.4: When spatial organisation integrates transparency, permeability and enclosure, it becomes porous, absorbent to a diversity of social experience, Ljubljana, Slovenia.

Spatial porosity refers mainly to the structural properties of transitional edges, highlighting the need for a socially absorbent structural realm capable of attracting and holding activity in such a way as to accommodate density without oppressive crowding. As we established in our earlier discussion about segments, long largely unbroken edges, which allow for little or no interaction across adjacent realms, have very limited capacity for social absorbency. This is principally because the spatial structure delivers emphatically directional experience with limited social width and locational significance. The spatial porosity of such a setting would be very limited indeed and in consequence one would not expect to find much in the way of stationary human occupation or activity along it. As the intensity of the segment type increases, however, so too in general does its spatial porosity as the directional emphasis gradually recedes, giving way to more locational significance amenable to stationary activity. Spatial porosity can be closely related to the properties discussed earlier as enclosure, transparency and permeability, and we can visualise this in terms of perforated boundaries. These tend to be associated with forms of urban structure that deliver a clear sense of proximity, or 'here', but which have sufficient open-ness to provide sensory and/or physical accessibility through to adjacent realms, or 'there'.

The kind of 'mutually dependent public performances' that make up everyday life, referred to by Stravides, are vividly played out along Sheffield's Eccleshall Road, for example, where linear and stationary spaces are separated yet connected allowing a well-ordered and complex range of social functioning to take place along its length (Figure 5.5). The porosity of Eccleshall Road is predominantly given by its capacity to maintain different kinds of moving and stationary street activity together, safely and efficiently within adjacent realms, while simultaneously allowing these to integrate freely across thresholds. Eccleshall Road is a predominantly directional environment: one mile of busy arterial traffic flow to and from the south-west of the city. Yet its diversely segmented edge, characterised by a highly transparent relationship of built form and adjacent public space, delivers a string of varying enclosures which attract and accommodate stationary activity as an integral part of the street's function as a vehicle and pedestrian movement corridor. Flexible, open frontages to shops, bars and restaurants provide a perforated edge blending together interior and exterior space, while their narrow terraces, raised and at street level, provide numerous opportunities for active and passive engagement between people passing by and those involved in stationary pursuits. The resulting ensemble provides a harmonious, dynamic and theatrical blend of movement, pause and occupation afforded by the spatially porous

Figure 5.5: Sheffield's Eccleshall Road. Predominantly a busy vehicle and pedestrian corridor made socially absorbent by its string of mainly low- and moderate-intensity segments.

transitional edge. Eccleshall Road is a magnet for people-watching due to its holistic blend of separation and connectivity across thresholds, providing a highly absorbent framework for the continuous and dynamic dance of social exchange along it.

Eccleshall Road provides an example of spatial porosity in a predominantly linear environment of relatively narrow spatial expansion, at least compared to the richness in variety of social activity it supports. A more expansive and architecturally

Figure 5.6: Chester's Rows. A three-dimensional grid of spatial volumes packed and interconnected in a network of territories which hold and express the city's diverse social identity.

more dramatic example of spatially porous urban form can be found in the historic Rows of the city of Chester (Figure 5.6). Chester's Rows are a unique type of urban form, thought to have evolved from the city's medieval origins, which today continue to support the city's commercial, retail and recreational core. The centre of Chester is characterised by its decorative building façades which give the streetscape a highly distinctive quality, but it is the spatial composition that we focus on here. The uniqueness of the Rows lies in their continuous covered, open-fronted, 'walkways', elevated above the now largely pedestrianised streets. In consequence, it provides an unprecedented assemblage of all segment types linked together in almost unbroken continuum throughout the core of the small city centre. In purely spatial terms, Chester's public urban fabric consists of a sequence of tightly defined, yet highly transparent, spatial enclosures packed together over two storeys and in some instances three, because of the contribution of semi-basement spaces. It is in spatial essence a three-dimensional grid-like structure, fractal-like in its integration of self-similarity and localised variation, arising from the plot-based arrangement of built form and the variations of decorative and functional expression it has received throughout its historic evolution. This spatial structure defines a highly porous interconnected arrangement of localised terri-tories into which the city's commercial and social life is projected delivering a richly varied yet coherent streetscape. The diversity of social opportunity that such an absorbent structure affords is evident in the variety of functions accommodated. It provides a compact, dense and widely adaptable framework for a wide range of retail, office and residential use, as well as supporting spontaneous and casual social gathering through use of its galleried display areas for watching street performance, or just people moving about, and the appropriation of quieter spots by groups of teenagers as sheltered social haunts.

Localised expression

[H]uman needs are sacrificed on the altar of design and aestheticism in many British towns ... People tend to go missing in the pristine imagery of archi-tecture and design where life's untidiness is regarded as an aesthetic intrusion.

(Worpole, 1998)

Spatial porosity is a structural quality which we associate with opportunity to optimise how social activity can be expressed and embodied in urban form.

Figure 5.7: Localised expression in the pageant of a Venice washday, and its antithesis in the form-dominant 'designer neatness' of Salford's Chimneypot Park development.

Chester's Rows and Eccleshall Road are examples of porous urban form within which their particular identities are captured and expressed in a mutually inter-dependent relationship of spatial and social order. For this to happen, localised expression needs encouragement and facility. Localised expression highlights that how transitional edges appear to us arises from the way that patterns of occupation and use become projected into the environment. How we perceive them is, therefore, at least as much a manifestation of what routinely takes place there as it is the material and spatial infrastructure that accommodates it. What we are trying to focus on here is that, when certain structural and social conditions prevail, people are more likely to feel encouraged and empowered to express their individual and collective identities, their activities and values, in their immediately adjacent surroundings. It is this that should be at least as significant in the way that we perceive our environment as that which has been introduced by profes-sional planning and design processes. We suggest that this is more likely to occur in socially active environments where social activity forms a strong part of the local identity. The characteristics of public–private gradient and hide and reveal, discussed earlier, for example, may well be those which, when present, create the kind of local conditions to encourage a greater diversity of individual and collective expression into the surrounding environment (Figure 5.8).

Figure 5.8: An open structure to gardens in Vastra Hamnen, Malmö, Sweden, allows the expressions of residents to contribute to the identity of the public realm while retaining control of their privacy and degree of exposure.

Spatial porosity is a quality of socially restorative urbanism that primarily addresses the structural characteristics of space in relation to optimising social potential. Within this structure, then, localised expression addresses how social processes relating mainly to territorial activity become activated to take on spatial and material form. It is, in essence, about how the lives of people can become a more visible part of urban form: a conspicuous lack of which Ken Worpole lamented in the epigraph at the head of this section. We have discussed earlier how encouragement to do so depends in large part on the opportunities people have to perceive, and then respond to, degrees of privacy and publicity. Where the public realm abuts the private one abruptly, the visibility of people's expressive action tends to extrude into the public realm minimally, if indeed at all. A residential area in the north of the Bo01 zone of the Vastra Hamnen development, Malmö, Sweden, provides an interesting example of seamless private to public gradient, in which the localised expressions of residents, through the arrangement of gardens and associated artefacts, characterise the publicly accessible adjacent landscape (although in reality this internally facing landscape is strictly more semi-public than public). In most instances, here, there is no formal boundary around the private gardens and so the overall effect is of a merging of private and semi-public realms, rather than a separation of them. What has been introduced through choices made by residents about the amount and extent of enclosure, boundary treatments, outbuildings, vegetation cover, as well as very personal touches in the form of garden ornamentation and seating, etc., is what largely defines the identity of this residential area. The lack of pre-given formal barriers has led to a highly varied and imaginative juxtaposition of features through which residents have retained a significant measure of control over how they define and control their privacy, and how much they reveal to neighbours and passers-by. In this way, spaces overlap between public, private and communal space: gardens are very much a part of the public realm and the public realm very much a part of the private garden experience in mutual interdependence.

A similar kind of localised expression can be found in the earlier, and arguably less gentrified, Homes for Change development, a part of the Hulme regeneration project, Manchester, of the early 1990s (Figure 5.9). The Homes for Change development is perhaps a more comprehensive example of localised expression in that it expresses both the lives of its residents and families through their occupation and use, but also that of the wider residents' cooperative set up to spearhead the design and development. A result of close collaboration between architects and the cooperative of prospective residents, the Homes for Change is a live–work development planned for 75 dwellings and units for 26 small businesses. The largely internal-facing residential/work-unit blocks enclose communal courtyard gardens which form a complex blend of private, semi-private and communal spaces set out at different levels. The material arrangement of internal block façades has been used in such a way as to give the development a human scale, a domestic feel. In

Figure 5.9: Homes for Change, Hulme, Manchester: a balance of form, place and understanding?

consequence, it has a much less mass manufactured appearance than many multi-storey residential blocks, which, along with its spatial organisation, encourages and accommodates a lively diversity of personalisation by residents with pot plants, storage devices, children's toys, outdoor seating and clothes drying apparatus. After more than 20 years of life, the identity of Homes for Change is not that of romanticised communal living: it has the texture of authentic lived experience which, through a combination of careful spatial design and resident management, seems to have evolved into a sustaining balance of individuality and communal interests. In Habraken's terms, there is plentiful evidence of place-making and common understanding contributing a unique sense of identity to the initial structural form.

Coherence and adaptation

> It is characteristic of people that they reflect and weigh alternatives before they act. People must choose; therefore, they must deliberate and achieve consensus for any act concerning more than one person. The Order of Understanding is primarily social.
>
> (Habraken, 1998, p. 11)

Finally, sustainable social absorbency must be recognised as something dynamic that depends on change and evolution. The literature supports that this involves the achievement of a balance between the maintenance of a sense of overall coherence, important to the establishment of enduring identity, familiarity and ultimately legibility, but which should in the finer grain of detail be amenable to acts of continual adaptation and change. One way to understand this in relation to how social behaviour is projected into the surrounding environment is in terms of how people try to balance self-assertion with the need for conformity. As discussed earlier, this seemingly contradictory human attribute is associated with intuitive territorial behaviour and is an important factor in the achievement of self-esteem. People must become aware of themselves as individuals, possessed of a sense of 'mine', but they also need to belong, and through this experience a sense of 'ours'. When conditions are appropriate, this dynamic exchange may well project into the environment as acts of expressive individualism, but ones which, for the most part, remain constrained within mutually accepted norms which deliver an overall sense of coherence and identity at the collective scale. Significant environmental attributes in this respect might include looseness and ambiguity, encouraging

Figure 5.10: Adaptability in produce display expresses the individuality of traders while contributing to the coherence of an Alexandrian street market.

individual interpretation, appropriation and adaptation, but which also encourage territorial negotiations which work towards an overall sense of belonging, mutual support and shared concern.

The dynamic, yet sustaining, inter-relationship of coherence and adaptability can be found on the island of Burano, in the northern Venetian lagoon (Figure 5.11). Originally settled by the Romans, Burano is today known for lace-making and its brightly coloured houses. In essence, Burano is a complex collective of small plot-based lots tightly packed adjacent to a network of canals and defining a sequence of small squares and courtyards. Although visually and spatially complex, Burano is structurally very simple owing to the repetition of very similar building types with slight localised variations in height, setback, colour and façade detailing, for example. Through use of this relatively narrow range of adaptation in built form and the spatial arrangement it defines, Burano is endlessly varied, yet entirely coherent in its structure. This provides a structural and spatial framework against which many acts of localised adaptation can be accommodated without breaking down the overall coherence. Burano's identity is sustained through the cooperation of its inhabitants to adhere to established controls over which colours are permitted to be used in particular lots. Although this represents a statutory control over the coherence of the settlement, it has not inhibited relatively idiosyncratic contributions, such as the photo on the right of Figure 5.11, which might stray close to the boundaries of communal accept-ability, but which add interest and individuality without breaking the balance of the whole.

Delivering coherence and adaptability in larger-scale developments brings particular challenges. Coherence in the form of large-scale blocks can often mean sterile monumentality where opportunities for adaptability are few because the infrastructure is not often readily amenable to change and people are discouraged because the environments they create are frequently not at a scale manageable for personal adaptation, especially outside. The Java Island residential development in the docklands of Amsterdam delivers a spatial infrastructure that goes some way to

Figure 5.11: Fine grain adaptability accommodated within strong overall coherence, Burano, Italy.

Figure 5.12: The larger scale of coherence delivered by the residential blocks of Java Island, Amsterdam, gradually gives way to a looser structure at smaller scales encouraging local adaptability.

responding (Figure 5.12). Essentially a linear development of large-scale residential blocks set out along the extent of the Java Island dock provides an overall sense of coherence to the development. The blocks define a series of enclosures which gradually reduce in scale into smaller communal and then individually scaled settings. The overall effect is rather like a set of nested settings which initially break the overall development into a series of neighbourhoods within which are smaller communally scaled settings, and within these, usually around the building edges, are individual or shared garden spaces at manageable scales for personal adaptations. At this level of scale, and because of the adaptive interventions of local groups and individuals, the environment has a much looser and more ambiguous feel. This delivers a form of coherence, arising largely from the collective impact of vegetation, small structures and boundaries at a more human scale, but a form of coherence that can be sustained through continuous adaptations within the overall development structure.

Vegetation plays a significant role in the coherence and adaptation of the Java Island development, at different levels of scale, from the structural which softens the large scale of built form through to the human scale of private gardens and communal areas. Much the same is evident in parts of the Hammerby Sjostad development to the south of Stockholm city centre (Figure 5.13). Located around Hammerby Lake, the development is Stockholm's largest urban development in many years and boasts a strong emphasis on ecology and environmental sustainability. In this case, the emphasis given to the establishment of green infrastructure contributes at least as much to the overall coherence of the development as does the built form. Hammerby's green infrastructure filters through into the development's many residential courtyard areas where, like Java Island, it contributes to the delivery of human-scale spatial organisation amenable to change and adaptation by the resident communities in the form of allotment gardens, play areas and other adaptable spaces. The naturalistic feel of much of the green infrastructure around Hammerby Sjostad creates a network of loose green margins throughout the development and especially along the lakeside, which captures and emphasises the adaptable and evolutionary qualities of the natural environment. This is a quality consistent with the development's environmental aspirations, but also helps to enhance social gains in the form of restorative benefits to residents through their routine encounter and interaction with the semi-natural landscape settings.

Figure 5.13: Green infrastructure contributes to the overall coherence of Hammerby Sjostad, feeding through into communal courts and loose green margins emphasising the adaptability and evolving nature of green open space.

Transitional edges, Habraken and Experiemics

We have now developed a more comprehensive understanding of the anatomy of transitional edges, consisting of strings of segments collectively acting on their laterality, extent and locality. We are also able to say that, in order to optimise the social absorbency of transitional edges, the strings of segments that constitute transitional edges must collectively deliver a spatially porous structure, facilitate and empower localised expression, and have overall coherence yet be adaptable and amenable to change. With this conceptual framework we can then return to the work of John Habraken (1998), who has focused his understanding of the structure of the ordinary built environment as a relationship of control levels that people are able to exert, or not exert, within the built environment they inhabit.

Harbraken's 'form' is essentially a structural concept and we have tried to demonstrate that what we see in much of contemporary urban design is a highly form-orientated approach which, arguably, places excessive amounts of control in the hands of specialised professional agencies. However, there must be form and, as Habraken points out, there must be professionals capable of delivering form that is structurally stable and enduring. We suggest here that if form can be delivered which has more of the characteristics of spatial porosity, as we envisage it here, then it may be reasonable to speculate that we may have form which is more, rather than less, amenable to achieving a re-balancing of form with Habraken's other two observations about control, those of place and understanding.

Place arises from processes of occupation, and in the terms we have developed here, this facilitates localised expression as space transforms into place through the meanings, values and uses that occupiers give it along with the way that those decisions and subsequent activities are expressed by them. Habraken then offers the level of control he calls understanding, an essentially territorial conception as people find ways to reflect their own individuality in their occupied places while recognising the constraining influence of others they share occupation with, as families, neighbours and communities. For this level of understanding to work, the environment in which it takes place must be able to be worked upon so that the expressions of individuality can become finely balanced with the mutual respect and conformity through which a sense of overall coherence can be sustained. In this way, and taking our lead from Habraken, we can demonstrate that, conceptually at the very least, a close bond of integration exists between decisions made at the level of structural fabrication and the extent to which these can be occupied and appropriated in socially beneficial ways driven by territorial negotiations.

Work that we will talk about in Part III highlights also the importance of understanding transitional edges as fundamentally interconnected systems. Our discussion of the anatomy and characteristics of transitional edges thus far has tended to focus on the way they define the interface of built form and adjacent open space as a fusion of spatial and social dimensions. While important and indeed intrinsic to the way edge environments appear in much of the wider literature, as discussed in Chapter 4, this does not perhaps pay sufficient attention to the nature of transitional edges to weave together forming larger spatial networks. As we have described, accumulations of segments form transitional edges and while low-, moderate- and high-intensity segments predominantly characterise attributes of a particular transitional edge, giving it localised identity, it is the portal segment that acts to connect it to other transitional edges. As an idealisation, then, by means of portal segments, transitional edges exist in mosaics of interconnectedness with the capacity to reach across large spatial areas.

This expanded conception of transitional edges has important potential to embrace other elements of the urban realm, architecturally less tangible perhaps, but nonetheless vital to spatial fabric and social value. Along with the connective function attributed to portal segments, other anatomical properties we have attributed to the transitional edge concept in this chapter, laterality and extent particularly, provide the means by which city communication networks can be incorporated into the same conceptual structure. We will highlight this in Part III with work focused on public transport systems in Sheffield. This illustrates in particular how the balance of MTOY relationships, which underpin the territorial balance we seek through the segment hypothesis, similarly applies beyond the specific context of the built form and open space interface.

So, just as Eccleshall Road, discussed above, is a transitional edge with relatively tightly packed segments largely experienced at either stationary or pedestrian pace, the wider public transport infrastructure can be thought of as having similar socio-spatial attributes, but much more stretched, characterised by more rapid movement and specific points of embarkation, which are in effect portal segments. Public transport networks can therefore be understood as particular categories of transitional edges that are stretched out and woven into the wider fabric of the urban realm at a larger scale. We believe this further demonstrates the need for a fusion of disciplinary boundaries so that the provision of urban public transport transcends merely the domain of traffic management agencies and highways planning and engineering. Just as we have discussed the social value intimately integrated with particular morphological properties in transitional edges at the building, open space interface, so too does social visibility, confidence and competence require similar consideration to be given to the more stretched out and spatially extensive transitional edges of public transport systems.

In Part III, then, we will talk about the development and application of a participative process called Experiemics. Initially conceived as an inclusive means to give voice to groups in society who traditionally are marginalised and in most cases, to all practical purposes, excluded from decision-making about places they use, Experiemics offers potential as a means to empower individuals and groups to regain some measure of control at Habraken's levels of place and understanding. We suggest that, especially in the spatially optimal circumstances that we now understand in terms of transitional edges, Experiemics can work in a complementary way to deliver social as well as material benefits through engagement with environments routinely used, including as we shall show, public transport provision, by working to overcome a present tendency to polarise the 'mine' and 'theirs', with a resurgent emphasis on the experience of 'ours': the sense of belonging that much of contemporary urban development has hitherto overlooked. The work done with our learning disability colleagues has helped to highlight that their sense of belonging at these transitional edges is crucial to the achievement of a sense of participation within the wider urban community. Done well, it can then expand their contribution and influence beyond the specific and relatively narrow range of locations with which they are usually associated.

Locality

In a typical UK city centre (Figure 5.14(a)) professional planning and design have given dominance to the flow of vehicular traffic, rather than the human use that activates urban spaces and streets. As such, there is little identifiable sense of *location* at the transitional edge. In Figure 5.14(b) we see how this detrimentally affects patterns of human occupation, illustrated both by the men to the left of the image and the women to the right who display considerable vulnerability, caught between multiple transport corridors. Here an individual's level of mine, or personal control over the environment, is exceedingly low, reduced to the narrowest of spatial margins. Where locational opportunity is absent, the negative result of such urban environments is socially significant, as users experience a noted decrease in individual confidence and competence.

Figure 5.14(a): Locality.   Figure 5.14(b): Locality.

Laterality

Photographs taken at eye level (Figure 5.15(a) and 5.15(b)) reveal an absence of *laterality* between the pavement and road at the transitional edge in this busy urban street. No spatial allowance has been made to develop a clear point of arrival and transition. Again transport movement is the dominant feature, but this time there is

Figure 5.15(a): Laterality.   Figure 5.15(b): Laterality.

added competition over edge ownership between private (parked cars) and public (buses) uses. Therefore the individual user experience of public transport (bus service) is made unecessarily difficult by a lateral blockage of private use (parked cars) which inhibits the fluidity of embarking and departing. The overall effect is a loss of laterality (both spatial and experiential) and ease of movement, which is felt acutely by the disembarking passengers.

Extent

Along a key pedestrian access route to a city centre public transport hub the stressful nature of urban life is intensified by limited *extent* (Figure 5.16(a)). Crucial views are constrained by solid edges (brick walls to either side), inappropriate location of street furniture and physical blockages (the portable toilet blocks in the background of the image). As a result, there is an intensified sense of human competition and congestion. No space to pause or gain bearings is given, which leaves pedestrians with no option but to continue forward at a pace dictated to them by their constrained environment. However, upon reaching the transport hub (Figure 5.16(b)), they are not rewarded for their excursions. There is little sense of arrival, extensive views continue to be compromised by hard edges, vehicular transport flow dominates and the environment presents few opportunities for human affordance.

Figure 5.16(a): Extent.   Figure 5.16(b): Extent.

PART III

EXPERIEMICS

Introduction

A central commitment in our research has always been to try to ensure that our theoretical stance provides the strong foundation from which our research-into-practice work can deliver social and environmental change in everyday environments. In order to help achieve this within our developing concept of socially restorative urbanism, we tried to show in Part II how an examination of transitional edges emphasises the need to understand their nature as being in a holistic socio-spatial relationship. The mutually interdependent contribution that spatial and social dimensions make to the manifestation of urban order appears to be especially heightened at transitional edges, and this requires some re-orientation in the approaches, professional and community, which need to be adopted in their delivery. This brings to focus attention on the relationship between spatial configuration and user participation. In this final section, therefore, we continue this journey from theory to practice and along the way explore the emerging capacity of Experiemics to catalyse the social action inherent in the socio-spatial manifestation of the transitional edge.

We therefore begin by examining the potential and current restrictions on the adoption of participative practice. In our research and practice in participatory approaches and the relationship this has to the delivery of both social benefit and environmental change, we have become increasingly aware that significant among these limitations is the absence of methods to include those who have been systematically alienated from the decision-making arena. One of the more frequently articulated criticisms of professionally led participatory practice is that it often tends to privilege, and therefore advantage, vocal and expressive minorities, perhaps leaving the voices of the majority unheard and unheeded. While many may exclude themselves from participatory processes because of apathy, reticence, lack of confidence, or time, there are many in society who do not have the opportunity to exercise such choice. For a wide range of reasons, perhaps relating to health, age at both extremes, social isolation, etc., active participation is not usually expected, or at times is not welcomed or facilitated because of particular challenges that are perceived to exist and that need to be overcome.

The outcome is that many people in society simply become excluded from even the most well-meaning of participative processes. From our point of view, this identifies a clear need for partnership working with certain excluded groups to develop more inclusive and effective approaches. Our work here, which we will discuss in Chapter 6, demonstrates that there is no need for 'special' processes that address excluded groups as unique social categories, but by working with them to develop methods and approaches that work for them we arrive at approaches that are inclusive and accessible to everyone. These approaches are key if participation is not to be restricted to mere involvement, but accepted as a means to ensure social transformation. This transformation returns us to Habraken's *form, place* and *understanding*, with the opportunity to tip the balance in favour of socially restorative urban design and development.

From a long-established research partnership working with disabled communities across the UK, the Experiemic Process emerges. In its seven stages, ownership, understanding and belonging are built. The framework of Experiemics is by no means static and, as we demonstrate, has been and continues to be shaped through the input of communities and individuals: it is above all a framework which is adaptive and evolutionary in its approach and application. These communities vary widely from people with learning disabilities to landscape architecture students across Europe to school staff, including dinner ladies, caretakers and teachers. Not least among these partners are children whose views are often overlooked in favour of adult assumptions but by whose actions the approach and methods of Experiemics have been greatly refined.

Experiemics may be applied in any everyday environmental situation that might benefit from increased professional understanding and collective belonging. Later, in Chapter 7, we will illustrate this through a number of examples. Whether employed to improve an individual's journey to work ('Excuse Me, I Want to Get

On!'; 'What's the Fuss, We Want the Bus!'), to create a plan for ownership and use of outdoor spaces ('Experiential Mapping') or to make playtime and lesson time a more enjoyable experience at school ('North-East of England School'; 'Experiential Learning from Children') (Chapter 8), Experiemics is a powerful tool. Its constant evolution and adaptability of application ensure that, especially when the socio-spatial properties we have associated with transitional edges occur, whatever the setting or population, change in favour of a more socially restorative environment can be achieved. Again, with reference to Habraken's concepts, when transitional edges have certain characteristics of 'form', then 'place' and 'understanding' have the potential to become more active in the realisation of urban order. Experiemics provides an effective means for this activation and therefore offers the potential to redress persistent imbalance of form, place and understanding in prevailing approaches.

Chapter Six

The need for participative processes

Introduction

> Excluding users in the design and planning process, based on the assumption that all people are the same, usually results in solutions that are totally uniform, in which everyone is assumed to have identical requirements.
>
> (Sanoff, 2000, p. 22)

Public participation has been promoted as a means of ensuring the production of user-friendly, sustainable, responsibly designed environments. This has been acknowledged at an international level through UNCED's Local Agenda 21, marking an important milestone regarding community involvement in neighbourhood and open space decision-making (UNCED, 1992). Defined as 'the act of sharing in the formulation of policies and proposals' (Skeffington, 1969), community participation has many well-recorded social benefits, including increased awareness of global environmental problems (Van Herzele *et al.*, 2005; Ohmer *et al.*, 2009) and development of greater community ownership leading to a reduction of negative social actions such as vandalism and anti-social behaviour. Where participatory processes are seen as transparent and inclusive, the number of positive social interactions increases, as does the sense of community (Speller and Ravenscroft, 2005). In times of economic constraint, community participation can also provide the opportunity to offset or accommodate public funding cuts through the volunteer involvement, such as special interest groups and in the UK and the USA 'Friends of' organisations.

Armed with considerable positive evidence to support the use of participatory practices, surely as professionals, we should now be in a strong position to employ community involvement as another tool of our trade, and include all in the design of the built and natural environment? It is true that we have more academic and practitioner guidance than ever before regarding possible participative methods (such as that produced by the Commission for Architecture and the Built Environment (CABE). Yet we are still in danger of ending up with uniform design solutions, spaces that lack place identity and do not meet the range of user requirements. Looking a little more closely, it becomes apparent that participation is not straightforward. Processes of participation can be complex. Challenges include management of vocal (and powerful) individual agendas which can override collectively agreed approaches, the worry for professionals and policy-makers regarding resourcing of time-consuming participatory practice and the sensitivity needed to manage community expectations. Among these, and central to our story, is the concern that many participative processes still exclude those who may gain most benefit from user-led design. These groups remain hidden through a lack of opportunities to engage in the design debate. One such group is people with learning disabilities (PWLD). To date, PWLD, a group who already experience considerable marginalisation and discrimination, have appeared almost invisible in the eyes of landscape design and architecture professionals (Mathers, 2008, after Imrie and Hall, 2001). Even within studies that aim to facilitate and understand environmental inclusion of disabled people, PWLD are segregated due to 'predicted' participation difficulties: 'mentally disabled were not interviewed, as it was considered too difficult to interview them' (Seeland and Nicolè, 2006). If participation is to be promoted as a means to readdress social problems in our public spaces, we cannot be exclusionary about whom we invite to participate. Participation should be a right for all. Understanding methods and processes to involve more hidden populations enables us to be responsive and inclusive of the diversity of people who share our everyday environments.

Exclusion in environment

To address the issue of the persistent absence of PWLD and other groups from participatory practice, we must first understand the context in which this has been justified and, second, look to create practice for its reversal. For PWLD, a key issue has been the general acceptance of PWLD as excluded 'rather than as experiencing material and representational discrimination and poverty ... to see them as not part of mainstream society, a situation that seems acceptable to many in society' (Hall, 2004, after Enable, 1999). PWLD have been labelled as *other* for centuries, generating unmerited isolation, fear and mistrust. Hall (2004, after Sibley, 1995) believes that in order for PWLD to become part of the accepted norm, with equal rights to oppose discrimination, PWLD would have to reflect what the majority sees in themselves and their daily experiences. This would encompass equivalent 'bodily behaviour and appearance, social location and/or economic engagement' (Sibley, 1995; Hall, 2004, p. 300). This is a normalcy that does not value diversity, substituting it for a more palatable fantasy as bland as it is unreal. Unfortunately this is being mirrored in our production of increasingly bland environments that seek to somehow accommodate the average person, if people are considered at all, and in this quest for the normal limit the participation of many.

Our public spaces should provide a level playing field, where the community may interact without social hierarchy or segregation. However, the 2002 Urban Green Spaces Taskforce report painted a very different picture. For example, in parks, daily nuisances caused by negative social interaction between different users due to prejudice and misunderstanding, were raised as an issue of great and current public concern (Urban Green Spaces Taskforce, 2002, p. 63). For PWLD, physical and behavioural differences have resulted in some people becoming targets of abuse. Studies by Todd (2000) and Ryan (2005) both recorded strong negative reactions to PWLD (children and adults) by other site users when out in public spaces. Through the seamless interaction of social experience and environmental form, which makes up our experience of place, many PWLDs are disabled by public environments, hindered by 'structural constraints, the attitudes and responses of others, the attitudes of the mothers and impairment effects' (Ryan, 2005, p. 68). Other authors working in disability geography also identify extreme difficulties for disabled people living in a 'non-disabled-centric' world. Work by Hansen and Philo (2007) has examined the experiences of disabled women dealing with impaired bodies in non-disabled spaces and the adjustments they are expected to make to become accepted. The women felt strongly that there was an 'unacceptability of their impaired bodies in many different social contexts and public spaces', which included – from the small to large spatial scale – shops, parks, streets, settlements and whole regions (ibid.). Hansen's participants were also acutely aware of how their difference was perceived and how their inclusion was only ever partial. Environmental adjustments purportedly designed to facilitate equality often appeared to be afterthoughts or add-ons.

To practically address this lack of understanding Hansen and Philo, among others, have called for the development of participatory practices involving and led by disabled people. For PWLD, this would provide a means to reverse a general lack of public understanding of hidden impairments and behavioural diversity, which has resulted in many PWLD retreating further down the path of segregation. In seeking security in environments, where they will not face confrontation, rejection and exclusion, PWLD are removed from the daily life of our public spaces to the detriment of society. In the next section we look to existing design practice and policy for answers. We ask, is focus on the design product (the constructed environment) enough to ensure inclusion? Or alternatively, should we be looking to evolve a more considered participatory process, as a means to imbue our urban environments with the opportunity for social restoration for all?

Development of social design strategies

The successful design of an environment results in a place where people are able to use the environment to its full effect and gain pleasure from that use. Designers must respond to the diversity of needs, and ways of being, within the user population in order for maximum inclusivity to be achieved. Research in the USA has focused on this issue through the concept of universal design. The term *universal design* was conceived by the architect and designer Ron Mace (1985), who defined the approach as follows: 'universal design is an approach to design that incorporates products as well as building features which, to the greatest extent possible, can be used by everyone' (Mace, 1988). One of the key aims of universal design is social inclusion. The US approach to universal design is a relatively recent idea, which has received great academic interest over the last two decades and has the potential for large techno-logical and academic investment and development. However, in other cultures such as India, academics recognise the historic, unlabelled existence of universal design (Balaram, 2001). Balaram gives the example of Indian everyday objects such as unstitched, uncut clothing (for example, the dhoti and sari) where society has naturally designed for diversity and equality. These garments (without extra cost or elaborate modification) may be worn by everybody, perform multiple tasks, be elegant and affordable to all. In Balaram's world-view of universal design, he acknowledges that the segregation and discrimination in society (which universal design aims to obliterate) may not be solved by technological invention alone. Instead, a more holistic approach must be considered, taking into account the following: societal attitudes, educating for the future, positive thinking by the user groups, networking and increasing usability range. Balaram (2001) cites communication methods as an integral tool for the acceptance and success of universal design by saying that 'in societies where illiteracy is dominant, oral, visual, and other forms of nonverbal communication can be employed effectively'.

Limitations of the US universal design approach have been criticised in the UK on the basis they do little to alter the disabled experience within society 'given that these attitudes are, at present, broadly discriminatory, there is no reason to suppose that technical adaptations, in and of themselves, will significantly change the lives of disabled people' (Imrie and Hall, 2001, p. 17). In other words, no matter how effective the design of physical product, the community in which it is situated, which observes and judges disabled users of the design, will remain unresponsive and unchanged. This has led to the rise and support of inclusive design. Inclusive design builds upon the ideology of universal design, but in addition values the design process and participation alongside the completed product. As described by the Disability Rights Commission, this is

the goal of creating beautiful and functional environments that can be used equally by everyone, irrespective of age, gender or disability, [and] requires that the design process must be constantly expanding to accommodate a diverse range of users, as we develop greater understanding of their require-ments, desires and expectations.

(DRC, 2003)

Involving and responding to all, this approach does not target disabled people as its audience, but foresees inclusion as a quality of life issue for all. In the UK, current disability legislation (DDA, 1995) does not yet achieve the ideal of inclusive design. The Americans with Disabilities Act is seen as the origin for the UK DDA with both reacting to mounting public awareness of the inequality in opportunities for disabled people in employment, provision of goods, facilities and services, and accessibility of buildings. The DDA has been described as 'grievance-led' legislation (Goldsmith, 1997) and has a somewhat additive approach to acces-sible design. This was evident in the run-up to enforcement of the DDA in 2004 when, with the fear of costly lawsuits looming, developers and architects set about making modifications to existing built form and seeking innovation for the incorporation of accessible features in new designs. Where the response has been additive introduction of these elements (ill-conceived ramps and inaccessible disabled toilets), inclusive design is far from achieved, ultimately engendering further discrimination and separation.

Participation within limits

Many PWLD have inherited a legacy of institutionalisation, extending to their lack of participation in the everyday life of public spaces. To date, there has been a tendency in research and practice to focus upon the rehabilitation or therapeutic benefits gained from the environment, rather than active involvement in environmental decision-making. In the UK, research conducted in association with the charitable organisation Thrive, sought to evaluate the benefits and limitations of Social and Therapeutic Horticulture (STH). This was achieved through assessment of the gardening project network established by Thrive. Thrive's aim of 'promoting and supporting the use of horticulture for vulnerable people' (Sempik *et al.*, 2005) involves many social groups, including PWLD. Through this research a number of themes were identified as important to the garden clients such as:

> nature, freedom and space; the social dimension of gardening projects; issues relating to work and employment; physical activity, health and well-being; development of self-confidence and self-esteem; the involvement of vulnerable clients in the research process; garden projects and environmental philosophies.

With specific reference to PWLD, the research cites how 'for particularly vulnerable adults, for example those with learning difficulties, the friendships formed while attending STH sessions are important because they often have limited opportunities to make new friends in their daily lives' (ibid., p. 66).

Following work by Sempik *et al.,* human geographer Hester Parr has written on the importance of 'particular human–nature relations ... in order to explore issues of human well-being' (Parr, 2007). Parr is far more critical regarding the personal and social benefits generated by gardening projects similar to those Sempik describes. She challenges whether activities undertaken within projects in removed (hidden) environments can been seen as truly transformative. In comparing the approach and aims of an allotment space in Nottingham, concerned solely with people with mental health problems, and a voluntary sector project in Glasgow with a range of volunteers including people with mental health problems, addiction problems and PWLD, Parr relays how the Nottingham project, although endeavouring to create a tranquil space for its volunteers, failed to further their social inclusion. She cites its removed physical location (separated from other allotment plots and the outside world by high hedges and a mazework of pathways), combined with a lack of formal training or qualification opportunities for its 'small group of volunteers ... who have not moved on to jobs' (ibid., p. 549). The second project provides a much more promising example of social change, whereby the volunteers are actively involved in a number of tasks, one of which is 'landscaping gap sites around the neighbourhood' (ibid., p. 551). Here Parr suggests 'there is a sense in which such schemes also facilitate "other" kinds of contributions in the making of participatory citizenship' (ibid., p. 552, citing Barnes, 1997, p. 169). As a result, the volunteers at this site benefit from a marked change in social status, frequenting local pubs, engaging the support of neighbours, sharing tools, gaining commission for work and forming casual friendships with the rest of the community.

The great difference between these examples is the territorial nature of their project locations. In Nottingham, the site continues a legacy of segregation by being a removed, private space. In contrast, the Glasgow project is located in the heart of the local neighbourhood, in plain view of all and where 'the gardening activities of the workers in this project create aesthetically pleasing and productive *public* spaces that are then available to be utilised by the wider community' (Parr, 2007, p. 552). Parr's message is clear, in order for the society to re-evaluate and redress their preconceived notions of marginalised communities (and witness the social contribution they have to offer), those who are marginalised, and their actions, must be made visible. Involvement must not be for involvement's sake. Widening participation must mean professional, political and community commitment to the development of shared aims that address shared issues, and to evolve a shared process where all benefit from development of a shared social capital. In the following sections, we describe the journey taken by public participation and ask whether a formal or informal approach is best employed to facilitate involvement by all.

Participation and professionalism

The twentieth century saw public participation become a statutory requirement in the UK (Skeffington, 1969). Early documentation of local-level public participation, such as the process to create the structure plan for the South Yorkshire region in the UK, revealed process aims which sought to 'involve the public from the outset of plan preparation in an open-ended discussion about problems and potentials' (Darke, 1975). However, local authority selection processes were still at work, resulting in only a small proportion of constituents' views being heard. More recently, alternative and additional methods of participation, such as those that involve forms of visual communication, have been employed to widen public participation and draw in views of more under-represented sections of the community, a well-known example being 'Planning for Real' which employs the use of 3D models (Gibson, 1981). This marked a new chapter in practitioner understanding, where it was acknowledged that to involve the public in the planning and design process of public spaces required methods of participation that bridged the gap between professional (design) knowledge and user experience, desires and understanding of a site. To be avoided were methods that were 'incomprehensible to the user, so the user fails to appreciate the relevance of the information provided' (Page, 1974).

If this understanding of participatory practice, as relevant and responsive to the user, has been with us for nearly 40 years, why is unification of what professionals design and what the community desires so problematic? In order to answer this, we must turn our attention to the culture of the professional (be it architects, landscape architects or planners) who are involved in shaping our environments. In 1976, planning author John Turner noted that:

> Paternalism and filialism ... are still very common attitudes in Britain. These are especially evident in the common assumption that the 'ordinary' citizen or 'layman', is utterly dependent upon the 'extraordinary' citizen or the 'professional', who cultivates the mystery of his or her activity in order to increase dependency and professional fees.
>
> (1976, p. 22)

The idea of elevated professions that separate extraordinary individuals from those around them is strongly supported by Habraken in *Palladio's Children* (2005), which considers the legacy of architecture through the ages. Habraken begins by tracing the chronological development of the architect and how this has resulted in today's profession. In architecture's evolution, Habraken identifies Vitruvius Pollio, Leon Battista Alberti and Andrea Palladio as key players in the historic definition of the discipline. Palladio, in particular, appears a catalyst, reconfiguring the role of the architect, where previously architectural styles bore reference to their geographical location and historic execution, i.e. Grecian or Roman architecture. In publishing *The Four Books on Architecture*, Palladio shifted the focus dramatically onto the individual architect, who now had the power to create buildings in an individual style, carrying an individual name. Palladio depicted his buildings as isolated monuments devoid of the everyday context and therefore not cluttered by normality. Through Palladio's work, architects became separated

> from the indissoluble unity of environmental form and culture that had until then brought forth buildings and entire urban fields, embodying skills and knowledge ... Everything else – the entirety of the ordinary built field where form, inhabitant and maker are functionally integrated and semantically joined – has remained obscure or self-evident. This has inevitably led to emancipation – and the isolation – of an entire professional culture from the integrated field of form and people.
>
> (Habraken, 2005, p. 28)

Today architects continue this legacy, both through their educational training and practice. However, the goal of creating monumental buildings sits at odds with the reality of the daily work of most architects. More regularly, they are called upon to design the everyday environments and contexts that Palladio chose to ignore. Yet through their training, international networks and professional publications, architects continue a love affair with the individual and their iconic creations. Most everyday streetscapes, the places and structures in which we live, work and socialise, are not a series of landmark buildings detached from one another. Most environments are made up of incremental developments that connect to, and overlap, one another (be it on a permanent or transitory basis). Understanding how these have come about, and the lives and needs of the people who will shape them in future, is the first step in participatory design practice. However, living with the goal of individualism, architects often find it difficult to relinquish the control that has been embedded through their profession's historic development. Recent research into the attitudes of landscape architects towards participation echoed this detachment and doubt:

> When working under pressure landscape architects often fall back upon the familiar and well proven approaches they developed during their professional

training and early practice. Study results indicated an uncertainty on the part
of the landscape architect about how to use input provided by participants
in the design process, which could cause problems when it comes to trying
out new aesthetical and practical solutions and ideas.

(Paget, 2008)

Architects, landscape architects, planners and the communities they serve are not
the only players in today's design systems. In the case of housing provision, Turner
revealed through his chapter 'Patterns of decision and control' how the majority
of 'centrally administered or heteronomous housing systems' (Turner, 1976, p. 29),
such as those that are evident in Britain, are primarily dictated to by regulators
or the public sector (governance). This governmental control occurs throughout
the planning, construction and management phases, with some input from the
suppliers or private sector (developers, architects and builders) during construction,
and at the bottom of the hierarchy, the users or population maintaining the least
level of control, only active during the management or maintenance phase. The
detrimental result of this centrally administered approach is clear:

> The difficulties and therefore rarity of the participation of users or even local
> institutions in the planning, construction and management of public housing
> programmes, needs no further emphasis. The consequences of this lack
> of participation provide material for an increasing literature on alienation
> experienced by modern housing users.
>
> (ibid., p. 42)

This model could be equally true of the way in which architects and landscape
architects practise, and how much input the community has into their designs
(over and above how much control is exerted from the public sector). In order
for community participation to be effective, Turner sees that systems must be in
place to allow a more locally self-governing or autonomous approach to be taken.
This would entail giving the community more control over planning, construction
and management, with the skills of the professionals utilised more responsively
during the construction phase, and government facilitating the community
through guidance and support. In association with this, Habraken recognises
another professional barrier, the existence and reliance on jargon, and is keen to
erode it through '[a] common professional language to research and report on

environment in terms of architecture need not eliminate poetic expression in favor of technical jargon, but it would establish separate more general terms of reference with which to build knowledge' (Habraken, 2005, p. 151). Therefore, for participation in control and decision-making to occur, we must break down not only the hierarchical systems that have constrained such an approach but also give due attention to the communication barriers that separate and divide one profession from another and one community from its local authority.

Social innovation

Moving forward from this premise with our own response we were also mindful of something that Habraken had drawn attention to in 1986, but increasingly evident more recently (Cuthbert, 2007; Mehaffy, 2008; Mehaffy *et al.*, 2010), that, particularly in environmental planning and design contexts, use of the word participation usually meant that users must participate in what professionals decide to do (Habraken, 1986). Despite an implication that participation is advocated by those who refuse the conventional paternalistic model, recognising instead the valuable experience and knowledge held by lay people, the question of who is invited to participate is usually tightly controlled from the outset by professional agencies. We would acknowledge that there are many sound reasons why this may be the case in environmental planning and design contexts, yet it serves to perpetuate a culture in which the lay public must almost inevitably accept their position as receivers of professional decision-making rather than as genuine participants in the determination of places they routinely use. As we discussed in Chapter 3, Axel Honneth (1995) has suggested that such subliminal external control can impact on the human capability to achieve and sustain a sense of self-esteem which, in the context of the disenfranchised experiences of many people, could have heightened impact on their well-being. According to Honneth (ibid.), the achievement of human self-esteem extends to a requirement for recognition that their actions have value within a particular cultural context. Against a background of concern, expressed by Habraken (1986) and others, about the professionalisation of participatory processes, Honneth's emphasis on the experience of recognition within a supporting community serves to highlight the importance of the social value of participation to which we subsequently sought to give greater prominence in the participatory process we developed.

Community capacity building and localism

> The language of community capacity building more often points to an explicit intention to improve the capacity of and within communities themselves, so there is a deliberate attempt to shape services and develop institutions that increase social capital, autonomy and the overall capacity to drive change from within a community.
>
> (Noya and Clarence, 2009, p. 28)

Since the late twentieth century, we have seen a national and international shift from government to governance, and an increase in neo-liberal energy behind community participation. Most noticeable is the form of partnership working where there is a shared responsibility (and resourcing) for a place or service. While governmental motivations driving this and the associated localism agenda are under increasing scrutiny, what emerges clearly is that political focus on participation is unlikely to fade in the near future.

Following the 2011 UK Localism Act and an onslaught of local authority spending cuts, questions of greater formalisation in UK public–community partnerships are now beginning to surface as a critical issue. Noticeable devolution of resources and control for open spaces to communities, through increased rights at the level of Community Assemblies and Area Panels, has the potential to shift power and control within public–community partnerships. Getting participation 'right' in times of economic constraint is therefore crucial. Discussing where power and control in participation now lie, entails a reflection on the individual partner capacities involved.

In the wider context, capacity may be defined as 'the power of containing, receiving, experiencing or producing' (*Concise Oxford Dictionary*, 1995) as well as a measure of ability to perform. Where environmental decision-making involves local authorities or other governmental bodies, capacity to participate is defined as 'the ability of the state to formulate and implement strategies to achieve economic and social goals in society' (Kjær *et al.*, 2002, p. 7). In times of economic constraint, the local authorities' capacity to resource and implement strategies may be reduced. This in turn raises questions as to how the community may be involved and can contribute.

As such, abilities of production and formulation also underpin interpretations of community capacity, which is a field of increasing academic interest and practical importance (Kretzman and McKnight, 1993; Fawcett *et al.*, 1995; Glickman and Servon, 1998; Noya and Clarence, 2009; Eichler and Hoffman, n.d.). As noted earlier in this chapter, when discussing the work of Hester Parr, being recognised for your contribution (through production or formulation) and being able to build on your capacity to do so, are especially important in the active involvement of traditionally less powerful communities. Within the arena of community capacity building, previous studies have therefore identified that for participative processes to be effective, resources in the form of skills and commitment (Meyer, 1994; Goodman *et al.* 1998), networks of relationships, leadership and support mechanisms for activation (Chaskin, 2001) are essential. This suggests the need for a participative framework that is adaptable (as the community capacity grows or changes) yet acknowledges the important existence of certain factors.

In this respect especially, grounds for optimism may be found in the recently published joint ResPublica and RIBA paper *Re-thinking Neighbourhood Planning* (Kaszynska *et al.*, 2012). Addressing specifically issues relevant to the resourcing and operationalisation of the UK Localism Act, particular focus is given to a need to move beyond a culture of consultation to more collaborative 'meaningful community participation' (ibid., p. 4). It is recommended that the demands of the Localism Act require a radical rethink of the way that community-led development is understood by policy-makers and the professional design community, giving greater value and resource to the shaping of towns and cities from the bottom up. This initiative explicitly links its benefits to better place-making with the mitigation of social ills, creation of stronger communities, generation of social capital and through this the delivery of better social health and well-being:

> Neighbourhood planning, underpinned by meaningful participation and engagement, can be an avenue for pre-empting the costly interventions of rectifying unsuccessful development and supporting fractured and deprived communities, but also generate positive social outcomes – social capital – through much improved social cohesion, trust and a sense of common purpose.
>
> (ibid., p. 7)

The recommendations of this document, if adopted and implemented, may well provide a policy foundation from which a dominance of *form*-orientated development can become rebalanced with a more explicit presence of community-led ownership and control, both in terms of processes of development through meaningful participation and also in terms of its occupation and use (*place* and *understanding*).

We conclude our thoughts on participation by reflecting briefly on the case we have made for a certain level of participatory formalisation and framework. Fundamentally, we see that without this, there is a danger that in circumstances of informal involvement, traditional territorial impulses and hierarchies may re-emerge, and those who are frequently absent or excluded from decision-making will remain so.

Summary

In this chapter we have seen how creating a positive participation process, where the hierarchical divide between professional and lay partners is bridged and community capacity built, relies upon an inclusive approach and an understanding that participatory support mechanisms must be in place. As we now move onto Chapter 7 we embark on a journey to address this, through the evolutionary development and application of the Experiemic Process. And finally as we leave this chapter, we identify a number of key points that we will take forward to ensure effective participation. These acknowledge that:

- *Communication:* plays a key role; and that professionals must avoid the use of specialised jargon and language.
- *Resources:* are required to support participatory practices in the form of skills (facilitation) and commitment.
- *Networks:* are key in building individual and partnership capacity.
- *Responsive and reflective methodologies:* are needed to facilitate the inclusion of different groups and sectors within the participation process.
- *Leadership:* is necessary to drive participation forward, but should be unbiased and in the form of facilitation.
- *External support mechanisms:* are in place and accessible, to ensure process activation and demonstrable results.
- *Value:* is placed on the participation and contribution of all partners, at whatever level this may be.
- *Transparency:* is essential in the partnership; all involved need to understand and communicate their motivations for participation.

- *Active inclusion:* participatory practices must seek to find ways to effectively involve those who have been traditionally marginalised or excluded, and make their actions visible.
- *Involvement must not be for involvement's sake:* participation must be relevant to the partners involved and not a mere public relations or 'tick box' exercise.
- *Development of shared aims to address shared issues:* widening participation means a professional, political and community commitment to develop a shared process where all benefit from development of a shared social capital.

Chapter Seven

Experiemic development

Introduction

At the close of Chapter 6 we set ourselves the task of delivering a participatory process capable of flexibility, reflection and evolution, but also structured in a manner to actively facilitate inclusion and empowerment. In this chapter we now examine how a longitudinal research approach has enabled us to produce such a process, hereafter referred to as the Experiemic Process.

The Experiemic Process is the means through which the practice of Experiemics aims to stimulate environmental and social change. The context in which the Experiemic Process may be successfully employed is the transitional edge, where environments have distinct spatial characteristics or opportunities, as argued for and outlined in Part II. Where these spatial attributes are present, the Experiemic Process catalyses action in order that the social value of transitional edges may be optimised. Returning to Habraken, where the form of the transitional edge has certain properties, Experiemics works to create an improved balance of place and understanding in order that seeding of affordances for social restoration may occur, take hold and be sustained.

Intrinsic within the workings of Experiemics is a commitment to recognise, understand and respond to, the territorial workings of MTOY (*mine, theirs, ours* and *yours*) as explored in Part II. In Experiemics we acknowledge that individuals involved in situations of collective decision-making will come to the table with their own agenda (mine). However, when there is a safe arena in which honest acknowledgement of individual agendas occurs from the start, we can reduce this scale of separation from theirs to yours. As a project progresses, methodologies are tailored to further reduce this divide, build trust and respect for one another's knowledge, be it professional or lay. Being invested together in the Experiemic Process produces outcomes that are beneficial to individual parties (gives you mine) but also evolves a sense of ours as professionals and communities arrive at collective solutions that bridge this divide.

In this chapter we work to develop the Experiemic Process from a position where research has identified that this gulf might have been previously at its potential maximum; between people with learning disabilities (PWLD) and environmental design professionals (such as architects, landscape architects and urban designers) (Imrie and Hall, 2001). This first of all involves an evolution of methodologies to actively include PWLD in environmental decision-making. This is followed by a refinement of these methodologies, or tools, in the structured development of the Experiemic Process through action research. This journey is not one we take alone. As the Experiemic Process simultaneously emerges and is employed, we see how the people who have shaped this process also change. We watch how individual and collective communicative competences and confidences are built, and with it evidence that broadening the spectrum of accepted professional communication can be an effective approach to creating inclusive, socially restorative urban environments.

A place to begin

In the educational training of today's design professionals, students are taught how to communicate their ideas using specific tools, such as Computer Aided Design (CAD) and Geographical Information Systems (GIS), and to represent their schemes through aerial plans, sections, 3D visualisations, axonometrics and isometrics. When professionals work directly with one another, this shared language built on an understanding of these representational tools can result in an open design dialogue both precise and technical, but also expressive and inspirational. However, as we alluded to in Chapter 6, such design communication methods are not always as effective when communities wish to take an active role. While professional knowledge regarding design specification, planning guidance and construction requirements is a necessary component of successful participatory projects, what is to be acknowledged is the tendency that 'today, wherever we work, architects [and other environment professionals] have no informed attitude toward the local' (Habraken, 2005, p. 169). As professionals become more globally oriented, there is a real danger that this gulf is set to grow. Without appropriate methods to facilitate a professional–lay dialogue, the understanding of what constitutes and catalyses a locally responsive and useable environment (such as those features found in the transitional edge) has the potential to go 'missing' along the way.

A responsive approach: 'Our Parks and Gardens'

To redress this imbalance, our initial work in Experiemics focused on developing communication methods in partnership with PWLD, whose exclusion from everyday decision-making is often a result of poor communication (Mathers, 2008). This involved taking a truly 'bottom-up' approach when working with two groups of PWLD in the UK over a longitudinal period from 2004–2007. In turn, this allowed our communication and participation toolkit to evolve in detailed response to the experiences of the individuals involved. Working in this way also avoided a generalisation of individual communication needs, reactions and relationships, in favour of a more meaningful in-depth analysis. This reactive and responsive approach is one that we have continued to build on when working with different communities throughout our Experiemic practice. Whether we are working with children, teachers, students or PWLD, we continue to be mindful of this emergent approach to information collection, participation and impact.

Our journey began early in 2004 in collaboration with a group of PWLD who attended a Yorkshire Day Service Centre.[1] In August of that year we created a research team under the moniker 'Our Parks and Gardens', named by the PWLD involved (Figure 7.1). This compromised ten men and women with learning disabilities, one member of support staff and a number of volunteers. The disabled people who participated had a range of physical, intellectual and sensory impairments, which for some resulted in limited verbal speech or written language. From the start, community ownership underpinned our approach, which led to a collective decision on project aims at our introductory planning day 'What Is a Park?' These were:

1. to discover what PWLD think about parks in their city and local area;
2. to create a way to share how PWLD use, and would like to use, parks with other people in the community;

3. to provide ways for the people who look after parks, to talk with PWLD and to include their needs and ideas in the future of parks.

Over a two-year period visiting five sites, 'Our Parks and Gardens' developed a seven-step visual communication toolkit (discussed in detail later), enabling the PWLD involved to explore and express their ideas regarding their experiences of public open space. Once developed, it was important to test the toolkit's application flexibility. Therefore, we facilitated a four-month trial during the spring and summer of 2006, working with students who attended a learning disability further education college in the North-East of England. Both these locations were chosen as a result of previous, personal involvement by co-author Alice Mathers, who had worked as a volunteer at the Day Service Centre, and been employed as an assistant tutor at the further education college. Finding an individual, and involving one, who can facilitate access to more hidden communities can often be time-consuming but is crucial in ensuring that participation is not restricted. Allowing adequate flexibility in your participation programme to develop such relationships and create a strong community conduit, is paramount if true inclusion and representation are to be achieved. This is a consideration we were mindful of as we moved forward with Experiemics.

Returning to 'Our Parks and Gardens' and the development of communication tools, it is important to note that during this early work the community did not

Figure 7.1: The 'Our Parks and Gardens' research team at work.

determine all the dimensions of the project. In 'Our Parks and Gardens', we established the project location, the community involved and the general focus (public open spaces), as this project was born out of a more traditional, qualitative research approach.[2] However, this position of predetermination altered as we became increasingly aware that the participation process we were developing was effective in enabling us to act in a predominantly facilitation capacity, while the community determined the project issue they wished to address. In 'Our Parks and Gardens' the PWLD involved aided this journey, through their active contribution to the development of project aims and refinement of project methods. This process of evolution occurred through weekly workshops, where together we explored the group's experiences of open spaces and honed communication approaches to dissemination of their findings. As a result, this three-year project produced a seven-stage toolkit with two key attributes:

1. It provided the means by which less visible and currently excluded communities could actively participate in environmental discussions with professionals.
2. It proved to be an implement of personal and collective change and empowerment, which became the central theme in the social activation of Experiemics at the transitional edge.

We now explore these two dimensions in further detail, beginning with the communication toolkit.

Inclusive methods: removing territorial hierarchy

By understanding that even within processes of participation, significant territorial impulses are at play, as represented by MTOY, creates from the outset a need for transparency, where the motivations of all partners can be openly communicated. Without this openness, we found that building a shared sense of ownership (towards an ours) was unlikely to occur and territorial impulses would remain unchanged, with mine, yours and theirs prevailing.

Figure 7.2 illustrates the participation toolkit we evolved together through 'Our Parks and Gardens'. To build this shared sense of ownership and openness (our practical foundation), we paid great attention to our communication of the project purpose and expectations of individual roles and responsibilities. Within the research context this first focused on how to create inclusion through informed consent.

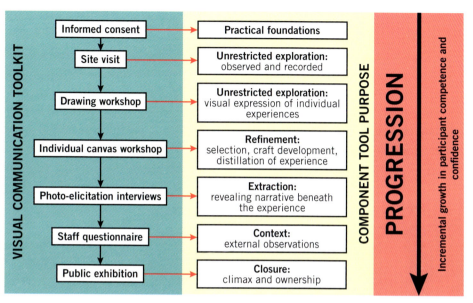

Figure 7.2: The 'Our Parks and Gardens' participation toolkit.

TOOL 1: Informed consent

Just as the toolkit as a collective entity aimed to break down participation barriers, the initial process towards securing informed consent[3] aimed from the outset to build project identity and partner trust. This meant that no one communication technique was relied upon to convey the project focus and scope. Instead a triangulation of methods was employed, including focus groups, presentations, written descriptions and workshops. These were tailored to reflect and respond to the requirements of the people involved, which resulted in project understanding being embedded from the start, instigating immediate development of community ownership.

TOOL 2: Site visits

In 'Our Parks and Gardens', communicating people's personal experiences of open spaces was greatly facilitated by first-hand contact with the environment. In qualitative research, mobile methods such as site visits or participant-led walks and 'go-alongs' (Carpiano, 2009) have gained favour in recent years, as they provide an informal method 'for exploring issues around people's relationship with space' (Jones *et al.*, 2008, citing Hein *et al.*, 2008).

In 'Our Parks and Gardens', use of site visits revealed that for the majority of people conceptualisation of new environmental experiences was closely linked to prior experience. In turn, this suggested that when communicating new environmental designs, professionals should pay attention to capturing and understanding existing environmental experiences, in order to provide a point reference for communities. For the people involved in 'Our Parks and Gardens', the site visits gave individuals the opportunity to have multi-sensory contact with an

Figure 7.3: Building a sense of mine (my own experience). Running through fountains during an 'Our Parks and Gardens' visit to the Peace Gardens, Sheffield, UK.

environment, through touch, sound, sight, smell and sometimes taste. As a result of this sensory contact, many of the group become more confident and competent in communicating their personal preferences.

The site visits also made use of another qualitative method to capture person–environment interactions, that of self-directed and observational photography. The use of photography is widely employed both by professionals, within the survey and analysis stage of design, and by social researchers interested in visual methods to capture human relations and responses (Banks, 2001). In 'Our Parks and Gardens', we encouraged the community to take photographs of their experiences in public spaces and later used these photographs to discuss how individuals perceived and experienced these places. As the project progressed and the group visited a wider variety of environments, for many people their personal interest in such places and the meaning they held for them intensified. Site visits were no longer about just seeing a space. As an individual's ownership over his or her own experience increased, a greater sense of mine was established, where before there was little attachment (Figure 7.3). This was reflected in the level of detail and information they were now interested in receiving before visiting a site, i.e. would there be water?; somewhere to sit?; toilets?; somewhere to eat?; who else might be there?

TOOL 3: Drawing workshop

As a participatory tool, the drawing workshops enabled an unpicking of the community's environmental experience to occur, without reliance upon traditional verbal or written communication methods. We found that drawing workshops were most effective if held shortly after the public open space visit. If too much time elapsed between this and a drawing workshop, the focus of the workshop became vague, and in the mind of the community actual memories and experiences were not as clear. The drawing workshops gave individuals the opportunity to express how they felt about different sites, using photographs they had taken on the day as a starting point. The workshops were not restricted to drawing alone, and a range of media was made available; for example, some people chose to write and others to collage their photographs. Individual work highlighted spatial qualities as well as moments of social interaction or experiential dimensions of place. In their art, a scale of territorial experiences was also reflected. This ranged from intimate moments of personal importance (mine), to observed experiences

Figure 7.4: Drawing by an 'Our Parks and Gardens' member of a local Sheffield park in autumn.

of others (yours), through awareness of, as yet, distant interactions (theirs) to that which was shared (ours) (Figure 7.4).

All work produced during the course of 'Our Parks and Gardens' workshops was kept within individual participant books. These books were important for a number of reasons. First, they gave ownership over 'Our Parks and Gardens' back to the individual, preserving a record of the personal journey made. Second, the books provided a useful reference point, alongside photographs, during semi-structured interviews (Tool 5).

TOOL 4: Individual canvas workshop

Following the site visits and drawing workshops, a canvas workshop was held to create a final, individual piece of work, which was displayed at the end of the project in a public exhibition. The canvas workshop had the aim of focusing and representing the key issues identified regarding the public open space studied. Completion of the canvas workshop signified the end of the community's production of physical work, or the survey stage in the project. In relation to each public space experience, this created a composite picture of what had occurred at the experiential transitional edge; what lay between the site's spatial organisation and its social occupation or use.

TOOL 5: Photo-elicitation interviews

Moving forward to an analysis of the information generated by earlier tools, the toolkit employed photo-elicitation interviews to reveal a deeper level of meaning beneath the previously identified environmental experiences. Photo-elicitation is a technique whereby photographs are used as tools to prompt contribution and memory awakening in conversation (Banks, 2001). First utilised by Yannick Geffroy in the 1970s (Geffroy, 1990), the merits of photo-elicitation are now well documented and include: memory stimulation, hierarchical equalisation (between interviewer and interviewee), presence of a neutral third party, reduction in the fear of being tested, and conversation initiation (Banks, 2001; Mathers, 2010). Whether in an individual or group situation, photo-elicitation reinforced community ownership over project direction. In interviews we discussed their photos, of subjects that had proven of interest to them, of sites they had visited. Again a sense of mine was strengthened.

TOOL 6: Staff questionnaire

In Experiemics we have set out to consciously develop methods to involve people who are currently absent from most environmental decision-making. However, this does not mean that the methods we employ are for exclusive use with these groups. Instead we see them as part of an adaptable participatory framework, to involve and give voice to diverse communities in circumstances of environmental change.

In accessing hidden populations, we have been critically aware of the 'gatekeeper' role played by learning disability support agencies and staff (Siegel and Ellis, 1985; Lennox *et al.* 2005). This gatekeeper issue extends to other vulnerable groups, be it older people, people with mental health conditions or young children. In 'Our Parks and Gardens', we found that, through extending an open invitation of participation to people's support organisations, multiple benefits were accrued. This included facilitating access to individuals and providing a level of historic insight into people's environmental reactions (Mathers, 2008). To capture this understanding further, the participation toolkit included a staff question-naire, which focused on themes emergent from the PWLDs' communication of their environmental experiences. In this way another dimension of understanding was added ('why an individual might have focused on a particular experience or element?') rather than a level of interpretation ('what the individual focused on?').

In work following 'Our Parks and Gardens' (described later in this chapter) this role and partnership with individuals and organisations that supported PWLD developed further. Through the employment of Experiemics, with the same PWLD over the course of a series of projects, it became clear that many people had as a result developed a high level of competence and confidence in self-advocacy. As a result, they no longer relied on advocates to the same degree. This observation led us to the conclusion that for the impact of Experiemics to be optimised, it should be employed over a longitudinal period, where there is the opportunity for empowerment to become truly embedded.

TOOL 7: Public exhibition

Working with communities and individuals (who in the eyes of many others may appear very vulnerable) in an intensive manner over an extended period of time required us to consider carefully how we would 'end' the project (Northway, 2000). Too often, participation, be it in research or practice, results in a report, publication or design, over which the community has little influence. In this way, participatory practice can be potentially damaging, undermining trust and leaving communities with little ownership and 'consultation fatigue', especially if the outputs are not directly accessible or useable to them.

In 'Our Parks and Gardens', the final tool we evolved in our toolkit was the orchestration of an exhibition. This had the dual purpose of preparing those involved in the project for the upcoming end and, in a highly visible manner, celebrating their work and input throughout. In both locations, the 'Our Parks and Gardens' group and students from the north-east college chose to hold public exhibitions in local cinemas and galleries, where their work could be openly viewed by the wider community (Figure 7.5). This illustrated the level of pride and accomplishment they now associated with their work. In both locations,

Figure 7.5: The further education students exhibit their work on public open space experiences across the North-East of England.

interviews and informal discussions with group members following the exhibitions, confirmed how this final stage in the toolkit had cemented their ownership over the project.

Building empowerment and competence

Through employment of the visual communication toolkit, we have shown how the methods involved have the capability to provide significant insight into the place perception of hidden communities. However, this work also uncovered a finer grain of experiential understanding regarding factors that inhibit or facilitate personal and social change through environmental interactions at the transitional edge.

This can be thought of as a journey comprising six key stages. Progression through these stages empowers an individual to become an included, valued

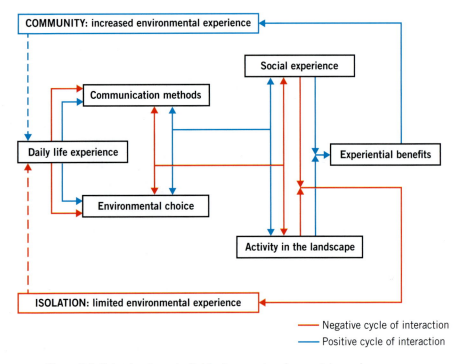

Figure 7.6: Releasing the potential for increased environmental experience.

community member who has access to the experiential benefits that their local environment has to offer (see Figure 7.6). Our work with different learning disability communities helped identify why this path to progression was not currently available to individuals, and the opportunities to alter this position.

Daily life experience

The current routine daily life experience of less empowered people (such as PWLD) is primarily restricted to assisted transference between a series of indoor environments, such as the home and school, day service centre or college. This routine does not generally include regular exposure to parks or other public open spaces. Therefore, breaking from this daily routine, which can be constructed over decades, may present a stressful experience. Our work with PWLD identified that a key factor in facilitating the transition for vulnerable individuals to expand their routine and include a greater range of environmental experiences was communication.

Communication methods

Use of accessible communication methods can, as we have shown, facilitate a stream of information to flow between parties in order that decisions are taken and choices made. Unfortunately many PWLD (and other groups) have limited access to information regarding the range of environmental experiences available to them, and where information is provided, it may not be in appropriate or accessible format. Similarly, if people wish to engage in environmental decision-making, existing communication barriers and imbalances in control and understanding may make this a frustrating process.

Environmental choice

Work with 'Our Parks and Gardens' revealed that even if accessible methods of communication are in place, PWLD may choose to seek out the safety of familiar landscapes, i.e. those environments that are part of their routine and easier to conceptualise. For people whose lives are marked more by dependency than independent choice, such decision-making may be beyond their immediate control. If self-advocacy[4] and independence are not actively encouraged, the incentive to explore and take ownership over new environments may not be there. Likewise by being unprepared, there is a danger that when individuals are presented with new environmental experiences, they may be more overwhelming than invigorating, with worries regarding personal behaviour, preparation, activities, access, facilities and other users.

Social experience

The social experience of public open spaces is also important in discouraging or encouraging people to continue to participate in the environment. Even if a space is familiar and has become part of a person's daily or weekly routine, negative social encounters may result in someone becoming uncomfortable when visiting the space. Where a severe negative social experience has occurred, such as bullying, individuals may naturally refuse to continue to use the space, or to experience similar spaces that they perceive to be sites of comparable danger. At this point, the negative cycle of limited environmental experience is enforced; individuals seek safety in their daily routine and remove themselves from the dialogue of new environmental choice.

Activity in the landscape

Progressing through this journey, we see how each factor impacts upon the next. By the time we reach activity in the landscape, the impact of social experiences that individuals have been involved with (either positively or negatively), has a considerable effect upon the activities in which they will participate. Other factors also affect this level of activity, however, such as age, health and well-being and gender. Yet, a negative cycle may still be broken at this point, if participatory processes are employed to encourage the individual to engage in open space activities, be it observational or physically interactive. This may be further facilitated through inclusive design of transitional edge environments, which then provide the affordance for individual needs.

Experiential benefits

If an individual does not experience public spaces as part of their routine, cannot communicate on an equal level with others to make new environmental choices, has only negative social experiences and does not participate in activity in the landscape, it is unlikely that they will gain the experiential benefits which such environments can provide. As such, they are caught in a cycle of limited environmental experience, which may be reinforced by the ageing process.

However, Figure 7.6 not only shows how these six factors can interact to produce a situation of limited environmental experience, but also that a positive outcome can occur: that of increased environmental experience. Increased environmental experience sees individuals participating in public open spaces as included and active members of their community. Therefore, if this is to occur, we recommend that the following must happen:

- Engagement with public open spaces becomes a regular feature in the daily life experience for individuals.
- Visual and alternative communication methods are widely adopted by environmental professionals, to facilitate access to information and participatory decision-making.
- Individuals are supported and encouraged to make new environmental choices and extend their collective public open space experience.
- Designers and planners of public open spaces are sensitive to the social needs of

different groups, and look to actively creating transitional edges where positive social interactions can occur.

• Designers and planners of public open spaces actively involve the community in the design process, not only at an aesthetic level but more importantly to discover how they would like to use a site and the types of activities they wish to engage in.

Summary

Our previous use of this communication toolkit has demonstrated its capacity to unlock experiential information previously hidden to professionals. However, there remain two significant implications for its application: that of resourcing and governance.

Aylott (2001) has written how it may be more financially palatable for governments and society to believe that certain individuals do not require a high level of support to actively participate. Yet, in order for emancipation to take place, resources must be invested so that communication and participation can be tailored to the individual where necessary. To do this, a longitudinal approach to participation and lasting commitment is required from the partners involved. In times of economic constraint, the need to demonstrate the wider impact of such approaches is never more apparent. Aligned closely to this argument for financial support is the need for a governmental and professional shift in control and understanding. In order to challenge professional attitudes that remain 'deeply embedded in routines of state procedure ... and privilege certain interests over others' (Healey, 1999, p. 1133), a social change is need. The visual communication toolkit facilitates one dimension of this, by providing the methods to encourage open dialogue. However, more is required. In Experiemics we have set out to address this. As such, we now move on to describe how by using this toolkit, we have developed a reflexive, participatory process with the ability to catalyse social change and increase a sense of ours. This is the story of the Experiemic Process, an activation framework for partnership at the transitional edge.

Moving into the edge: 'Excuse Me, I Want to Get On!'

In our search for socially restorative urbanism, we have identified how certain spatial arrangements, in transitional edge environments, have the capacity for activities to colonise and embed. These transitional edge environments are important by the nature of their very 'everydayness'. They are the interface between shop frontages and pavements, the alley ways to restaurant courtyards, where you put out your pots of plants or where you hang up your washing at the back of your apartment block. What we have tried to demonstrate throughout this book is that if, as professionals, we ignore the importance of these edge environments and do not plan for these spaces to occur and become occupied, we limit the richness of life that can take hold.

Through our research over a number of years, we have built our own library or catalogue of transitional edges, both good and bad. We used some of these to illustrate attributes of transitional edges in Part II. However, in parallel through our work with Experiemics, it became clear that communities already recognised the need for change at the transitional edge, especially regarding environments with which they had daily contact. Following the 'Our Parks and Gardens' project, members of Sheffield's learning disability community approached us to address issues they had regarding daily travel through the city. This identified a transitional edge environment (transport corridors) that was inherent to the social restoration of many urban locations. Transport corridors comprise a variety of transitional edges, between pavements and buildings, transport stops and the periphery of roads, transport vehicles and their departure and arrival nodes. Some of these edges have more temporal dimensions, while others are more spatially fixed. All have a strong socio-spatial dimension, where if the spatial arrangement does not allow for positive, shared use of the territorial space (creation of ours), negative social encounters can occur. These can be particularly alarming for vulnerable people, such as those with disability, effectively discouraging use and, with this, discouraging a presence and contribution to the wider urban community.

Without prior employment of the visual communication toolkit, which built individual and collective confidence, it seems unlikely that the community would have sought to directly address this issue, or to approach us in partnership to work with them. This therefore marked a key turning point for Experiemics, where the community became the project driver and our role became one of facilitation to activate action and change.

Seeding: building partnerships and ensuring understanding

Following the community's desire to improve their experience of travel throughout the city, in 2008 we sought and successfully obtained funding from the University of Sheffield's Knowledge Transfer Opportunities Fund. This provided the resources

Figure 7.7: Voices and Choices with the project banner/logo that they created for 'Excuse Me, I Want to Get On!'

for us to facilitate a six-month collaboration, working with individuals who had previously been involved in the 'Our Parks and Gardens' project. Since the completion of the 'Our Parks and Gardens' project, the group had evolved a broader self-advocacy focus and were now the self-named Voices and Choices group. As with the 'Our Parks and Gardens' project, we were committed from the start of the project to ensuring community ownership over the process and product. This began with the community identifying the project focus (travel on the local public tram system) and their naming of the project: 'Excuse Me, I Want to Get On!' (Figure 7.7).

Both we and the community recognised from the start that a wider partnership was needed, in order for 'Excuse Me, I Want to Get On!' to have real impact upon their experiences of tram travel. Therefore, the community invited managers from the Stagecoach Supertram company (who provided the tram service) to an initial meeting at their community centre (Figure 7.8). At this scoping meeting the community and transport provider agreed a series of project aims, which would deliver both individual (mine) and shared outputs (ours). These aims were:

1. to empower PWLD to access the Supertram safely and with growing confidence;
2. to make explicit good practice for support staff and the families of people with learning disabilities, so that they are able to best support their family member or person with learning disabilities to gain greater independence when travelling across the city;
3. to generate methods by which local service providers (Stagecoach Supertram) and policy-makers (Sheffield City Council) might make the city and its transport links more accessible and inclusive for people with learning disabilities.

Figure 7.8: Managers from Stagecoach Supertram participating in the project-scoping meeting with Voices and Choices.

Methodological evolution: capturing the ephemeral and kinetic

Following this meeting, with our facilitation, the community began to explore, through a series of workshops, the methods they believed would be effective in communicating their existing travel experiences and their aspirations for the future. This methodological exploration identified that the experience of travel was not a static entity and that kinetic and more ephemeral qualities needed to be recorded. In our facilitation role, we responded by providing information and guidance on the use of film to capture these dimensions. This resulted in the involvement of a local film company, Sheffield Independent Film (SIF), who provided expert facilitation to support this dimension of the project.

Within the local learning disability community, word of the project spread to other organisations, and the issue of travel emerged as one that held resonance with many groups and individuals. A sense of ours had begun to grow around 'Excuse Me, I Want to Get On!' In March 2008 (two months after the project commenced), the group were invited to meet with another Sheffield self-advocacy organisation, Speaking Up For Advocacy (SUFA). At this meeting, the catalytic effect of Experiemics was in evidence. As a result of transparent project focus and aims (driven by the community) and use of accessible communication methods, SUFA asked to join 'Excuse Me, I Want to Get On!' This gave strength to the community partnership and presence within the project. While a wider community ours was being built, SUFA were able to retain their sense of mine by choosing alternative communication methods to convey their travel experiences. As a group, they chose to focus on producing a piece of drama. This in turn inspired Voices and Choices to explore drama as an additional method in their project communication toolkit.

Over the course of six months Voices and Choices explored their experiences of using the Stagecoach Supertram and associated edge environments, through a diverse palette of person-led methods including film, photography, sound recording and written narratives. One of the most popular and effective methods, which the group had not used before, was film. Four members in the group, particularly inspired by the thought of capturing the changing experience of travel, chose to tell their individual stories through the making of a documentary film. In this film, each member had a different reason for wanting to use the Supertram (mine), but were united in their desire for greater independence through travel (ours). In each journey, the individual's experience of the spatial environment identified different design characteristics that either facilitated or inhibited use. These included the distance between crossing points, design of tram stops and seats, to the detailed arrangement of door buttons in the tram. While individual methods conveyed individual experiences, collective understanding was built through the continuation of regular group workshops, where members exchanged and developed ideas. Our facilitation of these workshops enabled more universal experiential themes to emerge, which could then be collectively evaluated.

Evaluation: a collective review

Review with the community of the emerging experiential themes distilled the project findings into three clear categories:

1. current problems experienced by passengers with learning disabilities;
2. current successful Stagecoach Supertram features which facilitate travel by passengers with learning disabilities;
3. future developments that would enhance the public transport experience of people with learning disabilities.

In turn, this aided identification of three transitional edge environments, which were to be found:

1. before reaching the tram stop;
2. at the tram stop;
3. on the tram.

Drilling down to a finer level of detail, within each of these transitional edges, the community identified a series of design and operational issues, which are summarised in Table 7.1. While some of these findings had clear spatial implications, many related to the current social dimension of travel, which required a social intervention to resolve. In order to do this, our workshops moved into a responsive stage, where we reviewed these findings and worked together to provide design and service recommendations to improve passenger experience for all (Table 7.2). This was very important to the group, as they saw travel on public transport as a shared experience, therefore recommendations were directed towards creating a socially restorative experience that could be seen as ours.

Table 7.1: Community findings regarding transitional edge tram travel.

Transitional edge environment	*Community findings*
Before reaching the tram stop	There are not always tram stops close to where people live. This discourages some people from using the tram.
	The tram doesn't currently travel to all the places people want to visit.
	It is difficult to get hold of accessible information on how travelling on the tram works, where it goes and when.
At the tram stop	The lack of seats at most tram stops makes waiting an uncomfortable experience for many people.
	The colour coding system of trams is confusing to many people. Although squares on the front of trams show the tram route colour, the overall painting of the trams in many colours confuses first time travellers in particular.
	The tram shelters are not enclosed and people are exposed to the cold and bad weather.
	The timetables are too high up for many people (especially those in wheelchairs) and are therefore difficult to read.
	People felt exposed at the tram stops to bullying. There was no obvious official protection in the form of staff, support or surveillance.
	The help points don't always work.
	Isolated tram stops are a target for vandalism. Glass on the floor made waiting a dangerous situation for people.
	The writing and numbers on maps and timetables are too small for many people to read.

▶

Transitional edge environment	Community findings
On the tram	Confusing buttons. Many people mistook the red colour of the help button for the stop request.
	Many disabled people have experienced being pushed and shoved at peak times.
	The tram doors close very quickly (which is particularly difficult for wheelchair users).
	Travelling by tram is expensive for those people who don't have a travel pass (such as carers and support workers).
	Getting the conductor's attention is difficult particularly at busy times.
	There is not enough luggage space.
	When the disabled seating is occupied, getting up the steps on the tram to find another seat is difficult for some passengers.
	The gap between some platforms and the tram varies and is too high at some points.
	Tram seatbelts would help disabled passengers feel more secure and steady.
	Anti-social behaviour by others (particularly teenagers) is intimidating.
	Non-disabled passengers who sit in the disabled seating. Disabled passengers do not always feel confident enough to tell passengers to move.
	When the tram is busy and noisy, it is difficult to hear the announcement or see the screen on the tram ceiling.

Table 7.2: Community recommendations regarding transitional edge tram travel.

Transitional edge environment	*Community recommendations*
Before reaching the tram stop	Extend tram routes to more residential areas. Highlight more of the city's attractions within a short range (walking distance) of the tram stops. These could include: • areas with services, such as post offices, the town hall, churches, banks, health centres, hospitals and libraries; • areas with amenities, such as shops, restaurants, cafes, pubs, cinemas, museums and theatres; • areas for healthy living and leisure, such as parks, swimming pools and gyms. Tie in tram travel to a wider *city legibility scheme (making the city more understandable)* through pictorial/photographic signs and way marking.
At the tram stop	Announcements at tram stops to tell you: where you are, when the next tram will arrive, where the tram is travelling to and from. Seats at all tram stops, to make the waiting experience more comfortable and accessible. Bigger print timetables. Positioned lower (or at different heights at the tram stop). Clearer maps with photographs, of recognisable landmarks at tram stop destinations and along the route. More staff to help passengers on and off the tram at tram stops.
On the tram	Clearer colour coding on trams (i.e. if the tram is running on the blue route, the entire tram could be blue). A less confusing button system (stop buttons only at doors, help buttons positioned in another obvious location). Subsidised fares for carers/support workers so they can accompany disabled people. Tram conductors to be more aware of the needs of disabled passengers, in order to support them more actively.

Evolution: dissemination and catalysation

Building upon methods we had employed in the participatory toolkit we had developed in the 'Our Parks and Gardens' project, we held a public dissemination day at the People's Parliament[5] in Sheffield Town Hall to disseminate our findings. Voices and Choices sent out targeted invitations to service providers (local transport companies) and policy-makers (the city council transport and mobility team) as well as to the regional learning disability community. The Parliament meeting took place on 17 July 2008 and was attended by over 100 delegates. Together with SUFA, Voices and Choices presented their findings, which included the first public showing of the documentary film. Following the event, the findings were made widely available in the form of an accessible project report, *Excuse Me, I Want to Get On: A Guide to Good Travel.*[6] Feedback, from a variety of local authorities and nationwide transport providers, regarding both of these dissemination methods highlighted their effectiveness in achieving social change and impact when used to do the following:

1. Give staff guidance regarding the needs of disabled passengers.
2. Aid development of best practice in terms of service delivery and environmental design.
3. Shape local policy strategies for inclusion, mobility and the avoidance of hate crimes.

This impact was reinforced by open invitations from transport companies to work with them to develop good practice:

> I showed your DVD to our General Manager and our HR Manager this morning. Both are keen to use it in our driver training. They have also offered for you to have access to our bus services if you'd like to do some filming on them.
>
> (Sheffield Community Transport Mobility Manager, 2008)

The dissemination day had a secondary purpose, as well as sharing project findings. It provided an opportunity to build upon the momentum that had developed behind 'Excuse Me, I Want to Get On!', and to identify with those present (practitioners, policy-makers and the community) other issues of local concern. Attendees were asked to complete feedback forms on the format and content of the day, but also to identify what other issues they had experienced as a result of living in an urban environment. Emerging from the feedback was the clear concern about wider issues of city travel, which reinforced our understanding of transport corridors as a key transitional edge.

Summary

'Excuse Me, I Want to Get On!' was a pivotal project for us on a number of levels. It was our first funded piece of knowledge transfer research, it was borne out of a community desire to address issues that affected them (not an academic research exercise) and it proved that our approach to, and methodologies for, participative practice were capable of activating real-world change. After 'Excuse Me, I Want to Get On!' it became clear that we needed to more formally harness the process by which Experiemics catalysed action in transitional edge environments. We saw this was necessary so that it could be utilised and adapted to suit a variety of contexts and be used by a spectrum of communities. This next section describes the formation of the Experiemic Process and how by working through its seven stages professionals and communities can arrive at collective solutions to deliver ours.

Employing Experiemics: 'What's the Fuss, We Want the Bus!'

Following the success of 'Excuse Me, I Want to Get On!', and building upon our previous participatory work with PWLD (Mathers, 2008) and children (Simkins, 2008), we were awarded a two-year research grant by the Leverhulme Trust (UK). This funding gave us the opportunity to facilitate an investigation of the wider issue of bus travel by PWLD across Sheffield (the city) and South Yorkshire (the region). Partnership commitment behind this new project, named by the community 'What's the Fuss, We Want the Bus!', was strong from the start. Within a few weeks of our announcing our intention to take this work forward, three learning disability support agencies, two national transport providers and the city council had volunteered to collaborate. Capturing how the momentum behind this partnership had been built formed our first step towards the creation of the Experiemic Process.

Understanding motivation: balancing mine, theirs, ours and yours

Earlier in this chapter we reflected on the resource and governance implications of taking a longitudinal, participatory approach to address socio-spatial issues. Through our experience facilitating a series of successive projects, from 'Our Parks and Gardens' to 'Excuse Me, I Want to Get On!' and 'What's the Fuss, We Want the Bus!', we would argue that the social impact of taking a longitudinal approach far outweighs the financial support required to resource such projects. With the commencement of 'What's the Fuss, We Want the Bus!', we observed how the community involved (particularly those members who had originally participated in 'Our Parks and Gardens') now took a much stronger, leading role; they were the experts in their own experiences. As such, they were able to clearly articulate their motivation for involvement (their mine): 'Buses, not always friendly with people with learning disabilities, bus drivers need training (to be more kind and considerate)' (Voices and Choices, 2008). Other community groups, who had been involved in 'Excuse Me, I Want to Get On!', were also able to communicate precise issues which they wished to resolve (developed from their experiences of the previous project workshops):

> We need prominent notices on the bus that at least one window be kept open explaining why. When all bus windows are shut, the air becomes stale and unhealthy and the heat overpowering (even in cold weather). When many people are confined in an enclosed space, it is a health hazard and a breeding ground for viruses and it's also nauseating. The windows are difficult to reach. Sometimes there is a risk of aggression if one tries to open one. Also the use of aerosols, which is a hazard especially to people with respiratory problems and allergies. Added to this is the constant use of facing seats as footrests. The buses are filthy and smell of food, hairspray and urine (this is not the fault of the bus company) but why is this behaviour tolerated? Issuing fines would surely be in the bus companies' and passengers' interests. Bus journeys can be a distressing experience for people, especially those who are susceptible to infections, travel sickness and hypersensitivity, which are common to people with disabilities. Also sufficient seats are needed at tram and bus stops. Again this lack affects the most vulnerable.
>
> (SUFA, 2008)[7]

Figure 7.9: The 'What's the Fuss, We Want the Bus!' community partners: Voices and Choices, SUFA and WORK Ltd.

For the final community group, who had attended the previous project dissemination day, but had not participated directly, involvement motivations focused on the opportunity to collaborate positively with others, which they had witnessed as a result of 'Excuse Me, I Want to Get On!', 'A number of us (trainees) use the bus to get to work. At the moment, travelling on the bus can be confusing and scary. We would really like to work with other organisations to make bus journeys easier, safer and a more enjoyable part of our day' (WORK Ltd, 2008)[8] (Figure 7.9).

Through our Experiemic facilitation of the project, transparent partnership working was actively encouraged and practitioners and policy-makers were invited to be frank regarding the individual gains they wished to achieve as a result. For the city council and the regional transport executive, these were very much policy-driven and focused on accessing a level of client experience they could not ordinarily reach:

> I'm delighted that we have been able to make contact with yourself and your colleagues and I look forward to being involved, where possible, with the future research project you describe. This ongoing area of work is very interesting and I'm sure will prove very useful to ourselves and our partner organisations.
>
> (South Yorkshire Passenger Transport Executive (SYPTE) Senior Network Accessibility Officer, 2008)[9]

> While initially we are looking at people who attend our services, we need to be aware of what else is happening in the city. Your project seems an ideal

opportunity to work together and share information and, if possible, we would really like to take part in any way we can. If we all work together, we can ensure that transport providers offer services to suit people in Sheffield and meet their individual needs.

(Sheffield City Council Mobility Manager, 2008)[10]

Figure 7.10: National transport providers (First buses) present their organisational interests to the WORK Ltd group.

Therefore, a collective will to create an ours that would deliver individual mines was strongly in evidence from the start. On this foundation we refined the communication methods and participatory approaches we had developed through the 'Our Parks and Gardens' and 'Excuse Me, I Want to Get On!' projects into a reflexive participatory framework that we call the Experiemic Process (Figure 7.12). We now describe how this was employed within the 'What's the Fuss, We Want the Bus!' project, how such a process activates social interaction in transitional edge environments, and the key findings and impact generated as a result of this project.

Figure 7.11: Policy partners (Sheffield City Council) present their organisational interests at a 'What's the Fuss, We Want the Bus!' interim project meeting.

THE EXPERIEMIC CODE A mechanism for evaluation of Information throughout the process	**1**	Establishing Project Context determined by client group/environmental and/or social context.
	2	Identifying Project Partners creating a network of equal partnership with community, service providers, policy makers, practitioners.
	3	Revealing the Issues facilitation sessions with project partners to reveal 'grass roots' issues of significance or concern within project context.
	4	Bringing together the Issues commonalities and differences identified in stage 3 are grouped to determine a project focus.
	5	Project Methods project focus explored through an inclusive process of participation using person-centred methods appropriate to the individuals and project brief.
	6	Representation and Evaluation tools of representation and evaluation identify and reveal project outputs.
	7	Findings and Recommendations project outputs framed to achieve: • understanding of issues from all partners perspectives. • identification of opportunities for change. • ownership of existing and aspirational project processes and outputs. • changes identified to generate socially restorative environment and fulfil the project brief.

EXPERIEMIC PROCESS MONITOR
The monitoring mechanism throughout the process
(monitors the growth in social capital against criteria for environmental competence)

Figure 7.12: The Experiemic Process.

The Experiemic Process

Establishing the project context

An important first stage in the Experiemic Process is to ensure that the issues to be investigated are grounded in the community, rather than imposed by external agencies, to begin the process of establishing ownership of the project context with those who have direct experience of it (Mathers *et al.*, 2012). This responds to and addresses Habraken's (1986) observation that participative processes are frequently those determined and framed by professional agencies.

In the case of 'What's the Fuss, We Want the Bus!', the project context was informed by previous work in 'Excuse Me, I Want to Get On!' This project had identified strengths and weaknesses in detailed aspects of a specific form of transport provision and highlighted where improvements could be made. 'What's the Fuss, We Want the Bus!' then built upon this original partnership and premise, to deliver greater social and environmental impact at a regional service provision, policy and practice level.

Identifying the project partners

Throughout Part III we have drawn attention to the need to reduce territorial hierarchies within processes of participation. When inviting partners to join us in employing the Experiemic Process, it is important that all are seen as equal contributors in order to create an ours. That individuals are recognised and valued for their own expertise (mine), be it for their personal understanding of transitional edges, their practical and professional knowledge or political overview. This follows Honneth's (1995) emphasis of the importance of achieving a context for recognition of the value of individual acts. Where the Experiemic Process is employed to facilitate partnership with traditionally less empowered communities, ensuring an increased primacy in ownership of the project context can create a more equal territorial balance.

In 'What's the Fuss, We Want the Bus!' the community context for involvement was very clear; the PWLD involved did not want to merely *identify* matters of concern, but to influence *change*. Accordingly, a network of project partners was created, including 24 members of the learning disability community who attended three learning disability support centres, policy-makers and practitioner agencies. The involvement of policy-makers from the local authority and key transport providers enabled this aim to change to be an attainable output and reality. As Experiemics shows, our role within the process focused on facilitating a programme of open communication between the partners, rather than directing the process formally. This catalytic role enabled the community to gain true ownership over the issue under study. Demonstration of community ownership evolved and became formalised in the later stages of the project when they began direction of methods used in the process's 'Representation and Evaluation' stage.

Revealing the issues

Once the project partners have been identified, focus groups are employed to establish specific aspects of project context, which the community wish to investigate in detail. This stage represents a framing of achievable tasks and again primacy is given to the

Figure 7.13: A SUFA member records her emerging bus transport issues.

community to express particular areas of concern arising from their own experiences, serving to reinforce their ownership (or mine) of the project.

The 'What's the Fuss, We Want the Bus!' focus groups made it explicit that all three community groups had a shared desire to be able to use bus services more freely. However, each group identified specific issues from their own experiences that made this difficult to achieve (Figure 7.13). These were: poor treatment of PWLD by bus drivers (Voices and Choices); feelings of insecurity and vulnerability arising from the behaviour of other passengers (SUFA); and confusing and fearful experiences that prevented safe and enjoyable bus travel (WORK Ltd).

Bringing together the issues

Through regular smaller and more informal group workshops, this stage of the process continues to establish a framework of common understanding within which each community member can have their own contribution recognised and valued. In this common framework, each group (especially when working on

Figure 7.14: WORK Ltd develop their project focus through regular group workshops.

large-scale partnership projects) retains ownership of their own particular area of interest (Figure 7.14).

In 'What's the Fuss, We Want the Bus!' the wider project context of bus travel was gradually brought into sharper focus through identification of a collective desire for all community members to be able to enjoy using buses safely and with confidence as part of daily life. This highlighted further implications for the policy and practitioner partners, which came to focus on driver training, passenger conduct policy and ensuring safety in everyday bus experiences. Through this refinement of the wider issue, four key project questions were identified: (1) what is it like getting to the bus stop?; (2) what is it like at the bus stop?; (3) what is it like on the bus?; and (4) what is it like getting off? How to answer these key questions catalysed a need to identify appropriate data collection methods.

Project methods

For every project that employs the Experiemic Process, the choice of methods should be adapted to address the project community and context. This means that while it is useful to have a methodological toolkit at your disposal, which does not rely on one form of communication alone (i.e. not just written or verbal), methodological choice should evolve in response to the requirements of the previous four process stages. A responsive approach should be employed throughout; as the project progresses and community ownership and confidence are built, these methods may themselves evolve.

Selection of 'What's the Fuss, We Want the Bus!' methods was agreed in collaboration with the community to reflect individual and group communication preferences, and to facilitate the phenomenological exploration of their public transport experiences. At each of the three community partner sites, a series of eight one-day workshops was held with eight participants over a five-month period, punctuated by a public intermediate project review meeting. The catalyst for the series of onsite workshops was an initial participant-directed bus journey, undertaken by each group in order to capture existing experiences through photography, sound recording and film. Each of the three participant groups then took part in a series of drawing, photo-elicitation, film and discussion workshops. Responsive development of these methods, to include participant-produced animation, for example, was facilitated at the request of one of the participant groups. This developed the static narrative of the participants' experiences

Figure 7.15: Voices and Choices animation workshops.

(captured through their drawings, photographs and words) into a sinuous representation of their person–environment interactions (Figure 7.15).

An intermediate public project review meeting was held at Sheffield Town Hall to facilitate dissemination of the research interim findings and to obtain feedback from the wider learning disability community, policy-makers and practitioners. Following evaluation of this public review, the community engaged in a further series of workshops to reveal their aspirational travel experiences, which subsequently formed the basis for engagement with policy and practitioner project partners. This approach, augmented by the use of visual methodologies and the creation of participant workbooks (to record thoughts and experiences), both provided a progressive structured record of relevant information in response to core questions and ensured individuals retained a sense of ownership over their own contribution (mine) and the value of this in relation to the collective task (ours).

Representation and evaluation

Within the project method stage of Experiemics, a rich and highly detailed range of information is likely to be produced, based on the authentic routine experiences of the community. Representing and communicating this effectively to diverse audiences presents particular and potentially polarising challenges. At one extreme is the need to effectively engage with other partners so that they can assimilate the implications of the project's outcomes within their existing professional structures. At the other extreme we must ensure that the community can retain ownership over the way their findings are communicated. Without this latter consideration, the Experiemic Process would risk repeating the limitations of conventional participatory practice, where communities simply deliver information into the hands of professional agencies for re-interpretation. During this stage, review and feedback sessions are therefore held with the community, during which their perspectives on central issues arising from the project, and how best to communicate them, are refined.

In 'What's the Fuss, We Want the Bus!' this enabled individual community groups to focus on a particular method or set of complementary methods to represent their findings in a manner they felt would have greatest impact. WORK Ltd, for example, organised and carried out interviews with representatives from the policy and practitioner project partners whom they identified as having an impact upon their current travel experiences (Figure 7.16). In addition, the Head Teacher and student representatives of a local college were interviewed to address issues arising from the intimidating behaviour of college students on buses used by WORK Ltd trainees. SUFA reviewed a bus journey to and from the city centre, and then wrote and performed a short drama to highlight, in particular: the need for safer crossings; difficulties getting buses to stop; condition of bus shelters and stops; passenger and driver attitudes. Finally, Voices and Choices chose to work with a professional animator to develop a script and learn various graphic and technical skills, which in turn enabled their production of a highly regarded animated film.

Figure 7.16: Members of WORK Ltd interview transport professionals and policy-makers.

Findings and recommendations

The final stage of the Experiemic Process involves a qualitative evaluation of the project's outputs using a specially developed coding system to establish core themes and make recommendations (Simkins, 2008). An important characteristic of this stage is to ensure that findings and recommendations remain accessible to the community and can be understood as inclusively as possible. Achieving this requires careful attention to the language used and methods of presentation to ensure that community ownership does not become compromised through, for example, translation of materials into excessively professionalised formats and specialised terminology. Throughout this stage, language used by the community to express their thoughts and ideas remains present, and the use of photographic and drawn images they have produced retains the essential personalisation of the project and makes its origins recognisable.

In 'What's the Fuss, We Want the Bus!' the evaluation resulted in the emergence of five key themes: social issues; safety; customer care; information; place and object issues. In relation to the five key themes outlined by the findings, a number of recommendations arose for policy and practice partners and these were delivered in the form of accessible reports and a DVD film documentary containing each of the participant group's chosen means of representation and a summary of the key findings from each (Table 7.3).

Table 7.3: 'What's the Fuss, We Want the Bus!' findings and recommendations.

Project theme	*Detailed description*
Social issues	*Issues*: Anti-social behaviour was of concern to many, which greatly affected their confidence when travelling. The need for personal space was raised, as well as a lack of respect by others, i.e. bullying, being pushed or sworn at. However, bus travel was also seen as a means to facilitate positive social experiences, with participants describing the potential for making new friends (increasing social contact) and developing confidence in independent travel. Travelling with friends was important to some individuals and a key reason why they currently didn't travel on public transport as their friends used the Community Transport service. Familiarity with other travellers and the transport staff were seen as having a potentially significant impact.

Project theme	Detailed description
Social issues	*Recommendations*: A greater civic authority presence (i.e. community officers) in public places would reduce fear of anti-social behaviour. Developing relationships through partnership between communities (such as schools and the learning disability community) and policy and practice is effective in addressing local issues. Further training opportunities for PWLD to learn to travel independently would facilitate self-esteem.
Safety	*Issues*: All groups expressed concerns about being able to safely get to the bus stop. The distances people needed to travel to bus stops (particularly from their homes) were seen as an issue of safety, convenience and accessibility. The current condition of some crossings was also highlighted. Those that did not sound when it is safe to cross were seen as potentially dangerous. Meanwhile the bars on buses were seen as a sign of safety and used by some as comfortable support for bumpy journeys. *Recommendations*: Local authorities should re-examine the relationship between road crossings and the position of bus stops, and consider more crossing points. The inclusion of both audio and visual signals at all crossing points should be a standard specification.
Customer care	*Issues*: Being able to sit down before the bus departure. The ability to draw attention to oneself and prompt the bus to pull into a bus stop was seen as a problem when more than one bus used the same stop. For many participants this led to frustration as well as missing the bus. Wheelchair users appreciated the driver letting down the ramp for their access. However, in many situations, the ramps were not clean or in good repair, which made individuals feel devalued. Having a priority disabled passenger space (particularly for wheelchair users) on the bus was important, yet this often led to conflict with pram users. *Recommendations*: Travel operators should consider the issue of stopping buses when more than one bus is at a stop. In association, driver training should develop awareness that disabled passengers find this difficult. There should be further training of transport staff to be respectful of all passengers. ▶

Project theme	Detailed description
Infor-mation	*Issues*: Methods of transport information were often confusing or difficult to read. This was brought up as an issue in relation to use of the 24-hour clock on timetables as well as the predominance of jargon on signage and timetables, i.e. the central bus station is known as the 'Interchange' yet for many people this wording had little obvious relationship to bus travel.
	Many people felt that the size of font used made information difficult to read and concerns were expressed with regard to the travel guides and website. The journey planner (a newly installed information device) was indecipherable and could not be described as 'user friendly'. The use of colours was seen as confusing in terms of the timetable routes (where these bore no correlation to the colour of the associated buses) and destination boards on buses. The position of timetables at bus shelters appeared illogical, as they were often located at the opposite end of the bus shelter to the direction from which the buses arrived. Participants who were wheelchair users expressed difficulties regarding timetables' positioning as these were at a height above eye level. Transport signs were viewed as confusing or not present at all.
	Recommendations: Use of the 12-hour clock on bus timetables, production of clearer maps and removal of jargon from infor-mation (in particular signage) should be implemented. Travel operators should ensure consistency in their use of colour between timetables, buses and the design of shelters in order to facilitate orientation and confidence in travel. There should be greater investment in communication and equality training of staff at travel centres, i.e. British Sign Language (BSL) and Makaton.

Project theme	Detailed description
Place and object issues	*Issues*: The condition of bus stops, shelters and buses was seen as significant in how people felt about a place or travel system and whether they chose to use it or not. Clean streets and bus stops were regarded as good. As well as maintenance, the provision and quality of objects such as seats were viewed as significant. Locating the central bus station was not a good experience for the participants. People were confused due to the lack of signage and discouraged by the condition of pathways, the number of steps (on the access route) and the amount of litter and graffiti. The apparent colour coding of shelters was also seen as confusing. Wheelchair users appreciated being able to face the direction that the bus was travelling in, so they could see when their stop was approaching. The choice of seating place varied. Some people preferred to be at the front so they did not miss their stop and also took comfort from being close to the driver. Others saw this as potential for crowding and preferred to be at the rear, however, departing the bus was then seen as sometimes challenging. *Recommendations*: There should be greater partnership between travel operators and local authorities to maintain buses, bus stops and the areas around bus stops. Seats at bus stops should be at an appropriate height for people to use easily and the local authority should consider footpath surfacing and handrails on sloping ground. The position and number of litterbins around bus stops should be reviewed and improvements to lighting in public places made to facilitate safer travel at night.

Process completion: end of the journey?

Among the rich diversity of detailed information to emerge from the 'What's the Fuss, We Want the Bus!' project there are two significant issues that we believe add weight to advocates of 'bottom-up' approaches to environmental planning and design. The first of these is that a significant majority of the recommendations that emerged from the process pointed toward the need for relatively minor adjustment and adaptation to the existing transitional edge environment. This suggests that substantial improvements could be made to the quality of experience that PWLD have of bus use, and with this their encouragement to use it more, through the accumulated impact of small interventions, most of which require no expensive infrastructural change and could be accommodated within routine maintenance, monitoring and training procedures.

The second relates to the presentation of findings. A common characteristic of conventional processes of participation tends to see outputs as a source of data, much like any other form of survey information gathered to inform the initial planning stages of a project. There are good reasons why, important to the subsequent justification of decisions made. However, and especially in the case of information derived from participation events, this process acts to remove the information from its context and detaches the authentic voices which initially gave it expression, recasting it in professionally specialised formats. Our previous research suggested that this process of professionalisation can have such a steri-lising effect on locally generated information as to make the important messages it contains almost inaudible in extreme cases.

In response, the findings from 'What's the Fuss, We Want the Bus!' were presented publicly at a dissemination event in July 2008 at Sheffield Town Hall at a special sitting of the regular People's Parliament event that many of the learning disability participants were familiar with attending from previous occasions. These familiar surroundings gave participants the opportunity to deliver their findings in person in the ways they had chosen for themselves; as an exhibition of canvases, a short drama performance, a presentation of the animation film, and other film- and image-based materials. An audience of over 150 people, including people with learning disabilities, the local authority and transport providers, attended the event (Figure 7.17). As a result of this direct communication, which retained the authentic voices of the participant groups, the recommendations of 'What's the Fuss, We Want the Bus!' have since been included in the 2010 Sheffield City Council Adult Social Care Mobility Strategy, while the transport providers have employed the project DVD as a staff training resource. Through the sharing of experiences, the project has built community empowerment and cohesion: proof that participation does have a place in affecting policy and practice and that partnership with communities can promote positive change.

Figure 7.17: The 'What's the Fuss, We Want the Bus!' dissemination day.

Summary

In this climate of professional dominance and local submission, the final product of participatory collaborations may more realistically be an interpretation of what professionals believe the public would want. At worst, a final design is produced based on a professional's personal preferences and desires for the site, with a footnote flagging up public consultation as part of the design process. The cities of today are diverse communities, comprising young and old, male and female, disabled and non-disabled, all who have unique personalities, needs and preferences. The design professional's ability to create landscapes in which people may live happily, work, socialise and relax relies upon their ability to release information about what these environments mean and could mean to every individual. Currently, many professional design tools do not adequately allow landscape architects and other design professionals to create such a dialogue with their communities. Without being versed in the language of such tools, members of the community are put at an immediate disadvantage. For those, such as people with learning disabilities, who have restricted verbal and written communication, the opportunity to participate in the design debate is beyond their grasp at present. Having never been consulted or involved in decision-making, the landscape-specific knowledge that people with learning disabilities possess lies dormant and concealed from general view. Without their contribution to the ongoing design debate, let alone the society in which it works, landscape architecture and other related disciplines can never claim to be inclusive.

We have sought to demonstrate that new forms of participatory process are required in order for the, hitherto unrecognised yet important, voices of under-represented groups in society to be heard and valued within professional agencies who influence the form and content of places they use. We have suggested that such processes have far greater potential than to simply provide an effective means whereby professional agencies can access the experiences of user groups, important though this is as an end in itself. Our research has shown that achieving empowerment can depend as much on the participatory process itself as on what it delivers to the decision-makers. By recognising that participation in actions seen to be making a valued contribution to an issue of shared concern within a mutually supporting community can raise levels of self-esteem and community cohesion, we assert that there are significant social as well as informational outcomes from participation. We believe that the former needs to be better understood and more explicitly incorporated into participatory processes used in environmental planning and design arenas, and that the potential this has for developing local social capital through inclusivity should be much more widely recognised as a desirable outcome in itself. Through conducting this research we hope to have been able to demonstrate that aspects of the disciplines of disability studies, participatory practices, and urban design theory can be mutually and beneficially informative and that this may help inform better urban place-making for the benefit of all in society.

One of the driving forces of Experiemics is to achieve positive change in the lives of the community through active contribution. The seven stages of the Experiemic Process place *control* over what is investigated, how it is done and finally how findings are represented and communicated firmly in the hands of those who have first-hand experience. It achieves this by stripping away the polarisation of 'expert' and 'lay' participants, a familiar characteristic of many participatory methodologies, recognising instead that all participants are differently expert, either by virtue of special training or by virtue of routine daily experience. Presently, most approaches to decision-making that affects the environments people routinely use are delivered in a top-down manner, in which professional agencies determine process and make master plans for implementation. Even in the more enlightened of these processes where public participation is sought and valued, this remains firmly a part of top-down decision-making as local experience is usually extracted from the context and recast as problems requiring professional solution, but through the Experiemic Process, this no longer needs to be the case.

Chapter Eight

Developing the practical application of Experiemics

Introduction

In this chapter we will extend consideration of the Experiemic Process with details of significant additional features of its operational capability arising from a number of other participative projects. Some of this work took place concurrently with the work in Chapter 7 and some subsequently. The central purpose of these activities was to provide us with the opportunity to apply and test various ongoing developments in the Experiemic Process evolution, especially those relating to inclusive and accessible methodologies, and particularly to try to concentrate on issues that might relate to its efficient application in conventional practice arenas. One of the key challenges that we wanted to confront in the development of the Experiemic Process is that of operational efficiency. Public consultation, and especially that which has a high degree of participative input, can be highly resource-hungry and in the competitive, commercially driven reality of practice, this can become a significant disincentive, even when there are statutory requirements in place. This can lead to tokenism and to ill-conceived and ineffective practices that at worst can do more harm than good. We have outlined some of the background to this tendency in Chapter 6 in our discussion about the need for participative processes.

Our claim for Experiemics is that it is an effective means by which to engage a wide range of groups in society in identifying issues of concern to themselves and then, empowered by the process, to establish fully inclusive and openly accessible ways to investigate the nature of these concerns and reveal proposals beneficial to all involved. This is what we mean by the capacity of the process to transform the polarising impacts of mine and theirs towards a more common framework of understanding and mutual benefit: the ours, or sense of belonging, that we explained earlier in the book as a cornerstone to the achievement of individual self-esteem. In a changing political climate concerned increasingly with local empowerment and personal responsibility, processes that can galvanise and catalyse community-led action effectively and efficiently are more important than ever. If our claim is to become a reality, then Experiemics needs to be more than theoretically well founded, it also has to be operationally efficient. The work outlined in this chapter, then, has helped reveal and develop further details of its application in various contexts, demonstrating above all the key significance of the following in particular, which give nuances of flexibility and adaptability to the structural framework of the Experiemic Process. To this end we are again grateful to the Leverhulme Trust and the University of Sheffield Knowledge Transfer Fund for the financial resources that made this work possible.

We will develop this chapter by going on to show, in particular, how a variety of operational issues arose and were developed through various projects. They are important issues embedded into the practice of Experiemics, but we believe they also highlight wider considerations that need to be thought about in all kinds of participative activity. They are founded on the core principles of empathy with all participant individuals and groups, a commitment to the development and application of inclusive practices, and processes of dissemination that can retain and express the authentic voices of all participant groups.

Case Study 1 Development of the 'Insight Method'

Some of these operational aspects have their formative roots in Ian Simkins' doctoral research which involved exploration of existing and aspirational place experiences of primary school children (Simkins, 2008). A central premise of the research programme was that, while children were commonly involved in processes of environmental improvement consultation, especially in relation to school grounds improvement work, this often meant following instructions brought into the setting by outside experts. While valuable in many ways, this approach seemed not always to be giving the children involved a sufficiently participative stake in how they communicated their feelings and ideas about places they used every day. The research programme developed sought to explore how to widen the empowerment of children by developing methods to give them a voice that would ordinarily be hidden from design and planning processes. Some 69 UK primary school children took part in three participatory phases of the research which aimed to understand their perceptions of their own neighbourhoods.

The research design was initially founded on traditionally accepted approaches to provide a robust academic and methodological structure consistent with a PhD research framework. A review of practice and literature led to a provisional framework of methodological tools for testing and developing in the participatory phases of the research. These included, for example, semi-structured interview models previously used in practice contexts at schools, cognitive mapping and drawing techniques, and photo-elicitation techniques. These methods provided a basis from which to begin the process of engaging with children and, in the context of the research objectives centred on improving the empowerment of children in the process, began to help highlight two key issues that would be important in the subsequent development of the Experiemic Process.

First, while most children were quite content to cooperate with these methods, it began to become clear that they did so with significantly varying levels of enthusiasm and confidence. The multi-method approach adopted was therefore becoming an effective means by which to show that account should be taken not only of the ability to communicate thoughts, but also of children's preferences about how they as individuals expressed them. Some children simply responded better when, seemingly irrespective of age, they were treated as co-participants in the creation of methods and not as simply responding to predetermined methods imposed from outside the context.

A second issue to quickly emerge at the formative stages of the research was the importance of inclusive language and, along with this, the capability for participant children to experience something of themselves within the process. Throughout the research phases this gradually evolved into what was to become known as 'now' and 'wish' phases of participatory activity. An adaptation of cognitive mapping developed a basis to allow children from a range of ages to map aspects of their own neighbourhood experience, first locating places of significance on a map which usually included their home, school and what they did outside. They would then become empowered to explore and express within this familiar framework more complex experiential aspects by concentrating first on what it was like 'now', personalising and evaluating their work by drawing themselves in the picture doing what they liked doing best outside at a preferred location. Once completed, the children then drew a second picture which would be their aspiration for their neighbourhood, a 'wish' picture.

It was found by this means that a staged process could be identified, centred initially on giving a degree of control to the children over what they actually did: by becoming a co-participant. Moving then to a process that initially allowed them to make a representation of what they, as individuals, understood as the most important constituent components of their neighbourhood, personalising it with images of themselves and then using this as a platform from which to express feelings and ideas about what was happening 'now' and then what they might 'wish' it to be like. This began to show how to make a fairly sophisticated evaluation and design process inclusive and accessible to even young children.

By using a version of a Leitmotif Code as a template, findings from this work could subsequently be coded. As a consequence, it was possible to identify broad categories within which the emergent place perceptions of the children could be grouped. The developed model identified five generic themes which were: (1) *place-specific experiences*; (2) *object-specific experiences*; (3) *feelings and emotional significance;* (4) *imagination and recollection aspects;* and (5) *interactions*. It was found that each of this study's five generic themes had a number of typologies and each typology was composed of a number of categories of elements.

The significance of the development of the themes and their constituent components, coded in terms of their hierarchy and relationships, was a crucial part of the study's development. It had demonstrated the possibility that by including participants in the design of methods that were to be used, levels of empowerment could be created that deepened and enriched the levels of experiential information that emerged, grounding it very specifically in its context of origin. Furthermore, this information could then be systematically coded and categorised to present a more generic or collective picture which similarly remained attached to the specific context.

A process of participation began to emerge, known then as the Insight Method and Code, that was empowering, inclusive and sufficiently informative as a collective that, when applied alongside the developing Experiemic Process, would help inform how its initial stages might be strengthened by emphasising the importance of a flexibly applied multi-method approach and the application of inclusive language. It also began to reveal the importance of adopting a highly reflective approach whereby subsequent stages of a participative process, which may be guided and planned at the outset, might need to remain open to adaptation and evolution informed by the preceding stages. This began to suggest a process of participatory action, grounded in its specific context, which required the evolutionary characteristic of in-situ adaptability. These would become important cornerstones of the operation of the emerging Experiemic Process. The developed model, embodied into the evolving Experiemic Process was summarised as shown below.

Stance

- principles of a longitudinal approach employing reflective practice; adaptation and being responsive;
- empathic;
- child-/person-centric;
- empowerment;
- ethical perspective of children's informed consent inclusion;
- multi-route facilitation.

Process stages

- research;
- plan;
- instigate;
- reflect;
- react;
- implement response.

Case Study 2 Research into practice: applying a person-centred process to environmental and social change in a primary school, North-East of England

This project, made possible by a grant from the UK Leverhulme Trust, provided an opportunity to further develop structural and operational aspects of the Experiemic Process in the field. In particular, it was instrumental in the further development of the methodological principles of 'now' and 'wish' that had proved to be especially successful in the academic research outlined above. It also provided a means by which to begin to see how another Experiemic concept, the mine, theirs, ours and yours (MTOY) relationships, discussed earlier, could be incorporated into a more unified operational structure. In this case we tried to engage with the whole school community rather than only the children. The point of this was: first, to recognise that there are many other groups that make up such a community, and it is therefore important to try to capture similarities and differences if subsequent processes of change are to reflect the different 'mines'; second, to find out what would happen when different elements of the Experiemic Process were applied to different groups and to establish what in situ adaptability might mean here. In keeping with the collaborative nature of the Experiemics application, discussions with the participating school developed a structure of workshop activities capable of engaging with the school community to create a sense of 'ours' and of 'our' ownership of any physical change within the school grounds as a product of the project.

For many years, research has been undertaken in children–environment relations, but despite the diversity of work in this field there remain concerns regarding the 'significant methodological difficulties in presenting research in such a way that it can be effectively and efficiently used by built environment professionals to improve the places inhabited (or not) by young people' (Kraftl *et al.*, 2007, p. 401). This project, therefore, was partly developed to show how research can be applied to encourage professional practice to better engage with and understand a community's perspectives. It demonstrated how doing this effectively can increase social cohesion and self-esteem in the participants as well as produce recommendations for environmental change.

With cost consciousness and practical application in mind, the project demonstrated how this limitation can be overcome by the application of appropriate steps and methods in the Experiemic Process undertaken to engage with a school community. The work was undertaken in two days using a variety of methods developed to work with adults and 69 children aged 3–5 years old to capture views and aspirations about the school nursery play area. The rich stream of information that arose was subsequently evaluated using the Insight Code framework of representation. This informed recommendations for improvement to the play area but also increased social cohesion and the sense of empowerment among participants through the capacity of the process to first reveal individual interests, or 'mines', but also to begin to make explicit how these could ultimately be accommodated and expressed within a wider sense of ours: in this case a sense of mutual understanding that had more of a social than a physical manifestation.

The school had concerns about the design of the nursery play area and what it facilitated as a resource for the staff and children. The school wished the children to experience the grounds as a play and learning resource. The staff comments to the original designers were apparently ignored and the dissatisfaction with what appeared to be a functional and aesthetic solution to the space was strongly felt. The research partnership we were able to establish with the school through the Experiemic Process was established on the basis that the children would be involved in participating in developing a new concept for the grounds. This concept could then be taken forward and implemented by a practitioner, but it would be one that the children had been involved in, rather than just the teaching staff. The participative spectrum was widened still further by a decision to try to use the Experiemic Process to address a rather strong sense of division between parents and teaching staff: parents seemed very protective of the school, for perhaps obvious reasons, yet felt excluded from thinking of the school as a theirs; they felt it was the territory of the teaching staff who had the power of exclusion.

Although this was beginning to become quite a complicated and multi-faceted project, we also wanted to address issues of efficient execution, to try to explore what could be achieved within relatively short, and therefore cost-effective, timeframes. We wanted to know if the Experiemic Process could demonstrate that it was possible to engage with a large number of individuals in a community, productively and efficiently, but quickly, without generating a sense of tokenism. The participation process was therefore designed to be carried out as a workshop over just two days: one day to engage with the children and another with parents, teaching and non-teaching staff.

In order to respond to the importance, highlighted earlier, of the need for a multi-method approach that would allow participants some measure of control over how they chose to capture and represent their feelings about 'now' and 'wish', a wide range of options were made available. In order to optimise the sense of involvement in children, in particular, these included interactive methods, such as self-directed photography, sound recording, observational walks, as well as games devised to re-enact issues considered important. In order to maintain the core principle of inclusivity, all of the findings from these processes were reviewed in situ by involving children placing expressive faces representing the way they felt about images produced. A 'wish' phase of the work followed a similar format, refined in consequence of what had been learned from the 'now' stage, which gave children the experience of comparing and contrasting their feelings about the existing 'now' situation with what their aspirations, or 'wishes' were. On the second day the adult participants followed a format of observations and conversations regarding the daily routine, from their perspective of what they did at school and what the children did (Figure 8.1).

Subsequent to these stages of the Experiemic Process, which are essentially focused on the collective determination of issues, methods of exploration and gathering of experiential information through their application, a process of evaluation centred on the Insight Code begins the process of categorising recurrent themes. In this particular case, six recurrent themes emerged as: Object; Place;

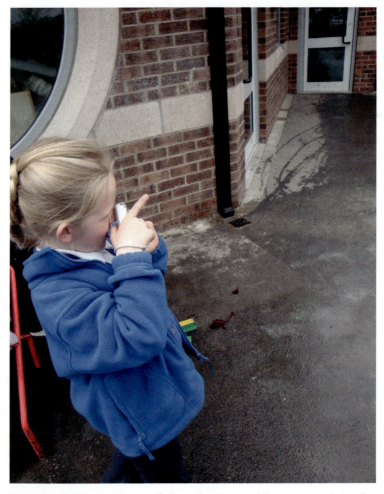

Figure 8.1: Children leading a self-directed walk around the nursery and recording their thoughts about 'now'.

Feelings and Emotions; Imaginings and Recollection; Interactions; and Sensory. Outputs were subsequently framed to achieve an understanding of project issues from all the partners' perspectives, particularly those who are usually under-represented (children). One of the most significant aspects of this was the production of a documentary-style DVD capturing the various stages of the process from the perspective of the participants. In this way, project outputs and dissemination continue to remain as inclusive as possible, thus retaining the authentic voices of those for whom this environment is their ours. Ultimately, this helped the school community to secure funding for the implementation of their plans, enabling the employment of a landscape design consultant to help them realise some of their aspirations. The redesigned yard was opened in a ceremony attended by staff, planners, children and parents.

Case Study 3 Playground and field project: primary school, North-East of England

One of the characteristics we wanted to build into the Experiemic Process was a capacity for continuity in practice. During the course of work with the learning disability communities, outlined in Chapter 7, it became apparent that the growing empowerment and confidence developed by participants not only instilled a desire to do more, but also a capacity to identify possible new project directions related to what they had previously done. This seemed to arise in part from a characteristic of the process, at the point of dissemination, to look forward to new possibilities as well as bring closure to the current project. This is meant to reflect the reality that both environmental improvement and social development are a continuous process and for this reason we wanted to try to build into the Experiemic Process a longitudinal dimension that could reflect this.

In respect of the school project described above, the inclusion of the school community and DVD production effectively became the catalysts which gave the school the confidence to expand their ambitions for the school environment with another, more extensive, project, which would explore the future potential of the school field and playground. In this second phase, 70 children took part in the process, as well as adult participants representing school staff and parents' interests. In this phase we tried to build further on the overall objective to explore the operational efficiency of the Experiemic Process. This involved the early stages of the Experiemic Process, in which methodological tools developed through partnership working with the school community, being orientated towards development of a working model of participatory methodologies that could be undertaken in a day, with one class. If this could be achieved, it would further demonstrate the efficient application of the Experiemic Process within professional practice parameters.

The workshops were organised in stages to find out what the children's thoughts were about 'now', and what their 'wish' ideas were for change (Figure 8.2). This inclusive system was expanded in this phase of the work with an 'action' stage, conceived primarily to test the relative viability of 'wish' ideas. This was then followed by participant involvement in a 'review' stage which contributes to the longitudinal characteristic of the Experiemic Process as a whole by providing for a continuous process of reflection and evaluation of both issues and the process itself. Actual activities involved in these stages followed developments and adaptations

Figure 8.2: Drawing 'wish' pictures and rating the most important wishes with a gold star.

of sound recording, self-directed photography, discussion groups, etc., used in the previous nursery area phase, but developed to reflect different age groups and the intentionally tighter timeframe.

The introduction of the 'action' stage in this phase of the work introduced a greater level of interactivity, providing the chance for participants to see some of their 'wishes' come true. After the 'wish' evaluation stage had been completed, each group chose two 'wishes' to test and build outside, constructing the 'wishes' using temporary structures, such as cones, sports equipment, string, canes and plastic sheets (Figure 8.3). The aim was for the children to experience and consider aspects such as size, three-dimensional enclosure, location, what they could see, hear, smell and touch at the location, what it felt like being there and what the experience of getting to and from it was like (Figure 8.4). They made drawn and written records of these experiences, personalising as before by introducing images

Figure 8.3: Chalking out 'wish' ideas in the 'action' stage: a pond with a fountain and fish.

Figure 8.4: Taking 'action' by building 'wishes' to test the ideas: a wendy house.

of themselves as present within the work and expressing their feelings about it through using expressive faces.

The culmination of this process was the identification of the group's preferences for which journey to and from the field and the playground they considered most important, bringing the process to focus on a collective ours. These were then tested by various means through which the children were able to bring aspects of their 'wishes' to life through various representational means including acting out aspects, creating sounds and otherwise trying to bring out 'virtual' qualities of their proposals which could then be shared with others to form a basis for evaluation. This is a form of inclusive dissemination of ideas created within the process that begins to move beyond the abstractions of representational forms like drawings and plans, by introducing a level of tangibility all participants could share that could be experienced first-hand, rather than be simply interpreted. An important element of the Experiemic Process is the recognition that different methodologies are necessary to facilitate inclusion of different groups of people. A similar process, but involving mapping and discussion-based methods, brought adult participants into the process as well.

This phase of the project concluded with an event at a sports day so that, as parents attended to watch their children engaging in a variety of outdoor activities, they too could be brought into the process as included participants. This succeeded in overcoming an initial reluctance on the part of parents to participate in other ways. Posters of all of the children's work were mounted inside the school hall and around the playground. Parents were proactively engaged to invite ideas and opinions about the playground and field. They were also asked to place stickers on large plans of the site, writing comments on them and placing them in the relevant location and rating them to reveal preferences.

Over the course of the two phases of the project, application of the evolving Experiemic Process helped the various factions of the school community to express their own thoughts and feelings about what the school environment meant to them and how they saw improvements being made. Through their partnership working to develop a wide range of inclusive methods for exploration of issues and representation and communication of potential solutions, all the school community had the opportunity to see and be involved in the creation of a shared vision. This level of inclusivity, embracing both the school and its wider community, began to bring together ideas about how the project might move forward through the collective endeavour to seek sources of funding and to embrace locally available skills and other resources that might assist in implementation. Here, again, the particular forward-looking characteristics of the Experiemic Process, to try to engage with the whole community by means of carefully developed inclusive dissemination, had helped to give forward momentum to the project as well as embed ownership of this within the locality.

Case Study 4 Development of the Experiential Landscape mapping methodology

As we have tried to outline in this chapter so far, inclusivity and accessibility are cornerstones of the Experiemic Process. Without these, no participative process can claim to be truly open to the involvement of all. Our work with both children's groups and people with learning disabilities reveals that age and ability are not in themselves barriers to the kind of active participation which can become a creative influence in both the development of social competence and cohesion and how this is then projected into environmental improvement proposals. As John Habraken (1998) has shown, the structure of the ordinary is a complex fusion of levels of control, some requiring specialised professional services, but not all. Some levels are an intrinsic part of all human territorial awareness and, as we have discussed, this is more or less a universal human characteristic.

The real barriers are more to do with access to, and then ownership of, the means through which people develop understanding of their surroundings, how they feel about it now and what they might wish to do to make changes which suit them as individuals and communities. From this follows the communication strategies with which information is shared and negotiated as part of the natural territorial balance of control. Without inclusive communication, those with privileged access to the most influential and usually specialist communication methods will generally prevail. We have suggested that, in many instances, conventional professionalised terminology creates such boundaries, privileging the influence and therefore control of a specialist minority. Our emphasis on trying to see human and environment relations as an interplay of mine, theirs, ours and yours, is an attempt to try to overcome this with a communication structure accessible to all. This is also why there is an emphasis in the Experiemic Process on partnership working to develop methods that are specific to a particular project, rather than have them imposed from outside the context.

One particular method arising from the fundamental principles of Experiential Landscape and its underpinning of socially restorative urbanism, both in relation to the transitional edge structure discussed in Part II, and its operationalisation as an evaluation and design tool, is experiential landscape mapping. As we outlined earlier in our development of the segment hypothesis, we have developed the experiential landscape as a holistic inter-relationship of four components, each conceptualising the inter-related spatial and experiential dimensions of human–environment relations. These are called centre, direction, transition and area, and the transitional edge structure discussed in Part II develops in particular from transition and how this is woven together with centre and direction with varying degrees of emphasis represented by the different segment types. Centre, direction, transition and area (CDTA) also provide the means by which the experiential landscape for individuals and groups can be mapped and then evaluated to augment conventional professional evaluation and design processes with specific experiential information not easily captured by other methods.

Our use of CDTA in both practice situations, as one of the foundation methodologies in Experiemics and in other research and teaching contexts in the UK and overseas, has helped to demonstrate that CDTA mapping is a viable, effective and flexible mapping methodology, easily assimilated and applied because its underpinning principles are relatively simple. However, despite this, CDTA remains itself a rather specialised concept and, although it is meant to capture the fundamental human experience of routine place use, its language and means of communication remain in the domain of specialised processes and, although originally rooted in the way people normally express their place experiences, it has developed into an academic and professionally orientated method. Within the context of the Experiemic Process, however, CDTA mapping, adapted to better reflect its roots in authentic experience in order to combine with other methodological aspects of the process, offers a potential means by which community groups could find effective ways to capture and communicate place experiences to professional audiences. In this sense it has potential as an abstraction that can bridge the gap between individuals and communities and the professional specialists they may use to help them realise their aspirations. To this extent, CDTA offers potential as a form of language that can contribute to the longitudinal objectives of the Experiemic Process, ultimately empowering communities with a self-directed means to maintain productive communication with a range of professional systems and processes.

A small grant from the University of Sheffield Knowledge Transfer Opportunities Fund provided the means to explore this development further and assess its effectiveness through a project with some of our learning disability partners. A vocational training centre called Spectrum Active, members of which had collaborated with us on work described in Chapter 7, had recently acquired new premises and land they wished to develop to secure the future of the site as a commercial, educational and recreational resource. By means of the partnership working which is central to the Experiemic Process, a project was devised to develop various aspects of the CDTA mapping methodology in phases over a four-month period. This involved participants, both staff and students at Spectrum Active, undertaking a variety of activities centred on CDTA principles to record, first, their perceptions of the site as it existed (now) and subsequently to express their aspirations for how it could be developed according to their own educational, recreational and development needs (wish).

The main outputs of this process were essentially twofold. By working through the stages of the Experiemic Process, this time centred on adaptations and expansions of the CDTA mapping tool as a means of capturing and representing present feelings and future aspirations, the Spectrum Active members produced a development plan and schedule of self-directed actions for work that could be undertaken on the site. A second output focused on the evolution of the CDTA process, its incorporation into the inclusive principles of now, wish, action and review, developed through previous projects, refinement of its terminology and process of application. The whole process culminated in the production of a project DVD which Spectrum Active then presented to an audience of local community members, university academic staff and practitioners, explaining how

Figure 8.5: Creating a 'wish map' using symbols to represent CDTA aspirations at specific locations.

they had been able to take ownership of the process, introduce refinements and adaptations to suit their needs and how this had helped them to develop and articulate their plans for the Spectrum Active environment (Figure 8.5).

This not only resulted in a programme of self-directed action for work on the site under the control of its members, but also helped the group to reach out to the neighbouring community, forging links with external organisations, including the local council, shops and neighbourhood groups. This enabled Spectrum Active to experience themselves as an active and productive part of a wider community, and to benefit from a range of locally available services, in the form of volunteer skills and discounts from local tool suppliers, for example. The use of and, more importantly, the localised development and refinement of CDTA as a process of inclusive communication had facilitated the personal responsibility for and control over physical changes that were then made to the Spectrum Active grounds through a phased sequence of work. It was a process that, again, reinforced the importance of inclusive language, derived from and developed within the local context, to drive physical and social developments forward through in situ adaptability which can then help to connect together various facets of a local community in activities of mutual interest and support: ultimately the delivery of a localised sense of ours, manifest in physical change but also in local social cooperation and support.

Summary

The operational principles we have highlighted in this chapter have been refined and extended in other work, and we have been privileged to have had the chance to work with other groups who have been generous in their willingness to take part in our evolving work and from whom we have been able to learn much. Another school project, for example, in South Yorkshire, allowed us to build on the work done with Spectrum Active in developing inclusive processes of communication, demonstrating clearly that when these are in place and under the ownership and control of the community, many different layers of expertise can be brought together to mutual benefit. In this instance, the school community, newly equipped with communication tools they had developed that could cross over from community to professional, would show that they, the community, were 'expert' in their own daily experiences, and how this could then be integrated with the technical and aesthetic 'expertise' of a professional landscape architect who helped by advising how to interpret their 'wishes'. In this way, a better balance of form, contributed by the professional, was able to be achieved with the territorial needs of the community to create new places and through this express the coherent understanding of their particular community.

Work with ARC Scotland, an organisation that supports providers of services for people with learning disabilities, provided an invaluable chance to explore how aspects of the Experiemic Process could be incorporated into training packages for service providers in this area. As with the work with Spectrum Active, the emphasis here was placed on exploring how effectively principles of the Experiemic Process could be brought into service provider training, stressing again the importance of inclusive communication strategies to its success. We are currently exploring effective means of CPD training in other contexts, notably with Movium, a school staff training and professional development organisation in Sweden. Similarly, a project involving the development of way-finding strategies within an NHS hospital environment, provided the opportunity to see how inclusive and adaptive communication and mapping methods could be used to help hospital patients, particularly children and their carers, navigate around. This has helped to reinforce our belief that it is possible and extremely necessary, to break out of discipline-specific communication systems if basic human needs, in this case simple orientation, are to be effectively met in cross-disciplinary environments that bring architecture, landscape architecture, interior design and health and well-being together in one place.

Through these accounts of a few of the practical applications that have influenced the development of the Experiemic Process, we have tried to explore what the kind of self-organisation envisaged in socially restorative urbanism might mean at the point of practice. Experiemics, at face value, could be interpreted as a fairly formal structure whereby communities of different kinds and in different contexts can: identify issues of common interest and concern to them; cooperate in partnership working with relevant stakeholders to determine methods that will best suit their means of exploring these concerns; and determine how their findings and views are to be communicated so that the authentic voices of the participants involved remains heard. To this extent, like other 'formal' processes of participation, it can therefore appear as a professionally derived sequence of activity that retains the balance of control with the professionals involved in directing the process through its stages and towards its conclusion. This would not be an accurate interpretation and this understanding is important to the way that Experiemics is operationalised in its intention as a catalyst for locally derived change, under the control of local participants, driven by methods and processes of inclusive communication rooted in the particular context of its application. We see, then, the Experiemic Process more as a framework for the localised adaptation of activity that has the potential to deliver both social and physical benefits through locally orientated partnership working. It is meant to be a framework for initiating processes of self-organisation, and in achieving this it must have both a formal and an informal side which needs to be recognised and understood if it is to be effectively applied. Its overarching framework is, therefore, flexible and adaptable in response to continuous processes of reflection throughout its application.

In Chapter 7 we outlined how the overall framework of the Experiemic Process gradually evolved into a seven-stage process and how this was used to successfully integrate the interests of three groups of PWLDs with those of public transport service providers in Sheffield. Through this account we hope to have been able to demonstrate that, not only is it possible for these hitherto disenfranchised groups to take part in decision-making processes, but that when processes of participation are inclusive and accessible to all stakeholders, they can influence policy development for the benefit of all in society. In the interests of clarity and continuity, we concentrated predominantly on our work with the learning disability community to trace the development of the Experiemic Process in Chapter 7. This helps to show how the structural framework of Experiemics came into being, but as this chapter shows, this is not by any means a complete picture. As we have shown here, the development of the process was and remains highly evolutionary and adaptive. We have learned along the way that this is not only necessary to the development of the process, but that in fact it is an intrinsic quality of the process itself. Our work in applying aspects of the developing Experiemic Process in various practice-related situations shows, among other things, how important it is to go into a live fieldwork situation with a clear and well-organised framework of participative activity, but that it is also crucial to the success of the process to remain extremely fleet-footed in order to respond effectively to circumstances, often entirely unforeseen at the outset, that change in situ and over time. These include, in particular:

- *The importance of a multi-method approach.* Every individual is, of course, different and we have learned that individuals will express their ideas and aspirations with greater ease and enthusiasm if they have some control over the way in which they can express themselves. Predetermined, often highly professionalised, participation techniques can, especially in the case of vulnerable groups, be intimidating, induce harmful competitiveness and ultimately be counter-productive.

- *Inclusive language is exceptionally important.* What is inclusive can be specific, even unique, to a particular context. Identifying such common communication frameworks is therefore the first step in the development of a sense of ours in a project context. One of the more successful developments in our work in this respect has been the embedding of the principles of now, wish, action and review, used in a range of contexts as a methodological foundation to frame the place perceptions and aspirations of groups of children from 3–11 years of age, adult care worker training and environmental improvement competence in adults with learning disability.

- *In situ adaptability is a core operational principle.* As indicated above, even the most rigorously planned and tightly controlled processes of participative activity will easily unravel due to the impact of site-specific untidiness and unpredictability. This can be frustrating for participants and can be wasteful of resources if it leads to failures in progress. Successful Experiemic application requires the capability and flexibility to make often many minor modifications to the process as it unfolds in situ.

- *Efficient execution in the field.* Again, as highlighted above, processes of participative activity will not be widely adopted if they are perceived as excessively time-consuming and costly. In order to try to respond to this, experimental practices have been developed and applied which show that effective participation can be achieved within the often short timeframes of specific contexts, for example, to operate around the tightly controlled programme of a primary school day.

- *Engaging the whole community.* A significant part of the Experiemic Process involves the early identification of 'the project partners'. This requires being aware of and responding to particular interest groups that form the whole community. In a school context, for example, this can mean children, parents, teachers and other school officials, such as the governing body, catering personnel, etc. Ways need to be found to include everyone. Again, this means first identifying the 'mines' and then working through the process to eventually deliver the common ground: the sense of ours.

- *Inclusive dissemination methods.* Closure of the process is important and there is a critical difference between the sense of closure, which can retain a sense of participation, and simply ending the process, which can often create the frustration of abandonment. Participation in exhibitions, performances, development of film recording and other forms of participative closure have been found to be an important way to retain the authentic voice of the participants and avoid this simply being extracted from the context and recast in external professional contexts.

• *Outreach staff training.* Widespread application of any process of participation requires that it can be relatively easily assimilated, interpreted and adapted in various contexts and this has implications for training. In this respect we have developed adaptive workshops to investigate to what extent and with what impact, the Experiemic Process can be taught and adopted by others. Its transferability is therefore a part of its wider inclusivity.

Chapter Nine

Conclusion

Life on the edge

We began this book with the intention of articulating a new conceptual framework, called socially restorative urbanism. The main aim is to draw on our research and experience to lay foundations for new avenues of thinking, research and practice, that might help to make urban place-making, including its management and adaptability, more firmly rooted in human–environment relations. In order to do this, we have suggested that two complementary aspects of urban place-making require particular attention. The first rests on aspects of spatial organisation which are associated with the social dimensions of urban order, here brought to focus on our exploration of the transitional edge as a socio-spatial component of urban form. The second concerns the nature of relations between professional processes of urban place-making and the participation of urban occupants in those processes. In this respect, the research which underpins the development of the Experiemic Process is an attempt, in part at least, to recognise the need for catalytic frameworks which are capable of empowering people to become active contributors in processes that bring change to places they use. Experiemics and its relationship to the spatial structures inherent in our concept of transitional edges reflect the need to recognise the importance of achieving a better balance of top-down professionalised decision-making with community-led bottom-up participation. We have argued here that this is especially important as societies begin to further explore the implications of a more localised approach to service delivery and environmental management.

We have tried to highlight that getting the spatial arrangement right 'by design' can only go so far in the delivery of socially sustainable solutions. The making and managing of our routinely used urban environment is not entirely an issue of professionalised problem-solving. At worst, this can create an alienating, disenfranchising impact, which diminishes the control people have over the places they occupy and use, in its extreme form with detrimental consequences for self-esteem. Participative practices are also not, *per se*, a sufficient solution either. At some extremely hard-to-define point in the delivery of spatial arrangement, and the participation of occupants and users in that delivery, a fusion of some kind needs to happen, and we have tried to argue that one thing preventing this fusion from becoming effective is communication. Discipline-specific terminology can be just as divisive in well-meaning processes of participation as not doing it at all. The early stages of the Experiemic Process are designed to overcome these barriers by seeking to identify common ground and mutually inclusive communication strategies as the foundations for effective partnership working. This can be significantly strengthened through focus on the *mine, theirs, ours* and *yours* (MTOY) relationship, a common framework of understanding which has simplicity and almost universal accessibility as a means of structuring territorial relationships of all kinds. Its great strength is that it helps to overcome the conventional primacy on design solutions and physical change, an essentially material concern, with the aim of delivering an ours, the sense of belonging, a predominantly social concern.

MTOY, its role in the Experiemic Process and in the socio-spatial structures of transitional edges, begins to help overcome the boundary between the spatial and social. It provides an accessible and inclusive means within almost any context to talk about environmental change from an essentially territorial perspective, where each individual can maintain self-identity and self-interest but with awareness of the need for the mutually supportive structure of ours. This makes the sense of belonging a central goal for socially restorative urbanism and the cornerstone from which comes adaptive and evolutionary environmental change driven by locally orientated partnership working. Throughout the book we have had the good fortune to have been able to anchor these socially orientated concepts firmly in the structure of the built environment through the work of John Habraken. Because Habraken has shown how the structure of the ordinary is essentially a matter of control, rather than 'design', it becomes possible to understand the necessary fusion of the social and spatial through the medium of territorial activity, and from this to understand more clearly the aspects of territorial formation that must remain professionally led (form), those that require more collaboration (place) and ultimately those that must be occupant-led (understanding). The central concern of socially restorative urbanism, to deliver the sense of ours, or belonging, as an essential social gain, requires us to build in ways that restore the balance of form, place and understanding. Doing so requires the delivery of spatial infrastructure more amenable than is often the case at present to occupant participation and expression: in essence, an approach, driven by a fusion of spatial and social dimensions of urban form.

If the concept of socially restorative urbanism, as a way of thinking about the human–environment relationship in the processes of urban design, is to develop, then we are suggesting that this must begin with something of a mental re-orientation that is better able to embrace such a socio-spatial fusion. Our contribution here is to assert that this might begin with a refocus on the components of urban form particularly associated with urban social life. We find here that this rests, not on buildings, or streets, or public open spaces, or any other discrete element of urban assemblage, but on where these fuse together melding seamlessly from one into the other as transitional edges. We have tried to show that, when we do bring transitional edges into sharper focus, as components of urban form in their own right and not just as what happens where 'in' meets 'out' and where social action meets material form, we can begin to identify something of their anatomy. This is what we sought to develop in Part II, showing how transitional entities called segments can accumulate in ways that allow us to see how different social potentials can be catalysed through their varying relationships of directional and proximate emphasis, spatial enclosure and connectivity. To this extent, with their roots in the phenomenological principles underpinning Experiential Landscape, segments are as much social as they are spatial, and as such provide us, at least as an abstract approximation, with the beginnings of a socio-spatial structure capable of integrating social processes and spatial organisation.

Segments and their accumulation as transitional edges can, therefore, be a focus for design attention. They provide a structural framework amenable to conventional design decision-making processes that can, in optimal circumstances, deliver spatial porosity which then encourages and supports localised expression, coherence and adaptability. To this extent segments cross the divide between the structural and social in a blend of the two: they can be designed, but only to a certain extent, beyond which their form becomes dependent on the social processes that take place there. In Habraken's terms, then, segments give the professional design fraternity the potential to make socially optimal form. We suggest in the interests of stimulating further debate and inquiry that it may be here, in the design of segments and their accumulation as transitional edges of different kinds, that we arrive at the elusive realm where professional interventions need to begin to recede to make way for urban form to be enriched by social processes. We imagine here that occupant and user self-organisation, encouraged and sustained by the inherent human scale of the segment hypothesis, acts then to enrich the framework of segments through the infusion of place (processes of occupation) and understanding (individual and collective expression).

Having reached this elusive realm, we have then to face how we might understand this gradual release of professional levels of control towards those of occupants within the context of practice. This is inevitably a complex matter intrinsically related to the infinite breadth of human variability and how its purposes, meanings and associations are projected into the environments we share. Perhaps an oversimplification, but in developing the concept of socially restorative urbanism, we have chosen to focus in this respect on human territorial instinct, particularly on how this seems to relate to the achievement of self-esteem. In principle, this appears to hinge on achieving a delicate balance of self-assertion, the need to recognise and value, or at least tolerate the assertions of others and conform to the norms of the collective to which we belong. In pursuit of as inclusive a means of communication as possible, we have developed this idea of territoriality in the Experiemic Process by representing it in terms of the relationship of MTOY. We have tried to use this, first, to demonstrate that prevailing professionally dominant practices tend to deliver solutions which are tipped towards polarisation of mine and theirs and often make it difficult for communities to develop the necessary sense of ours, or belonging. Second, we have incorporated the ethos inherent in this territorial relationship into the Experiemic Process with the explicit aim of delivering an inclusive way of partnership working that works towards the identification and establishment of the sense of ours, by seeking out common understandings within specific human–environment contexts.

By doing so we are not suggesting that the Experiemic Process is, in itself, a *necessary* prerequisite to the delivery of better balanced MTOY relations. When spatial and other circumstances are optimal, MTOY relations in community establishment and development can maintain balance through natural and usually subliminal processes of human self-organisation as it plays out through routine life. However, as we describe through the work with our learning disability and children participants, this natural balance is not always a possibility. Age and disability, as well as other social and economic circumstances, are not the only reasons for environmental disenfranchisement, though. Our critique of prevailing approaches to regeneration and design in our urban environments highlights that such approaches themselves are capable of detaching people from control and influence over places they use. The balance of MTOY relations does seem to have become out of kilter in many contemporary urban settings, making this imbalance a wider societal problem and not one confined to those on the fringes of society. The Experiemic Process, as an inclusive human-orientated approach to partnership working, has a significant role to play in helping to redress the MTOY balance where this is found to be needed, and in so doing helps deliver both social and environmental benefits, acting to catalyse the social dimension of segments.

The research and practice we described in Chapters 7 and 8 have been instrumental, not only in the development of the Experiemic Process and its operational characteristics, but also in providing the opportunity to explore how its application in different contexts gives rise to both social and environmental benefits. It is this particular quality of the Experiemic Process that integrates it into the concept of transitional edges as having mutually interdependent social and spatial dimensions. Making this work in practice also involves consideration of ways to effectively communicate the principles of socially restorative urbanism to potential practitioner audiences. With this in mind we would like to conclude the book by looking at some of the issues that might be brought to its further development in education and practice. By doing so, we take perhaps the first tentative steps towards the development of a re-orientated, or possibly even new, disciplinary position focused on the socio-spatial significance of transitional edges to the delivery of urban social sustainability. Clearly, this is a complex aspiration beyond the scope of this book, but we may begin to give a flavour of what this might involve through reference to a student project undertaken at the Department of Landscape, University of Sheffield in 2011 (Figure 9.1).

The project involves students evaluating socially orientated aspects of the extensive urban river corridor regeneration that has been taking place in the city of Leeds over the past three decades, developing design proposals in response to their findings. This forms part of a wider research-led teaching programme designed to engage post-graduate landscape architecture students with emerging developments and ideas in urban landscape design. In this instance, a project was designed with two specific aims in mind. The first was to investigate ways in

Figure 9.1: A vision of socially restorative urbanism at the edge of the River Aire, Leeds City, by Will Pendred, Peter Robinson and Madoc Hill, Masters in Landscape Architecture students at the University of Sheffield, 2011.

which the core principles of socially restorative urbanism might be interpreted for delivery to students with some background in the built environment disciplines within a relatively short timeframe, to see how quickly and effectively these could be assimilated by students working in small groups. The second was to see what effect this new line of thinking might have on their design decision-making. In addition to the hope that this would provide a worthwhile and rewarding research-orientated educational experience, we wanted also to begin to look at ways to communicate socially restorative urbanism to practitioner audiences with the specific intention of cutting across traditional disciplinary boundaries. Students involved came from a variety of backgrounds including architecture, landscape architecture and planning, and the idea was to build on this inter-disciplinary mix by giving the project a focus outside of their discipline-specific backgrounds, specifically by making transitional edges the focus for design attention, and a strong social emphasis through making the territorial experiences of authentic site users the main influence on design decisions.

Along with introductory and instructional lectures, a site visit and a resource pack of selected relevant information with reading recommendations delivered in the first week, the main components of the six-week process involved role play and site investigation, three-dimensional design exploration and resolution, including model-making. Because of practicality and time constraints, the students were not able to become involved with actual site users to inform their investigation and so replicated this with fictional characters who might typically use the site area for various reasons. These formed a 'virtual' community of users whose territorial habits could be brought to life through story boards that made explicit their characteristics, relationships and daily routines. Their 'nows' and 'wishes' could then be explored through an adaptation of the Experiemic Process to form foundations for design development of the sites they inhabited. An important element of the process is for students to work on design exploration in three dimensions throughout. This makes it possible to ensure that decisions are always informed by the human scale and to stress the importance of spatial containment and its adaptability through use. It also makes it more possible for design development drawings to be continuously populated with scale figures, emphasising that what people do is as much a part of the urban landscape as the material fabric. Physical, and in some cases digital, model-making to communicate the final design proposal maintains this emphasis.

Figure 9.2 shows one particular design solution from this project that exemplifies some of the qualities of socially restorative urbanism. At present the site is a semi-derelict river's edge courtyard bounded by the River Aire and an abandoned Victorian mill building. The students envisaged a live–work community in occupation of the site and set about developing proposals that would enable the community to accommodate a wide diversity of social activity by optimising the potential for spatial variation with the minimum of financial investment. This would centre on the identification of four key structural interventions that would give the site its framework of form. In this way the presently minimal levels of spatial porosity were significantly increased with a series of enclosing spaces that connected and blurred the distinction between interior and exterior realms and allowed for the differentiation of living accommodation and small workshops and stalls. Optimal flexibility of use in this small courtyard was achieved by making many of these structural frameworks adaptable and changeable so that the community could control its form and function according to what they wished to do, as individuals and as a collective. The mines and yours are thus retained, yet within the mutually supportive framework of ours, given in part by the adaptable structures which could be moved and reshaped according to the community's various living, working and recreational needs, and in response to seasonal variations. An overall sense of coherence remains evident, giving the courtyard a recognisable identity, driven entirely by the specific requirements of the community involved, while maintaining the capacity for localised expression and adaptation.

By means of this very simple design studio we can begin to draw out three significant issues that are important to the practice of socially restorative urbanism. The first, and possibly the most important, is that the process is informed throughout by the authentic lived experience of the people who inhabit the site, their interactions with one another and with the material and spatial structure (albeit in this studio version via role play). The role of the professional in this is to facilitate the expression of this 'life' through the stages of the Experiemic Process which then becomes the driver for socially orientated change. The second issue brings this change to focus on transitional edges as components of the urban realm which fall outside of the traditional disciplinary boundaries, requiring thought

Figure 9.2: Simple 'bolt-on' structures increase the spatial porosity of this transitional edge. Their adaptability enables this live–work community to change the physical form of this riverside courtyard to accommodate a wide diversity of social activity. Design work and model building by Rosie Loveridge, Patrick Conn and Sam Breed, students of the MLA Landscape Architecture, 2011.

processes that are cross–disciplinary, even if this may be at a relatively superficial level in the context of a short academic project. A third issue lies with the emphasis on three-dimensional working, and particularly three-dimensional modelling. As well as providing a means to retain the sense of human scale and human habitation throughout the process, this form of representation is also much closer to the craft of making and adaptation which are central to the ethos of socially restorative urbanism. We would suggest that this return to an emphasis on human social functioning and its translation in spatial form through transitional edges may characterise a new generation of practitioners better equipped to respond to socio-spatial issues in urban design decision-making (Figure 9.3).

Much more, of course, will be required than experimental design studios can deliver if the principles of socially restorative urbanism are to progress. As we have discussed throughout the book, our underlying aspiration is to try to find a means whereby the current form-dominant approaches to urban design can be rebalanced by returning aspects of control to urban inhabitants in the determination of how places they use are shaped and evolve. With increasing international and national focus on localism, this is now becoming an increasingly important issue in the determination of policy and if this is to be effective in the long term, ways will need to be found to enable appropriate re-orientation of professional practice and,

Figure 9.3: A new generation of practitioners better equipped to respond to socio-spatial issues in urban design decision-making.

by extension, the education of practitioners. As we have discussed in this book, we believe that this needs to involve a shift away from the large-scale and rapid delivery pace characteristic of much contemporary urban regeneration and design, towards a longer-term and more time-conscious approach which will need to be informed through new avenues of research.

We hope to have made a contribution to beginning this process by asserting, through our discussion about transitional edges and the participatory process of Experiemics, that fruitful avenues of inquiry might focus in particular on the relationship between social process and spatial organisation. Much has already been done in this respect, of course, but it seems that whatever understandings we have acquired thus far are being hindered in their effective application, partly by sustaining disciplinary divisions and partly because of communication between professional specialists and those who live with the consequences of their decisions. Perhaps the further development of new readings of the environment and the relationship people have with it in terms which can be accessed by all may ultimately begin to break down the professional–lay divide. We have found that talking about the human–environment relationship through the interconnected territorial language of MTOY offers benefits in this respect, and we hope to have been able to demonstrate that this approach has the capacity to give influence and control to even the most voiceless members of society.

Socially restorative urbanism is, then, rather more of an agenda than a solution. It presents an alternative approach to urban place-making and management which has explicit socio-spatial foundations. Optimising its application requires professional design action to become more focused on transitional edges as coherent components of the urban realm. Importantly, this means recognising transitional edges as having integrated spatial and social dimensions: the former understood in terms of their constituent segments; the latter in terms of associated territorial expressions which can be catalysed by the Experiemic Process. In its essence, then, socially restorative urbanism is a fusion of spatial arrangement, territorial expression and the inclusive communication strategies which encourage these to be directed to the delivery of a sense of ours, or belonging. An agenda for further development of socially restorative urbanism might, therefore, include the following considerations:

- *a more explicit understanding of the human–environment relationship* at the heart of approaches to research, teaching and practice underpinned especially by phenomenological perspectives, which provide foundations from which to see such relationships as mutually interdependent and mutually transforming;

- *recognition of the interdependency of urban morphology and social processes*, especially how these can better inform an integration of professional, top-down processes with community-led bottom-up processes in urban place-making and its management and adaptation;
- *the primacy of transitional edges, as socio-spatial components of urban order,* within research, education and practice, especially their key significance to the social life and vitality of the urban realm, the well-being of urban inhabitants and users, and the nature of their socio-spatial organisation to that significance;
- *emphasis on the need for accessible and inclusive forms of communication* capable of overcoming professional and community boundaries and discipline-specific boundaries;
- *development of cross-disciplinary research, education and practice* that can define and operationalise the better integration of built environment disciplines with psychology and sociological principles in particular, focused on the social and spatial dimensions of transitional edges;
- *development of new readings of the urban realm* more closely related to territorial functioning and in particular the need for a better balance between professional intervention and occupant self-organisation;
- *re-orientation of practice and policy to be more localised and context specific,* emphasising the importance of longitudinal, time-sensitive partnership working.

This implies quite a different kind of professional disciplinary position than that offered by current specialist provision and makes us consider what the nature of the professional role should be in the application of socially restorative urbanism. This highlights not just the relationship between processes of professional intervention and the participation of those who inhabit and use its outputs, but also the need for cross-disciplinary relations capable of overcoming the divisions evident in the currently prevailing disciplinary boundaries. If the socio-spatial foundations that lay behind socially restorative urbanism can be accepted, and there seems to be compelling reason in both theory and practice that they should be, then this requires more than a closer relationship, or indeed full integration of, the built environment professions, particularly architecture, landscape architecture, and urban planning and design. If even this interdisciplinary stance can be achieved, we can certainly conceive of a disciplinary position with the knowledge and skill sets to transcend the interior and exterior duality in the material realm, but this may not in itself ensure that resulting decisions are necessarily any better sociologically or psychologically informed. As we discussed earlier in the book, Alexander Cuthbert (2007) has explicitly raised similar issues in consequence of a review of urban design theory, suggesting that the way forward toward the delivery of urban realm with genuine social relevance needs to be much better informed by social processes than it is at present. We are not suggesting that socially restorative urbanism presents a solution to Cuthbert's evaluation, but we do hope and believe that it may offer a step in the same direction with at least some of the means by which to discuss ways in which social processes and human experience may be restored to urban place-making and the sense of belonging with it.

Notes

1 New Age-ing Cities

1   A wide-ranging review of literature relevant to this is outlined in Chapter 4.

7 Experiemic development

1   In the UK context the term 'Day Service' refers to a community-based centre, traditionally set up by the local authority to support vulnerable members of the community.

2   This project formed co-author Alice Mathers' doctoral study 'Hidden voices: the participation of people with learning disabilities in public open space' (University of Sheffield, 2008).

3   Informed consent was required as the community partners were PWLD, who have been identified as a vulnerable social group.

4   Self-advocacy is defined as 'an individual's ability to effectively communicate, convey, negotiate or assert his or her own interests, desires, needs, and rights. It involves making informed decisions and taking responsibility for those decisions' (Van Reusen *et al.*, 1994).

5   The People's Parliament is a bi-monthly, regional meeting of PWLD run by PWLD. It provides the setting where issues affecting PWLD can be discussed and fed back to the local authority (through the Learning Disability Partnership Board) and other public bodies.

6   Available for free download at: www.elprdu.com/projects.html#excuseme.

7 SUFA is a self-advocacy organisation involved in the provision of advocacy services for people with learning disabilities including: self-advocacy, citizen or one-to-one advocacy, crisis advocacy and peer advocacy.

8 WORK Ltd is a registered charity established in 1995 which trains and educates young people and adults with learning difficulties within a real-life working environment, to enable them to obtain work experience and to promote independent living and personal development.

9 The SYPTE is the coordinating body responsible for the development of public transport across the South Yorkshire region.

10 The Sheffield City Council Mobility Strategy Team are a division of Sheffield City Council Adult Services responsible for providing services to people who need support to live independent lives.

Bibliography

Alexander, C. (1979) *The Timeless Way of Building*. New York: Oxford University Press.

Alexander, C. (2002) *The Nature of Order: An Essay on the Art of Building and the Nature of the Universe. Book Two, The Process of Creating Life*. Berkeley, CA: The Center for Environmental Structure.

Alexander, C., Ishikawa, S., Silverstein, M., Jacobson, M., Fiksdahl-King, I. and Angel, S. (1977) *A Pattern Language*. New York: Oxford University Press.

Altman, I. (1975) *The Environment and Social Behaviour: Privacy, Personal Space, Territoriality and Crowding*. Monterey, CA: Brooks/Cole.

Appleton, J. (1996) *The Experience of Landscape*, 2nd edn. Chichester: Wiley.

Aylott, J. (2001) 'The new learning disabilities White Paper: did it forget something?' *British Journal of Nursing*, 10(8): 5–12.

Balaram, S. (2001) 'Universal design and the majority world', in W.F.E. Preiser and E. Ostroff (eds) *Universal Design Handbook*. New York: McGraw-Hill, 31–42.

Banks, M. (2001) *Visual Methods in Social Research*. London: Sage Publications Ltd.

Barnes, C. (1997) *Care, Communities and Citizens*. Harlow: Longman.

Bentley, I., Alcock, A., Martin, P., McGlynn, S. and Smith, G. (1985) *Responsive Environments*. London: The Architectural Press.

Berleant, A. (1997) *Living in the Landscape: Toward an Aesthetics of Environment*. Kansas: University Press of Kansas.

Berlin, I. (1965) 'Herder and the Enlightenment', in E.R. Wasserman (ed.) *Aspects of the Eighteenth Century*. Baltimore, MD: The Johns Hopkins University Press, 47–104.

Biddulph, M. (2007) *Introduction to Residential Layout*. Oxford: Butterworth-Heinemann.

Bonnes, M. and Secchiaroli, G. (1995) *Environmental Psychology: A Psycho-social Introduction*. London, Sage.

Bosselmann, P. (2008) *Urban Transformation: Understanding City Design and Form*. Washington, DC: Island Press.

Buchanan, P. (1988) 'A report from the front', in M. Carmona and S. Tiesdell (eds) (2007) *Urban Design Reader*. London: The Architectural Press, 204–208.

Cameron, D. (2010) 'Our "Big Society" plan', manifesto speech to the Conservative Party, 31 March 2010. Available at: www.conservatives.com/News/Speeches/2010/03/David_Cameron_Our_Big_Society_plan.aspx.

Canter, D. (1977) *The Psychology of Place*. London: The Architectural Press.

Carmona, M., Heath, T., Oc, T. and Tiesdell, S. (2010) *Public Places, Urban Spaces: A Guide to Urban Design*, 2nd edn. London: The Architectural Press.

Carpiano, R.M. (2009) 'Come take a walk with me: The "Go-Along" interview as a novel method for studying the implications of place for health and well-being', *Health & Place*, 15(1): 263–272.

Chalfont, G. (2005) 'Building edge: an ecological approach to research and design environments for people with dementia', *Alzheimer's Care Quarterly*, 6(4): 341–348.

Chaskin, R.J. (2001) 'Building community capacity: a definitional framework and case studies from a comprehensive community initiative', *Urban Affairs Review*, 36(3): 291–323.

Chermeyeff, S. and Alexander, C. (1963) *Community and Privacy: Toward a New Architecture of Humanism*. New York: Doubleday.

Cooper-Marcus, C. and Barnes, M. (eds) (1995) *Gardens in Healthcare Facilities: Uses, Therapeutic Benefits and Design Recommendations*. Martinez, CA: Centre for Health Design.

Cooper-Marcus, C. and Francis, C. (1997) *People Places: Design Guidelines for Urban Open Space*, 2nd edn. New York: Van Nostrand Reinhold.

Cooper-Marcus, C. and Sarkissian, W. (1986) *Housing as if People Mattered: Site Design Guidelines for Medium-Density Family Housing*. Berkeley, CA: University of California Press.

Cullen, G. (1971) *The Concise Townscape*. Oxford: The Architectural Press.

Cuthbert, A.R. (2007) 'Urban design: requiem for an era – review and critique of the last 50 years', *Urban Design International*, 12: 177–223.

Darke, R. (1975) *The Context for Public Participation in Planning, South Yorkshire*. Sheffield: Sheffield Centre for Environmental Research.

Day, C. (2002) *Spirit and Place: Healing Our Environment: Healing Environment.* Oxford: The Architectural Press.

Day, C. (2004) *Places of the Soul: Architecture and Environmental Design as Healing Art,* 2nd edn. Oxford: The Architectural Press.

Dee, C. (2001) *Form and Fabric in Landscape Architecture: A Visual Introduction.* London: Spon Press.

de Jonge, D. (1967) 'Applied hodology', *Landscape,* 17(2): 10–11.

Department for Transport (2007) *Manual for Streets.* London: Thomas Telford Publishing.

Disability Rights Commission (2003) *Creating an Inclusive Environment.* Available at: www.drc.org.uk/library/publications/services_and_transport/creating_an_ inclusive_environm.aspx last (accessed 4 June 2007).

Dovey, K. (1993) 'Putting geometry in its place: toward a phenomenology of the design process', in D. Seamon (ed.) *Dwelling, Seeing and Designing: Toward a Phenomenological Ecology.* Albany, NY: State University of New York Press, 247–270.

Dovey, K. (2005) 'The silent complicity of architecture', in J. Hillier and J. Rooksby (eds) *Habitus: A Sense of Place,* 2nd edn. Farnham: Ashgate, 283–296.

Dovey, K. (ed.) (2010) *Becoming Places: Urbanism/Architecture/Identity/Power.* London: Routledge.

Dovey, K. and Polakit, K. (2010) 'Urban slippage: smooth and striated streetscapes in Bangkok', in K. Dovey (ed.) *Becoming Places: Urbanism/Architecture/Identity/ Power.* London: Routledge, 167–184.

Dovey, K. and Raharjo, W. (2010) 'Becoming prosperous: informal urbanism in Yogyakarta', in K. Dovey (ed.) *Becoming Places: Urbanism/Architecture/Identity/ Power.* London: Routledge, 79–101.

Eichler, M. and Hoffman, D. (n.d.) *Strategic Engagements: Building Community Capacity by Building Relationships.* Boston, MA: Consensus Organizing Institute.

Enable (1999) *Stop It! Bullying and Harassment of People with Learning Disabilities.* Glasgow: Enable.

Epstein, R. (1998) *Principles for a Free Society: Reconciling Individual Liberty with the Common Good.* Reading, MA: Perseus Books.

Fawcett, S., Paine-Andrews, A., Francisco, V.T., Schultz, J.A., Richter, K.P., Lewis, R.K., Williams, E.L., Harris, K.J., Berkley, J.Y., Fisher, J.L. and Lopez, C.M. (1995) 'Using empowerment theory in collaborative partnerships for community health and development', *American Journal of Community Psychology*, 23(5): 677–697.

Fernando, N.A. (2007) 'Open-ended space: urban streets in different cultural contexts', in K.A. Franck and Q. Stevens (eds) *Loose Space: Possibility and Diversity in Urban Life*. London: Routledge, 54–72.

Franck, K.A. and Stevens, Q. (eds) (2007) *Loose Space: Possibility and Diversity in Urban Life*. London: Routledge.

Frank, L. (2010) 'Streetscape design: perceptions of good design and determinates of social interaction', M.A. thesis, University of Waterloo, Canada.

Geffroy, Y. (1990) 'Family photographs: a visual heritage', *Visual Anthropology*, 3(4): 367–410.

Gehl, J. (1977) *The Interface Between Public and Private Territories in Residential Areas*. Melbourne: Department of Architecture and Building, University of Melbourne.

Gehl, J. (1986) '"Soft edges" in residential streets', *Scandinavian Housing and Planning Research*, 3(2): 89–102.

Gehl, J. (1996) *Life Between Buildings: Using Public Space*, trans. J. Koch. Copenhagen: Arkitektens Forlag, Danish Architectural Press.

Gehl, J. (2010) *Cities for People*. Washington, DC: Island Press.

Gehl, J. and Gemzoe, L. (2000) *New City Spaces*. Copenhagen: Danish Architectural Press.

Gehl, J. and Gemzoe, L. (2004) *Public Spaces, Public Life*. Copenhagen: Danish Architectural Press.

Gerlach-Spriggs, N., Kaufman, E. and Bass Warner, S. (1998) *Restorative Gardens: The Healing Landscape*. New Haven, CT: Yale University Press.

Gibson, T. (1981) *Planning for Real*. London: HMSO.

Glickman, N. and Servon, L. (1998) *More Than Bricks and Sticks: Five Components of CDC Capacity*. New Brunswick, NJ: Rutgers Center for Urban Policy Research.

Goldsmith, S. (1997) *Designing for the Disabled: The New Paradigm*. London: The Architectural Press.

Goodman, R.M., Speers, M.A., McLeroy, K., Fawcett, S., Kegler, M., Parker, E., Smith, S. R., Sterling, T.D. and Wallerstein, N. (1998) 'Identifying and defining the dimensions of community capacity to provide a basis for measurement', *Health Education and Behavior*, 25(3): 258–278.

Grabow, S. (1983) *Christopher Alexander and the Search for a New Paradigm in Architecture*. Stocksfield: Oriel Press.

Habraken, N.J. (1986) 'Towards a new professional role', *Design Studies*, 7(3): 139–143.

Habraken, N.J. (1998) *The Structure of the Ordinary: Form and Control in the Built Environment*. Cambridge, MA: MIT Press.

Habraken, N.J. (2005) *Palladio's Children*. London: Taylor & Francis.

Hagerhall, C.M., Laike, T., Taylor, R., Küller, M., Küller, R. and Martin, T. (2006) 'Fractal patterns and attention restoration: evaluations of real and artificial landscape silhouettes', paper presented at the International Association of People–Environment Studies Conference, Environment, Health and Sustainable Development, Alexandria, Egypt, 11–16 September.

Hall, E. (2004) 'Social geographies of learning disability: narratives of exclusion and inclusion', *Area*, 36(3): 298–306.

Hall, E.T. (1959) *The Silent Language*. New York: Doubleday.

Hall, E.T. (1963) 'System for the notation of proxemic behaviour', *American Anthropologist*, 65: 1003–1026.

Hall, E.T. (1966) *The Hidden Dimension*. New York: Doubleday.

Hansen, N. and Philo, C. (2007) 'The normality of doing things differently: bodies, spaces and disability geography', *Royal Dutch Geographical Society*, 98(4): 493–506.

Hartig, T. (2004) 'Restorative environments', in C. Spielberger (ed.) *Encyclopedia of Applied Psychology*, vol. 3. San Diego, CA: Academic Press, 273–279.

Hartig, T., Mang, M. and Evans, G.W. (1991) 'Restorative effects of natural environment experiences', *Environment and Behaviour*, 23: 3–26.

Healey, P. (1999) 'Deconstructing communicative planning theory: a reply to Tewdwr-Jones and Allmendinger', *Environment and Planning A*, 31: 1129–1135.

Hein, J.R., Evans, J. and Jones, P. (2008) 'Mobile methodologies: theory, technology and practice', *Geography Compass*, 2(5): 1266–1285.

Hillier, B. and Hanson, J. (1984) *The Social Logic of Space*. Cambridge: Cambridge University Press.

Honneth, A. (1995) *The Struggle for Recognition: The Moral Grammar of Social Conflicts*. Cambridge: Polity Press.

Hoogland, C. (2000) 'Semi-private zones as a facilitator of social cohesion', M.A. thesis, Katholieke Universiteit Nijmegen.

Imrie, R. and Hall, P. (2001) *Inclusive Design: Designing and Developing Accessible Environments*. London: Spon Press.

Jacobs, A. and Appleyard, D. (1987) 'Toward an urban design manifesto', *Journal of the American Planning Association*, 53(1): 112–120.

Jacobs, A.B. (1993) *Great Streets*. Cambridge, MA: MIT Press.

Jacobs, J. (1961) *The Death and Life of Great American Cities*. London: Jonathan Cape.

Jones, P., Bunce, G., Evans, J., Gibbs, H. and Ricketts Hein, J. (2008) 'Exploring space and place with walking interviews', *Journal of Research Practice*, 4(2), Article D2. Available at: http://jrp.icaap.org/index.php/jrp/article/view/150/161 (accessed 16 August 2011).

Jorgenson, A. and Keenan, R. (2008) *Urban Wildscapes*. Sheffield: University of Sheffield and Environment Room Ltd.

Kaplan, R. and Kaplan, S. (1989) *The Experience of Nature: A Psychological Perspective*. New York: Cambridge University Press.

Kaplan, R., Kaplan, S. and Ryan, R.L. (1998) *With People in Mind: Design and Management of Everyday Nature*. Washington, DC: Island Press.

Kaszynska, P., Parkinson, J. and Fox, W. (2012) *Re-thinking Neighbourhood Planning: From Consultation to Collaboration*. London: ResPublica/RIBA.

Kjær, A.M., Hansen, O.H and Thomsen, J.P.F. (2002) *Conceptualizing State Capacity*. DEMSTAR Research Report No. 6. Aarhus: Department of Political Science, University of Aarhus.

Korosec-Serfaty, P. (1985) 'Experience and the use of the dwelling', in I. Altman and C.M. Werner (eds) *Home Environments*. New York: Plenum Press, 27–42.

Kraftl, P. (2007) 'Children, young people and built environments', *Built Environment*, 33(4): 399–404.

Kretzman, J.P. and McKnight, J. (1993) *Building Communities from the Inside Out: A Path Toward Finding and Mobilizing a Community's Assets*. Evanston, IL: Institute for Policy Research, Northwestern University.

Lennox, N., Taylor, M., Rey-Conde, T., Bain, C., Purdie, D.M. and Boyle, F. (2005) 'Beating the barriers: recruitment of people with intellectual disability to participate in research', *Journal of Intellectual Disability Research*, 49(4): 296–305.

Lewis, S. (2005) *Front to Back: A Design Agenda for Urban Housing*. Oxford: The Architectural Press.

Llewelyn-Davies (2000) *Urban Design Compendium*, vol. 1. London: English Partnerships.

Lopez, T.G. (2003) 'Influence of the public–private border configuration on pedestrian behaviour: the case of the city of Madrid, PhD thesis, La Escuela Técnica Superior de Arquitectura de Madrid.

Lozano, E.E. (1990) *Community Design and the Culture of Cities: The Crossroad and the Wall*. Cambridge; Cambridge University Press.

Lynch, K. (1960) *The Image of the City*. Cambridge, MA: MIT Press.

Macdonald, E. (2005) 'Street-facing dwelling units and liveability: the impacts of emerging building types in Vancouver's new high-density residential neighbourhoods', *Journal of Urban Design*, 10(1): 13–38.

Mace, R. (1985) *Universal Design: Barrier Free Environments for Everyone*. Los Angeles: Designers West.

Mace, R. (1988) *Universal Design: Housing for the Lifespan of All People*. Washington, D4C: U4S4 Department of Housing and Urban Development.

Madanipour, A. (2003) *Public and Private Spaces of the City*. London: Routledge.

Martin, M. (1997) 'Back-alley as community landscape', *Landscape Journal*, 15: 138–153.

Maslow, A.H. (1968) *Towards a Psychology of Being*. Princeton, NJ: Van Nostrand Reinhold.

Mathers, A.R. (2008) 'Hidden voices: the participation of people with learning disabilities in the experience of public open space', *Local Environment*, 13(6): 515–529.

Mathers, A.R. (2010) 'Road to inclusion', *Learning Disability Today*, 10(9): 34–36.

Mathers, A.R., Thwaites, K., Simkins, I.M. and Mallett, R. (2011) 'Beyond participation: the practical application of an empowerment process to bring about environmental and social change', *Journal of Human Development, Disability and Social Change*, 19(3): 37–57.

Mehaffy, M. (2008) 'Generative methods in urban design: a progress assessment', *Journal of Urbanism*, 1(1): 57–75.

Mehaffy, M., Porta, S., Rofe, Y. and Salingaros, N. (2010) 'Urban Nuclei and the Geometry of Streets: The "emergent neighbourhood" model', *Urban Design International*, 15(1): 22–46.

Mercer, C. (1975) *Living in Cities: Psychology and the Urban Environment*. Harmondsworth: Penguin.

Merleau-Ponty, M. (1962) *Phenomenology of Perception*. London: Routledge & Kegan Paul.

Meyer, S. E. (1994) *Building Community Capacity: The Potential of Community Foundations*. Minneapolis, MN: Rainbow Research Inc.

Moughtin, C. (2003) *Urban Design: Street and Square*, 3rd edn. Oxford: The Architectural Press.

Nenci, A., Troffa, R. and Carrus, G. (2006) 'The restorative properties of modern architectural styles', paper presented to the International Association of People–Environment Studies Conference, Environment, Health and Sustainable Development, Alexandria, Egypt, 11–16 September.

Newman, O. (1972) *Defensible Space: Crime Prevention Through Environmental Design*. New York: Macmillan.

Newman, O. (1976) *Design Guidelines for Creating Defensible Space*. Washington, DC: National Institute of Law Enforcement and Criminal Justice.

Newman, P. and Kenworthy, J. (1999). *Sustainability and Cities: Overcoming Automobile Dependence*. Washington, DC: Island Press.

Nooraddin, H. (2002) 'In-between space: towards establishing new methods in street design', *GBER*, 2(1): 50–57.

Norberg-Schulz, C. (1971) *Existence, Space and Architecture*. London: Studio Vista.

Northway, R. (2000) 'Ending participatory research?' *Journal of Learning Disabilities*, 4(1): 27–36.

Noya, A. and Clarence, E. (2009) 'Putting community capacity building in context', in A. Noya, E. Clarence and G. Craig (eds) *Community Capacity Building: Creating a Better Future Together*. Paris: OECD, 67–81.

Ohmer, M.L., Meadowcroft, P., Freed, K. and Lewis, E. (2009) 'Community gardening and community development: individual, social and community benefits of a community conservation program', *Journal of Community Practice*, 17(4): 377–399.

Page, J.K. (1974) *On the Design of Systems for Effective User Design Participation in Urban Designs*. Sheffield: Sheffield Centre for Environmental Research.

Paget, S. (2008) 'Aspects of the professional role of the landscape architect: exemplified through the development of school grounds', doctoral thesis, Uppsala, Swedish University of Agricultural Sciences.

Parr, H. (2007) 'Mental health, nature work, and social inclusion', *Environment and Planning D: Society and Space*, 25(3): 537–561.

Porta, S. and Renne, J.L. (2005) 'Linking urban design to sustainability: formal indicators of social urban sustainability field research in Perth, Western Australia', *Urban Design International*, 10: 51–64.

Porta, S. and Romice, O.R. (2010) *Plot-Based Urbanism: Towards Time-Consciousness in Place-Making*. Glasgow: Urban Design Studies Unit, University of Strathclyde.

Project for Public Spaces (2011) *An Idea Book for Placemaking: Semi-Public Zone*. Available at: http://www.pps.org/archive/semi_public_zone/ (accessed 10 October 2011).

Proshansky, H.M., Fabian, A.K. and Kaminoff, R. (1983) 'Place-identity: physical world socialization of the self', *Journal of Environmental Psychology*, 3(1): 57–83.

Punter, J. (2011) 'Urban design and the English Urban Renaissance 1999–2009: a review and preliminary evaluation', *Journal of Urban Design*, 16(1): 1–41.

Rajala, E.M. (2009) 'Between you and me: we: an architecture of interaction' *M.ARCH*. University of Cincinnati.

Rudlin, D.J.E. and Falk, N. (1999) *Sustainable Urban Neighbourhood: Building the 21st Century Home*, 2nd edn. Oxford: The Architectural Press.

Ryan, S. (2005) '"Busy behaviour" in the "Land of the Golden M": going out with learning disabled children in public places', *Journal of Applied Research in Intellectual Disabilities*, 18(1): 65–75.

Sanoff, H. (2000) *Community Participation: Methods in Design and Planning*. New York: John Wiley & Sons, Ltd.

Schumacher, E.F. (1973) *Small is Beautiful: A Study of Economics as if People Mattered*. London: Blond and Briggs.

Scopelliti, M. and Giuliani, M.V. (2004) 'Choosing restorative environments across the lifespan: a matter of place experience', *Journal of Environmental Psychology*, 24(4): 423–437.

Seeland, K. and Nicolè, S. (2006) 'Public green space and disabled users', *Urban Forestry and Urban Greening*, 5(1): 29–34.

Sempik, J., Aldridge, J. and Becker, S. (2005) *Health, Well-Being and Social Inclusion: Therapeutic Horticulture in the UK*. Bristol: The Policy Press.

Sibley, D. (1995) *Geographies of Exclusion: Society and Difference in the West*. London: Routledge.

Siegel, P.E. and Ellis N.R. (1985) 'Note on the recruitment of subjects for mental retardation research', *American Journal of Mental Deficiency*, 89: 431–433.

Simkins, I.M. (2008) 'The development of the Insight Method: a participatory approach for primary school children to reveal their place experience', unpublished PhD thesis, University of Sheffield.

Skeffington, A.M. (1969) *People and Planning: Report of the Committee on Public Participation in Planning.* London: HMSO.

Speller, G. and Ravenscroft, N. (2005) 'Facilitating and evaluating public participation in urban parks management', *Local Environment*, 10(1): 41–56.

Stravides, S. (2007) 'Heterotopias and the experience of porous urban space', in K.A. Franck and Q. Stevens (eds) *Loose Space: Possibility and Diversity in Urban Life.* London: Routledge, 174–192.

Sundstrom, E. (1977) 'Theories in the impact of the physical working environment: analytical framework and selective review', ARCC Workshop on the Impact of the Work Environment on Productivity, ARCC, Washington, DC.

Tenngart, C. and Hagerhall, C.M. (2008) 'The perceived restorativeness of gardens: assessing the restorativeness of a mixed built and natural scene type', *Urban Forestry and Urban Greening*, 7(2): 107–118.

Thwaites, K., Porta, S., Romice, O. and Greaves, M. (2007) *Urban Sustainability through Environmental Design: Approaches to Time–People–Place Responsive Urban Spaces.* London: Routledge.

Thwaites, K. and Simkins, I.M. (2007) *Experiential Landscape: An Approach to People, Place and Space.* London: Routledge.

Tibbalds, F. (1992) *Making People-Friendly Towns.* London: Longman Group UK.

Todd, S. (2000) 'Working in the public and private domains: staff management of community activities for and identities of people with intellectual disability', *Journal of Intellectual Disability Research*, 44(5): 600–620.

Tuan, Y.F. (1977) *Space and Place: The Perspective of Experience.* Minneapolis, MN: University of Minnesota Press.

Tuan, Y.F. (1980) 'Rootedness versus sense of place', *Landscape*, 24: 3–8.

Turner, J.F.C. (1976) *Housing by People: Towards Autonomy in Building Environments.* London: Marion Boyars Publishers Ltd.

Ulrich, R.S. (1979) 'Visual landscapes and psychological wellbeing', *Landscape Research*, 4: 17–23.

Ulrich, R.S. (1984) 'View through a window may influence recovery from surgery', *Science*, 224(4647): 420–421.

United Nations Conference on Environment and Development (UNCED) (1992) *Agenda 21: Earth Summit.* Rio de Janeiro: The United Nations Programme of Action.

Urban Green Spaces Taskforce (2002) *Green Spaces, Better Places*. London: Department for Transport, Local Government and the Regions.

Urban Task Force (1999) *Towards an Urban Renaissance: Final Report of the Urban Task Force*. London: Urban Task Force.

Van Herzele, A., Collins, K. and Tyrväinen, L. (2005) 'Involving people in urban forestry: discussion of participatory practices throughout Europe,' in C.C. Konijnendijk, K. Nilsson, T.B. Randrup and J. Schipperijn (eds) *Urban Forests and Trees: A Reference Book*. Berlin: Springer Verlag, 32–45.

Van Reusen, A.K., Bos, C.S., Schumaker, J.B. and Deshler, D.D. (1994) *The Self-Advocacy Strategy for Education and Transition Planning*. Lawrence, KS: Edge Enterprises.

Westphal, J.M. (2000) 'Hype, hyperbole and health: therapeutic site design', in J. Benson and M.H. Roe (eds) *Urban Lifestyles: Spaces, Places, People*. Rotterdam: A.A. Balkema, 19–26.

Whyte, W.H. (1980) *The Social Life of Small Urban Spaces*. New York: Project for Public Spaces.

Whyte, W.H. (1988) *City: Rediscovering the Centre*. New York: Doubleday.

Worpole, K. (1998) 'People before beauty', *The Guardian*, 14 January.

Index

Abdel-Hadi, A. and Hawas, K. xvi, 20, 25, 27
active edges 8, 28, 29
Albert Dock, Liverpool 21
Alexander, C. 7, 15, 33–4, 39, 59, 69, 80, 84, 89, 91, 95
Alexander, C. and Chermeyeff, S. 34, 83
Alexandria 25, 124
Altman, R. 47, 84, 86, 96–8
Amsterdam xvi, 4, 19, 125–6
anthropology 34, 76
Appleton, J. 80
appropriation 22, 25, 31, 33, 98–9, 101–2, 113, 119, 124
Architectural Institute of Korea xvi, 19
Attention Restoration Theory 57
attention span 52

beach culture 46
being away, extent, fascination, compatibility 56–7
belonging xiii, 4, 9, 10, 16–17, 37, 41, 45, 48–50, 52, 64–5, 67, 124, 130, 134, 196, 217–19, 225, 227
Bentley, I. 15, 88, 91, 92, 97, 98
Berleant, A. 69
Berlin, I. 67
between-ness 22–3, 27, 75

Biddulph, M. 84, 88, 93, 95, 97, 98
Borgianni, S., Setola, N. and Torricelli, M.C. xvi, 20, 25, 27
Borneo 99
Bosselmann, P. 80
bottom-up xiii, 18, 70, 154, 191, 216, 226
Burano, Italy 77, 124–5

Cairo 25, 27
capacity building 10, 148–51
Castello, L. xvi, 20–7, 41
Castlefields, Manchester 40
CDTA: centre, direction, transition, area 7, 208–11
Chester 39, 47, 118–20
Chimneypot Park, Salford 120
Clarence Dock, Leeds 19
coherence 35, 45, 112, 128, 223
coherence and adaptability 25, 114–15, 123–7, 218
communication 2, 47, 59–64, 89, 98, 129, 141, 144, 147, 150, 153–9, 163, 168, 171, 180, 183, 190, 207–17, 225–6
community cohesion 51, 86, 154
community landscapes 65
Concise Townscape, The 95
continuity 35, 103, 112–13, 203, 213
continuous building line 89–91

control, balance of 19, 37–50, 59, 93, 208, 212
Cooper-Marcus, C. 55, 88–91, 96, 98
Copenhagen 79, 80, 87
Cullen, G. 15, 69, 95, 105, 109, 111, 114
cultural expression 18, 26
Cuthbert, A. 1, 2, 14, 23, 35, 39, 147, 227

Daegu, South Korea xv, xvi, 16, 18–19, 218
de Jonge, D. 80
Death and Life of Great American Cities, The 33, 71
defensible space 96
Dehli, India 4, 85
directional 105–9, 111, 116–17, 218
disability studies ix, 41, 194
Dovey, K. 7, 31, 75–6
Dovey, K. and Polakit, K. 100
Dubrovnik, Croatia 45

Eccleshall Road, Sheffield 117–18, 120, 129
edge settings 5, 8, 21, 23, 32, 52, 73, 78, 80
Edwards, J. xvii, 78
effortless attention 57
empowerment, local xiii, 196
enclosure 35, 66, 79, 81–91, 96, 101, 109, 112, 115–19, 121, 126, 205, 218
environmental competence xi, 10, 60, 181
environmental psychology i, ix, 51, 53
Epstein, R. 93
evolutionary urban morphology 38–42
Exchange Square, Manchester 44
Experiemic Process xi, xvi, 8, 10, 38, 61, 66–7, 71, 134, 152–3, 167, 177, 180, 182–91, 194–215, 216–25
Experiential Landscape ix, x–xi, 1–2, 5, 7, 8, 23, 71, 73–4, 102, 110, 207–9, 218

fine grain adaptability 125
form, place and understanding 3, 37–8, 42–50, 53, 71, 122, 134–5, 218

Franck, K. and Stevens, Q. 15, 22, 31, 80, 82, 84, 89, 93, 99, 100

Gehl, J. 1, 7, 8, 15, 29, 34, 40, 41, 53, 69, 80–2, 84, 86, 88, 91, 93, 95, 105
Gemzoe, L. 34
geometric space 76
Grabow, S. 34
Greek asklepieia 54
green infrastructure 127
Greenwich Village, London 97

Habraken, N.J. xvi, 2–3, 6–8, 15, 23, 29, 37–49, 59, 64, 69–72, 73–5, 78, 84, 88–93, 96, 97–8, 100, 123, 128, 130, 134–5, 144–7, 152–4, 182, 208, 217–18
Hall, E. 34, 76, 88–9
Hammerby Sjostad 56, 127
Hartig, T. 52, 55
here and there 105
Hidden Dimension, The 88
hide and reveal 65–6, 79, 85–7, 101, 113, 115, 120
Hillier, W. and Hanson, J. 29, 35, 59, 88, 92
Homes for Change, Hulme, Manchester 122–3
Honneth, A. 49, 52, 66–7, 147, 182
Hoogland, C. 82, 86, 96, 97–8
human habitation xiii, xiv, 5–6, 43–4, 70, 74, 224
human restoration 5, 58
human well-being 37–8, 98, 142
human–environment relations 4–7, 19, 20, 33–4, 59, 75, 208, 216, 218, 225

Image of the City, The 33
in-between 14, 32, 96
inclusive communication 60–7, 208, 211–13, 217, 225
inclusive design 41, 141–2, 166
inclusive language 52, 197–8, 211, 214
inclusivity 5, 140, 194, 201, 207, 215

International Association of People-
Environment Studies 19
intimacy gradient 84
Islamic paradise gardens 54

Jacobs, J. 1, 7–8, 15, 29, 33, 38, 44, 53, 71,
76–7
Jacobs, A. 85, 86, 89, 94, 95
Jacobs, A. and Appleyard, D. 13, 96
Jakriborg, Sweden 92
Java Island, Amsterdam 19, 125–6, 127

Kaplan, S. and Kaplan, R. 52–3, 55, 57

landscape architecture xvii, 20, 32, 78, 134,
193, 212, 220, 221, 223, 226
laterality 110–13, 115, 128–32
Leverhulme Trust x, xvi, 177, 196, 199
Lincoln 42, 74
Lisbon 83
liveable cities 14
lived space 76
Ljubljana, Slovenia 116
local identity 26, 112, 114, 120
localised adaptability 112, 125, 213
localised expression 25, 114–15, 119,
120–2, 128, 218, 223
localism 26, 10, 16, 38, 51, 59–60, 148–9,
224
locality xiii, 21, 110, 113, 115, 128
loose form 100
loose green margins 127
loose meanings 100–1
loose practices 100–1
loose space 22, 31, 99–100
looseness 79, 99–101, 112–13, 115, 123
Lord Rogers of Riverside 2, 13
Lynch, K. 8, 15, 33, 34

Madanipour, A. 84, 93, 100
mapping methodology, experiential 7,
207–11
margins xii, 6–7, 37

Marr, A. 1, 2, 17–18, 20
Martin, M. 65, 67, 86
megacities 2, 17–18
mental fatigue 52, 54–5, 58
Merleau-Ponty, M. 7, 76
Milan 24, 47, 94
MTOY relations 6, 8, 10, 71, 129, 219–20
MTOY: mine, theirs, ours, yours 4, 152,
156, 199

natural surveillance 95
'New-Ageing Cities' (symposium) 26–8,
41
Newman, O. 88, 95–6, 98
Nooraddin, H. 87, 88, 92, 93, 97
Norberg-Schulz, C. 7, 33–5, 88

occupation, processes of 6, 16, 23, 70, 78,
128, 219

Palladio's Children 144–5
Palladian, post 3
Parga, Greece 44
participatory processes 2, 9, 27, 53, 70, 73,
134, 137–51, 182, 195
people with learning disabilities (PWLD)
138–43, 153–6, 162, 164–5, 170, 182,
184, 189, 192, 213
perforated boundaries 177
permeability 79, 91–3, 94, 96, 101, 109,
113–17
personalisation 3, 47–8, 88–9, 91, 96–9,
113, 123, 188
phenomenological 7, 33, 59, 74–8, 102,
185, 218, 226
placeleaks 21, 24
plot-based urbanism xv, 77–8, 119, 125
Porta, S. xv, 20, 23, 35
Porta, S. and Renne, J. 88–9
private–public gradient 86
professional interventions 28–9, 32, 70,
219, 226
professionalism 60, 143–7

Project for Public Spaces 95
prospect and refuge theory 80
proximity 82, 112–13, 117
psychological centrality 47–8
psychology 14, 32–3, 226
public-ness and private-ness 34, 84
Punter, J. 14, 35, 38

recognition 49, 64, 66–7, 147, 182, 207, 226
restorative environments 5, 11, 51–2, 55, 57–8
Robinson, J. xvi, 20, 26–7
Roman valetudinarium hospitals 54
Romanticism 55
Rome 58, 105
Romice, O. xv, 19, 23, 77

Salford Quays, Manchester 15
Schumacher, E.F. xi
Scopelliti, M. and Giuliani, M.V. 57
segment 7–9, 73, 110–19, 128–9, 208, 218, 225
segment hypothesis 101–9
self-assertion 4, 123, 219
self-esteem xii, 4, 6, 9, 37, 42, 49, 52, 57–9, 67, 69, 123, 142, 147, 189, 194, 196, 200, 219
self-organisation xiii, 2, 10, 29, 31, 38, 77, 110, 212–13, 219, 226
self-worth 10, 42, 57–9
social absorbency 8, 20, 52, 88–9, 105, 113, 116, 123, 128
social activity xiii, 8, 20, 28, 35, 59, 70, 75, 79–81, 82, 90–1, 93, 95–6, 101–2, 107, 113, 115, 118–19, 120, 222–3
social capital xi, 51, 60, 143, 148–9, 151, 181, 194
social depth 105–9
social exclusion 4, 59
social forces 3, 20, 22, 45, 102
social innovation 10, 18, 147

social interaction 35, 57–8, 79, 81–3, 84–5, 88–9, 91, 99–101, 108, 113, 115, 137, 139, 159, 167, 180
social organisation 67, 69, 71, 75
social processes 3, 8–9, 20, 27, 31, 33, 39, 46, 53, 70, 74–5, 121, 218–19, 226, 227
social restoration 59, 140, 152, 168
social sustainability 6, 11, 21, 23–4, 29, 31, 33–5, 40–1, 220
social value 2, 6, 8, 19–21, 28–9, 32, 39–40, 59, 129–30, 147, 152
societal processes 14, 22
sociology ix, 32
socio-spatial xiv, 1–2, 5–8, 11, 21, 23–8, 36–40, 53, 71, 73, 78, 101–9, 111, 113–15, 133–5, 168, 178, 216–20, 224–6
socio-spatial anatomy 5, 27, 115
socio-spatial structures 2, 21, 27–8, 217
spatial dimension 19, 34–5, 37, 49, 52, 71, 75–6, 88, 102, 168, 220, 226
spatial expansion 79, 87–9, 91, 101, 113, 115, 118
spatial extent 103, 110
spatial organisation xv, 6, 22, 26–8, 33, 37, 42, 53–4, 59, 67, 69, 75
spatial porosity 24, 114–15, 118–19, 121, 128, 218, 222–3
Spinningfield, Manchester 22
St Paul, Minnesota 27
stationary activity 101–11, 116–17
Stockholm, Sweden 48, 56, 127
streetscape indicators 35
Structure of the Ordinary, The 3, 6, 23, 37, 45, 128, 208, 217

territorial behaviour 3, 44–5, 59, 86, 102, 123
territorial depth 84, 98
territorial experience 3, 9–10, 23, 41, 47, 49, 74, 159, 221
territorial expression 6, 24, 29, 37, 45, 48–9, 78, 107, 225

territorial scale 63–4
territoriality 5, 42–8, 60–1, 79, 88, 91, 96–8, 101, 113, 115, 219
territory, primary 47, 96
territory, public 47
territory, secondary 48, 96, 98
threshold 25, 29, 89, 95, 98, 100, 102–3, 106–7, 110, 117–18
time-conscious xii, 19, 76, 225
top-down xiii, 2, 18, 70, 194, 216, 226
transitional edge, socio-spatial 101–9
transitional edges, anatomy 110–27
transitional edges, Habraken and Experiemics 128–32
transitional edges, phenomenology 74–7
transparency 65, 79, 92–3, 94–6, 101, 113–17, 150, 156
triangulation 82, 157

Ulrich, R. 52–3, 55
Uppsala 4, 50

Urban Design Studies Unit, University of Strathclyde xv, 23, 77
urban design theory 14, 29, 33, 35, 41, 73, 194, 227
urban habitat xv, 1, 4, 9, 11, 19–20, 27, 71
urban morphology xii, xv, 2, 20, 23, 33, 35, 37–9, 53, 71, 106, 226
urban place-making xii, 1–3, 9, 13–16, 29, 31, 59, 70, 194, 216, 225–7
urban regeneration 1, 3, 15, 25, 35, 46, 53, 225
urban renaissance 13, 35, 38, 238
urban restorative experience 53
urban social sustainability 31–4, 40, 220
Urban Task Force 1, 2, 14, 35, 40

Vastra Hamnen, Malmo 66, 121
Venice 54, 120
Victoria Quays, Leeds 40

World Health Organization 53
Worpole, K. 119, 121